HOLT McDOUGAL

Africa

Christopher L. Salter

HISTORY™

HOLT McDOUGAL

HOUGHTON MIFFLIN HARCOURT

Author

Dr. Christopher L. Salter

Dr. Christopher L. "Kit" Salter is Professor Emeritus of geography and former Chair of the Department of Geography at the University of Missouri. He did his undergraduate work at Oberlin College and received both his M.A. and Ph.D. degrees in geography from the University of California at Berkeley.

Dr. Salter is one of the country's leading figures in geography education. In the 1980s he helped found the national Geographic Alliance network to promote geography education in all 50 states. In the 1990s Dr. Salter was Co-Chair of the National Geography Standards Project, a group of distinguished geographers who created *Geography for Life* in 1994, the document outlining national standards in geography. In 1990 Dr. Salter received the National Geographic Society's first-ever Distinguished Geography Educator Award. In 1992 he received the George Miller Award for distinguished service in geography education from the National Council for Geographic Education. In 2006 Dr. Salter was awarded Lifetime Achievement Honors by the Association of American Geographers for his transformation of geography education.

Over the years, Dr. Salter has written or edited more than 150 articles and books on cultural geography, China, field work, and geography education. His primary interests lie in the study of the human and physical forces that create the cultural landscape, both nationally and globally.

ISBN-13 978-0-547-48488-4

9 10 0868 19 18 17 16 15

4500550063   C D E F G

Reviewers

Academic Reviewers

Elizabeth Chako, Ph.D.
Department of Geography
The George Washington
    University

Altha J. Cravey, Ph.D.
Department of Geography
University of North Carolina

Eugene Cruz-Uribe, Ph.D.
Department of History
Northern Arizona University

Toyin Falola, Ph.D.
Department of History
University of Texas

Sandy Freitag, Ph.D.
Director, Monterey Bay History
    and Cultures Project
Division of Social Sciences
University of California,
    Santa Cruz

Oliver Froehling, Ph.D.
Department of Geography
University of Kentucky

Reuel Hanks, Ph.D.
Department of Geography
Oklahoma State University

Phil Klein, Ph.D.
Department of Geography
University of Northern Colorado

B. Ikubolajeh Logan, Ph.D.
Department of Geography
Pennsylvania State University

Marc Van De Mieroop, Ph.D.
Department of History
Columbia University
New York, New York

Christopher Merrett, Ph.D.
Department of History
Western Illinois University
Pennsylvania

Thomas R. Paradise, Ph.D.
Department of Geosciences
University of Arkansas

Jesse P. H. Poon, Ph.D.
Department of Geography
University at Buffalo–SUNY

Robert Schoch, Ph.D.
CGS Division of Natural Science
Boston University

Derek Shanahan, Ph.D.
Department of Geography
Millersville University
Millersville, Pennsylvania

David Shoenbrun, Ph.D.
Department of History
Northwestern University
Evanston, Illinois

Sean Terry, Ph.D.
Department of Interdisciplinary
    Studies, Geography and
    Environmental Studies
Drury University
Springfield, Missouri

Educational Reviewers

Dennis Neel Durbin
Dyersburg High School
Dyersburg, Tennessee

Carla Freel
Hoover Middle School
Merced, California

Tina Nelson
Deer Park Middle School
Randallstown, Maryland

Don Polston
Lebanon Middle School
Lebanon, Indiana

Robert Valdez
Pioneer Middle School
Tustin, California

Teacher Review Panel

Heather Green
LaVergne Middle School
LaVergne, Tennessee

John Griffin
Wilbur Middle School
Wichita, Kansas

Rosemary Hall
Derby Middle School
Birmingham, Michigan

Rose King
Yeatman-Liddell School
St. Louis, Missouri

Mary Liebl
Wichita Public Schools USD 259
Wichita, Kansas

Jennifer Smith
Lake Wood Middle School
Overland Park, Kansas

Melinda Stephani
Wake County Schools
Raleigh, North Carolina

Contents

References

Available @

↗ **hmhsocialstudies.com**

- Facts About the World
- Regions of the World Handbook
- Standardized Test-Taking Strategies
- Economics Handbook

HISTORY™ is the leading destination for revealing, award-winning, original non-fiction series and event-driven specials that connect history with viewers in an informative, immersive and entertaining manner across multiple platforms. HISTORY is part of A&E Television Networks (AETN), a joint venture of Hearst Corporation, Disney/ABC Television Group and NBC Universal, an award-winning, international media company that also includes, among others, A&E Network™, BIO™, and History International™.

HISTORY programming greatly appeals to educators and young people who are drawn into the visual stories our documentaries tell. Our Education Department has a long-standing record in providing teachers and students with curriculum resources that bring the past to life in the classroom. Our content covers a diverse variety of subjects, including American and world history, government, economics, the natural and applied sciences, arts, literature and the humanities, health and guidance, and even pop culture.

The HISTORY website, located at **www.history.com**, is the definitive historical online source that delivers entertaining and informative content featuring broadband video, interactive timelines, maps, games, podcasts and more.

"We strive to engage, inspire and encourage the love of learning..."

Since its founding in 1995, HISTORY has demonstrated a commitment to providing the highest quality resources for educators. We develop multimedia resources for K–12 schools, two- and four-year colleges, government agencies, and other organizations by drawing on the award-winning documentary programming of A&E Television Networks. We strive to engage, inspire and encourage the love of learning by connecting with students in an informative and compelling manner. To help achieve this goal, we have formed a partnership with Houghton Mifflin Harcourt.

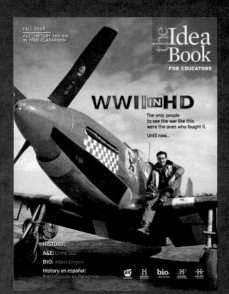
The Idea Book for Educators

Classroom resources that bring the past to life

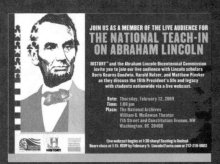
Live webcasts

HISTORY Take a Veteran to School Day

In addition to premium video-based resources, **HISTORY** has extensive offerings for teachers, parents, and students to use in the classroom and in their in-home educational activities, including:

▶ *The Idea Book for Educators* is a biannual teacher's magazine, featuring guides and info on the latest happenings in history education to help keep teachers on the cutting edge.

▶ **HISTORY Classroom (www.history.com/classroom)** is an interactive website that serves as a portal for history educators nationwide. Streaming videos on topics ranging from the Roman aqueducts to the civil rights movement connect with classroom curricula.

▶ **HISTORY email newsletters** feature updates and supplements to our award-winning programming relevant to the classroom with links to teaching guides and video clips on a variety of topics, special offers, and more.

▶ **Live webcasts** are featured each year as schools tune in via streaming video.

▶ **HISTORY Take a Veteran to School Day** connects veterans with young people in our schools and communities nationwide.

In addition to **HOUGHTON MIFFLIN HARCOURT**, our partners include the *Library of Congress*, the *Smithsonian Institution, National History Day, The Gilder Lehrman Institute of American History,* the *Organization of American Historians*, and many more. HISTORY video is also featured in museums throughout America and in over 70 other historic sites worldwide.

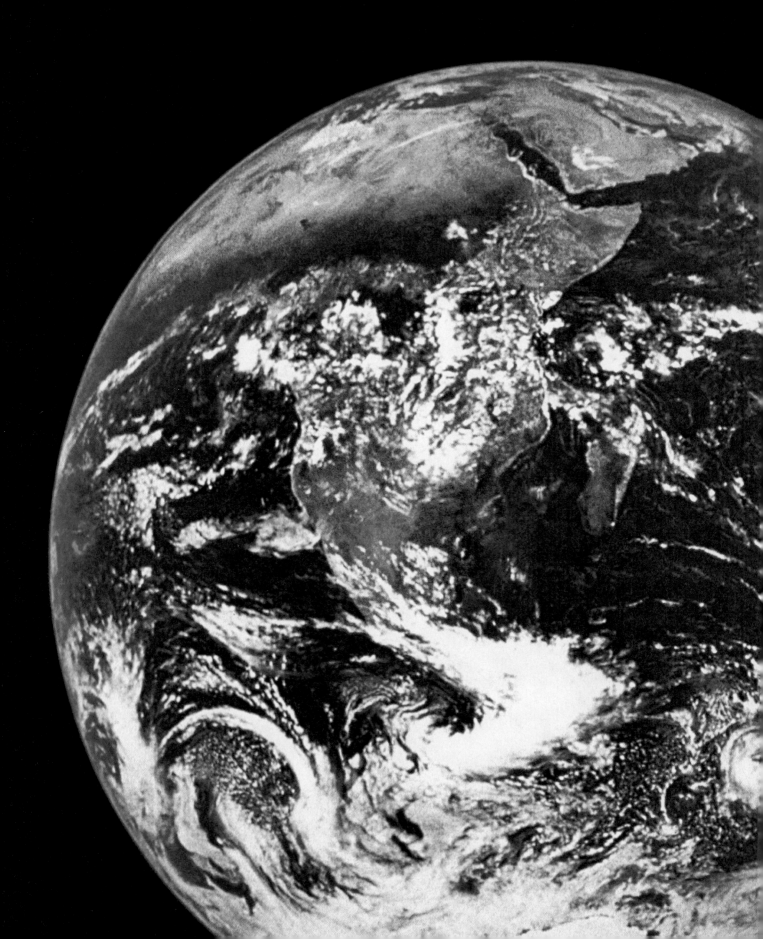

Geography and Map Skills Handbook

Contents

Throughout this textbook, you will be studying the world's people, places, and landscapes. One of the main tools you will use is the map—the primary tool of geographers. To help you begin your studies, this Geography and Map Skills Handbook explains some of the basic features of maps. For example, it explains how maps are made, how to read them, and how they can show the round surface of Earth on a flat piece of paper. This handbook will also introduce you to some of the types of maps you will study later in this book. In addition, you will learn about the different kinds of features on Earth and about how geographers use themes and elements to study the world.

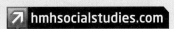 INTERACTIVE MAPS

Geography Skills With map zone geography skills, you can go online to find interactive versions of the key maps in this book. Explore these interactive maps to learn and practice important map skills and bring geography to life.

You can access all of the interactive maps in this book through the Interactive Student Edition at

hmhsocialstudies.com

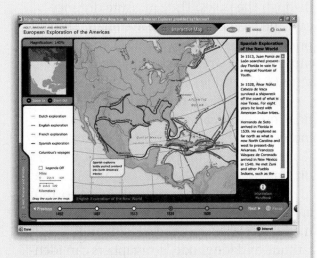

Mapping the Earth
Using Latitude and Longitude

A **globe** is a scale model of the Earth. It is useful for showing the entire Earth or studying large areas of Earth's surface.

To study the world, geographers use a pattern of imaginary lines that circles the globe in east-west and north-south directions. It is called a **grid**. The intersection of these imaginary lines helps us find places on Earth.

The east-west lines in the grid are lines of **latitude**, which you can see on the diagram. Lines of latitude are called **parallels** because they are always parallel to each other. These imaginary lines measure distance north and south of the **equator**. The equator is an imaginary line that circles the globe halfway between the North and South Poles. Parallels measure distance from the equator in **degrees**. The symbol for degrees is °. Degrees are further divided into **minutes**. The symbol for minutes is ´. There are 60 minutes in a degree. Parallels north of the equator are labeled with an N. Those south of the equator are labeled with an S.

The north-south imaginary lines are lines of **longitude**. Lines of longitude are called **meridians**. These imaginary lines pass through the poles. They measure distance east and west of the **prime meridian**. The prime meridian is an imaginary line that runs through Greenwich, England. It represents 0° longitude.

Lines of latitude range from 0°, for locations on the equator, to 90°N or 90°S, for locations at the poles. Lines of longitude range from 0° on the prime meridian to 180° on a meridian in the mid-Pacific Ocean. Meridians west of the prime meridian to 180° are labeled with a W. Those east of the prime meridian to 180° are labeled with an E. Using latitude and longitude, geographers can identify the exact location of any place on Earth.

Lines of Latitude

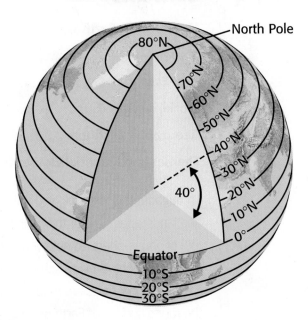

Lines of Longitude

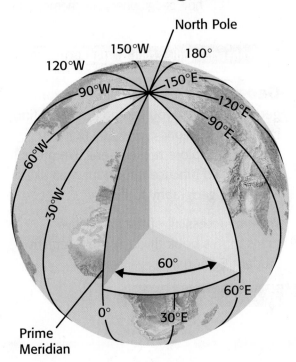

Northern Hemisphere

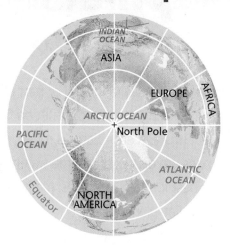

The equator divides the globe into two halves, called **hemispheres**. The half north of the equator is the Northern Hemisphere. The southern half is the Southern Hemisphere. The prime meridian and the 180° meridian divide the world into the Eastern Hemisphere and the Western Hemisphere. Look at the diagrams on this page. They show each of these four hemispheres.

Earth's land surface is divided into seven large landmasses, called **continents**. These continents are also shown on the diagrams on this page. Landmasses smaller than continents and completely surrounded by water are called **islands**.

Geographers organize Earth's water surface into major regions too. The largest is the world ocean. Geographers divide the world ocean into the Pacific Ocean, the Atlantic Ocean, the Indian Ocean, the Arctic Ocean, and the Southern Ocean. Lakes and seas are smaller bodies of water.

Southern Hemisphere

Western Hemisphere

Eastern Hemisphere

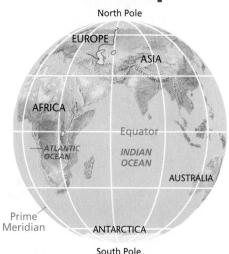

Mapmaking
Understanding Map Projections

A **map** is a flat diagram of all or part of Earth's surface. Mapmakers have created different ways of showing our round planet on flat maps. These different ways are called **map projections**. Because Earth is round, there is no way to show it accurately on a flat map. All flat maps are distorted in some way. Mapmakers must choose the type of map projection that is best for their purposes. Many map projections are one of three kinds: cylindrical, conic, or flat-plane.

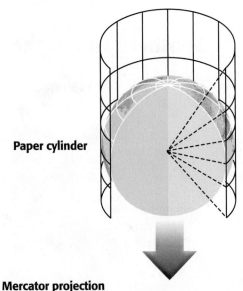

Paper cylinder

Cylindrical Projections

Cylindrical projections are based on a cylinder wrapped around the globe. The cylinder touches the globe only at the equator. The meridians are pulled apart and are parallel to each other instead of meeting at the poles. This causes landmasses near the poles to appear larger than they really are. The map below is a Mercator projection, one type of cylindrical projection. The Mercator projection is useful for navigators because it shows true direction and shape. However, it distorts the size of land areas near the poles.

Mercator projection

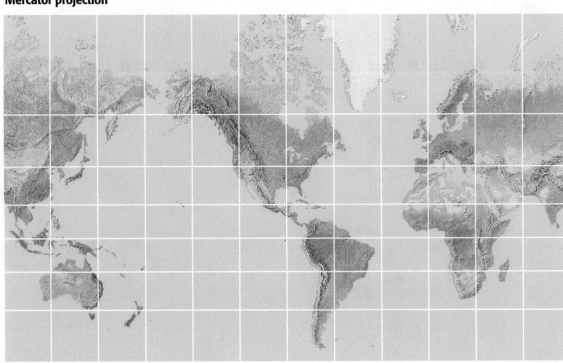

Conic Projections

Conic projections are based on a cone placed over the globe. A conic projection is most accurate along the lines of latitude where it touches the globe. It retains almost true shape and size. Conic projections are most useful for showing areas that have long east-west dimensions, such as the United States.

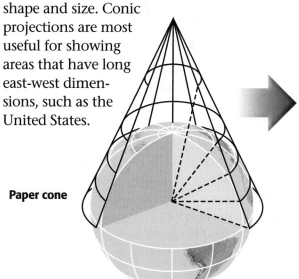

Paper cone

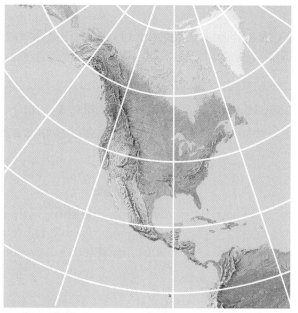

Conic projection

Flat-plane Projections

Flat-plane projections are based on a plane touching the globe at one point, such as at the North Pole or South Pole. A flat-plane projection is useful for showing true direction for airplane pilots and ship navigators. It also shows true area. However, it distorts the true shapes of landmasses.

Flat plane

Flat-plane projection

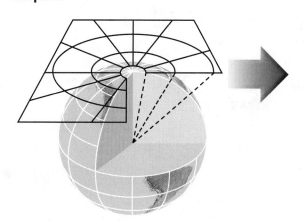

Map Essentials
How to Read a Map

Maps are like messages sent out in code. To help us translate the code, mapmakers provide certain features. These features help us understand the message they are presenting about a particular part of the world. Of these features, almost all maps have a title, a compass rose, a scale, and a legend. The map below has these four features, plus a fifth—a locator map.

❶ Title

A map's **title** shows what the subject of the map is. The map title is usually the first thing you should look at when studying a map, because it tells you what the map is trying to show.

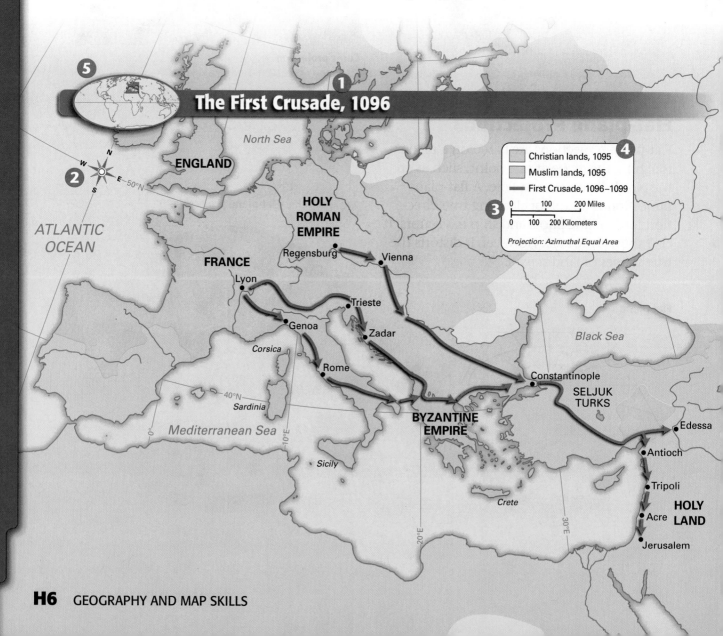

The First Crusade, 1096

North Sea

ENGLAND

ATLANTIC OCEAN

HOLY ROMAN EMPIRE

FRANCE

Lyon

Regensburg

Vienna

Genoa

Trieste

Corsica

Zadar

Rome

Sardinia

Sicily

Crete

BYZANTINE EMPIRE

Mediterranean Sea

Constantinople

Black Sea

SELJUK TURKS

Edessa

Antioch

Tripoli

Acre

HOLY LAND

Jerusalem

Christian lands, 1095
Muslim lands, 1095
First Crusade, 1096–1099

0   100   200 Miles
0   100   200 Kilometers

Projection: Azimuthal Equal Area

50°N

40°N

GEOGRAPHY AND MAP SKILLS

❷ Compass Rose

A directional indicator shows which way north, south, east, and west lie on the map. Some mapmakers use a "north arrow," which points toward the North Pole. Remember, "north" is not always at the top of a map. The way a map is drawn and the location of directions on that map depend on the perspective of the mapmaker. Most maps in this textbook indicate direction by using a compass rose. A **compass rose** has arrows that point to all four principal directions.

❸ Scale

Mapmakers use scales to represent the distances between points on a map. Scales may appear on maps in several different forms. The maps in this textbook provide a **bar scale**. Scales give distances in miles and kilometers.

To find the distance between two points on the map, place a piece of paper so that the edge connects the two points. Mark the location of each point on the paper with a line or dot. Then, compare the distance between the two dots with the map's bar scale. The number on the top of the scale gives the distance in miles. The number on the bottom gives the distance in kilometers. Because the distances are given in large intervals, you may have to approximate the actual distance on the scale.

```
0     100    200 Miles

0   100   200 Kilometers
```

❹ Legend

The **legend**, or key, explains what the symbols on the map represent. Point symbols are used to specify the location of things, such as cities, that do not take up much space on the map. Some legends show colors that represent certain features like empires or other regions. Other maps might have legends with symbols or colors that represent features such as roads. Legends can also show economic resources, land use, population density, and climate.

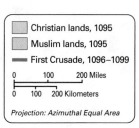

Christian lands, 1095
Muslim lands, 1095
First Crusade, 1096–1099
```
0     100    200 Miles

0   100   200 Kilometers
```
Projection: Azimuthal Equal Area

❺ Locator Map

A **locator map** shows where in the world the area on the map is located. The area shown on the main map is shown in red on the locator map. The locator map also shows surrounding areas so the map reader can see how the information on the map relates to neighboring lands.

Working with Maps
Using Different Kinds of Maps

As you study the world's regions and countries, you will use a variety of maps. Political maps and physical maps are two of the most common types of maps you will study. In addition, you will use special-purpose maps. These maps might show climate, population, resources, ancient empires, or other topics.

Political Maps

Political maps show the major political features of a region. These features include country borders, capital cities, and other places. Political maps use different colors to represent countries, and capital cities are often shown with a special star symbol.

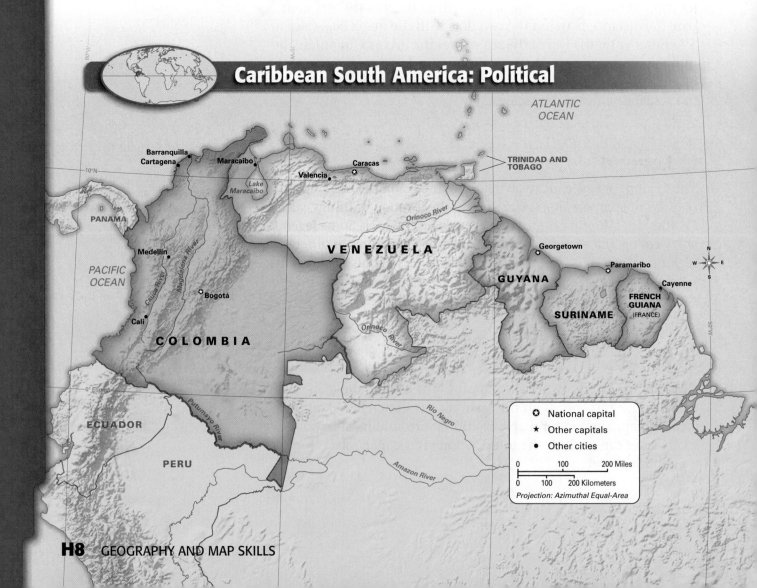

Caribbean South America: Political

ATLANTIC OCEAN

Barranquilla
Cartagena
Maracaibo
Caracas
Valencia
TRINIDAD AND TOBAGO

PANAMA

Lake Maracaibo

Orinoco River

Medellín

VENEZUELA

Georgetown

Paramaribo

PACIFIC OCEAN

Magdalena River

Cauca River

GUYANA

Cayenne

Bogotá

SURINAME

FRENCH GUIANA (FRANCE)

Cali

COLOMBIA

Orinoco River

ECUADOR

Putumayo River

Rio Negro

PERU

Amazon River

Legend:
- ✪ National capital
- ★ Other capitals
- ● Other cities

0   100   200 Miles
0   100   200 Kilometers
Projection: Azimuthal Equal-Area

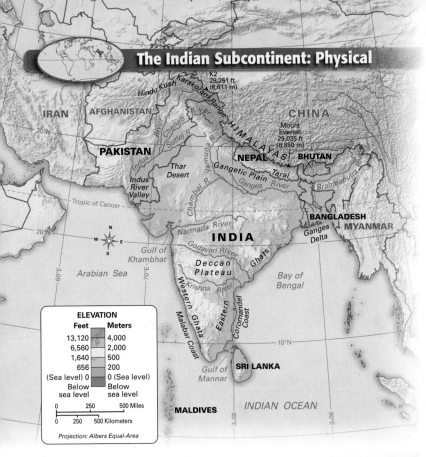

The Indian Subcontinent: Physical

ELEVATION

Feet	Meters
13,120	4,000
6,560	2,000
1,640	500
656	200
(Sea level) 0	0 (Sea level)
Below sea level	Below sea level

0   250   500 Miles
0   250   500 Kilometers
Projection: Albers Equal-Area

Physical Maps

Physical maps show the major physical features of a region. These features may include mountain ranges, rivers, oceans, islands, deserts, and plains. Often, these maps use different colors to represent different elevations of land. As a result, the map reader can easily see which areas are high elevations, like mountains, and which areas are lower.

Special-Purpose Maps

Special-purpose maps focus on one special topic, such as climate, resources, or population. These maps present information on the topic that is particularly important in the region. Depending on the type of special-purpose map, the information may be shown with different colors, arrows, dots, or other symbols.

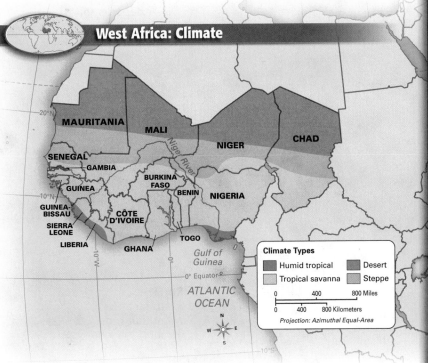

West Africa: Climate

Climate Types: Humid tropical, Desert, Tropical savanna, Steppe

0   400   800 Miles
0   400   800 Kilometers
Projection: Azimuthal Equal-Area

Using Maps in Geography The different kinds of maps in this textbook will help you study and understand geography. By working with these maps, you will see what the physical geography of places is like, where people live, and how the world has changed over time.

Geographic Dictionary

OCEAN
a large body of water

CORAL REEF
an ocean ridge made up of
skeletal remains of tiny sea animals

GULF
a large part of
the ocean that
extends into land

PENINSULA
an area of land that sticks
out into a lake or ocean

BAY
part of a large
body of water
that is smaller
than a gulf

ISLAND
an area of land
surrounded entirely
by water

ISTHMUS
a narrow piece of land
connecting two larger
land areas

DELTA
an area where a
river deposits soil
into the ocean

STRAIT
a narrow body of
water connecting two
larger bodies of water

SINKHOLE
a circular depression
formed when the roof
of a cave collapses

WETLAND
an area of land
covered by
shallow water

RIVER
a natural flow of
water that runs
through the land

LAKE
an inland body
of water

FOREST
an area of densely
wooded land

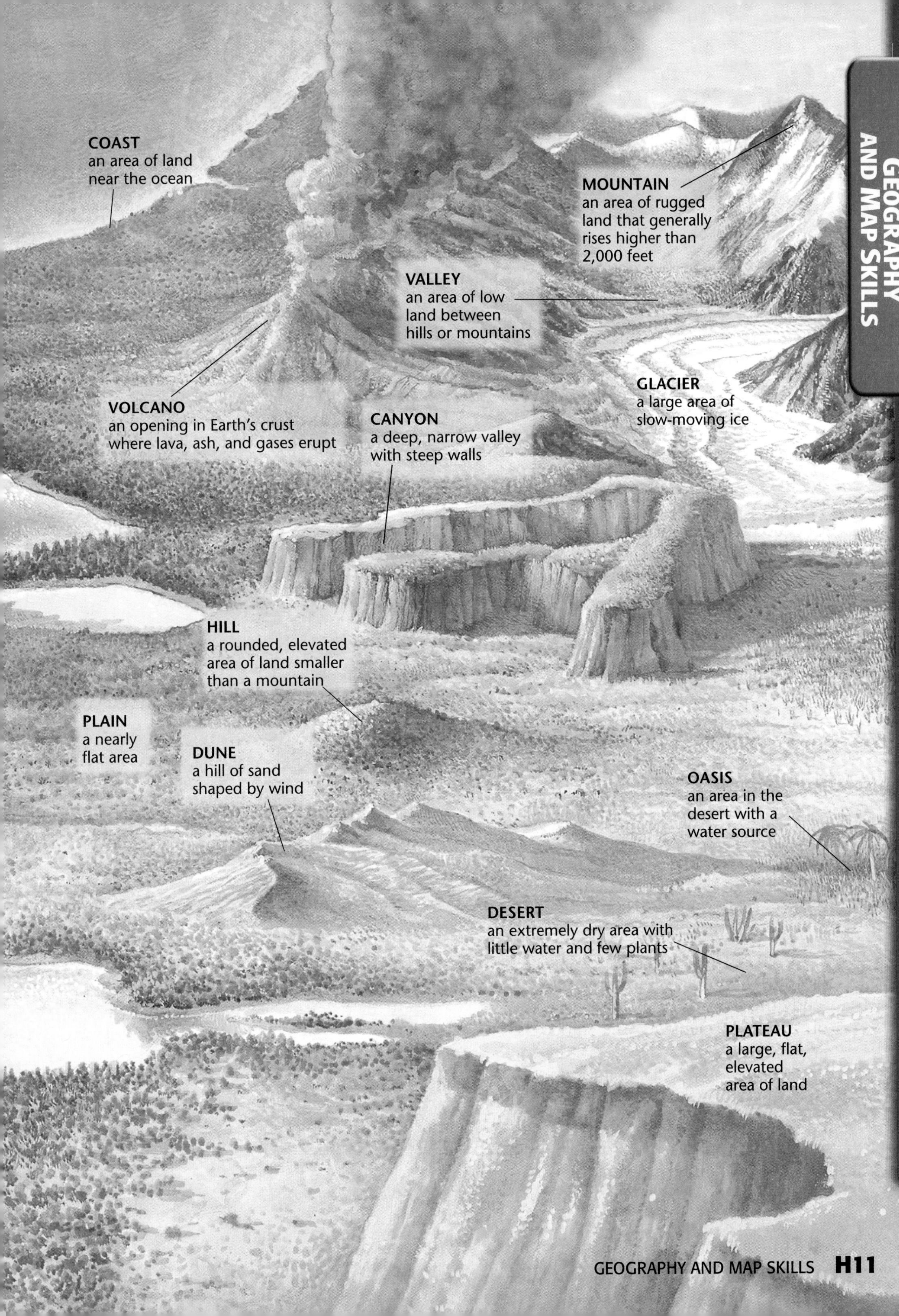

COAST
an area of land
near the ocean

MOUNTAIN
an area of rugged
land that generally
rises higher than
2,000 feet

VALLEY
an area of low
land between
hills or mountains

GLACIER
a large area of
slow-moving ice

VOLCANO
an opening in Earth's crust
where lava, ash, and gases erupt

CANYON
a deep, narrow valley
with steep walls

HILL
a rounded, elevated
area of land smaller
than a mountain

PLAIN
a nearly
flat area

DUNE
a hill of sand
shaped by wind

OASIS
an area in the
desert with a
water source

DESERT
an extremely dry area with
little water and few plants

PLATEAU
a large, flat,
elevated
area of land

Themes and Essential Elements of Geography

by Dr. Christopher L. Salter

To study the world, geographers have identified 5 key themes, 6 essential elements, and 18 geography standards.

"How should we teach and learn about geography?" Professional geographers have worked hard over the years to answer this important question.

In 1984 a group of geographers identified the 5 Themes of Geography. These themes did a wonderful job of laying the groundwork for good classroom geography. Teachers used the 5 Themes in class, and geographers taught workshops on how to apply them in the world.

By the early 1990s, however, some geographers felt the 5 Themes were too broad. They created the 18 Geography Standards and the 6 Essential Elements. The 18 Geography Standards include more detailed information about what geography is, and the 6 Essential Elements are like a bridge between the 5 Themes and 18 Standards.

Look at the chart to the right. It shows how each of the 5 Themes connects to the Essential Elements and Standards. For example, the theme of Location is related to The World in Spatial Terms and the first three Standards. Study the chart carefully to see how the other themes, elements, and Standards are related.

The last Essential Element and the last two Standards cover The Uses of Geography. These key parts of geography were not covered by the 5 Themes. They will help you see how geography has influenced the past, present, and future.

5 Themes of Geography

Location The theme of location describes where something is.

Place Place describes the features that make a site unique.

Regions Regions are areas that share common characteristics.

Movement This theme looks at how and why people and things move.

Human-Environment Interaction People interact with their environment in many ways.

6 Essential Elements

18 Geography Standards

1. How to use maps and other tools
2. How to use mental maps to organize information
3. How to analyze the spatial organization of people, places, and environments

I. The World in Spatial Terms

4. The physical and human characteristics of places
5. How people create regions to interpret Earth
6. How culture and experience influence people's perceptions of places and regions

II. Places and Regions

7. The physical processes that shape Earth's surface
8. The distribution of ecosystems on Earth

9. The characteristics, distribution, and migration of human populations
10. The complexity of Earth's cultural mosaics
11. The patterns and networks of economic interdependence on Earth
12. The patterns of human settlement
13. The forces of cooperation and conflict

III. Physical Systems

IV. Human Systems

14. How human actions modify the physical environment
15. How physical systems affect human systems
16. The distribution and meaning of resources

V. Environment and Society

17. How to apply geography to interpret the past
18. How to apply geography to interpret the present and plan for the future

VI. The Uses of Geography

Become an Active Reader

Did you ever think you would begin reading your social studies book by reading about *reading*? Actually, it makes better sense than you might think. You would probably make sure you knew some soccer skills and strategies before playing in a game. Similarly, you need to know something about reading skills and strategies before reading your social studies book. In other words, you need to make sure you know whatever you need to know in order to read this book successfully.

Tip #1

Read Everything on the Page!

You can't follow the directions on the cake-mix box if you don't know where the directions are! Cake-mix boxes always have directions on them telling you how many eggs to add or how long to bake the cake. But, if you can't find that information, it doesn't matter that it is there.

Likewise, this book is filled with information that will help you understand what you are reading. If you don't study that information, however, it might as well not be there. Let's take a look at some of the places where you'll find important information in this book.

The Chapter Opener

The chapter opener gives you a brief overview of what you will learn in the chapter. You can use this information to prepare to read the chapter.

The Section Openers

Before you begin to read each section, preview the information under What You Will Learn. There you'll find the main ideas of the section and key terms that are important in it. Knowing what you are looking for before you start reading can improve your understanding.

Boldfaced Words

Those words are important and are defined somewhere on the page where they appear— either right there in the sentence or over in the side margin.

Maps, Charts, and Artwork

These things are not there just to take up space or look good! Study them and read the information beside them. It will help you understand the information in the chapter.

Questions at the End of Sections

At the end of each section, you will find questions that will help you decide whether you need to go back and re-read any parts before moving on. If you can't answer a question, that is your cue to go back and re-read.

Questions at the End of the Chapter

Answer the questions at the end of each chapter, even if your teacher doesn't ask you to. These questions are there to help you figure out what you need to review.

Tip #2

Use the Reading Skills and Strategies in Your Textbook

Good readers use a number of skills and strategies to make sure they understand what they are reading. In this textbook you will find help with important reading skills and strategies such as "Asking Questions," "Summarizing," and "Using Word Parts."

We teach the reading skills and strategies in several ways. Use these activities and lessons and you will become a better reader.

- First, on the opening page of every chapter we identify and explain the reading skill or strategy you will focus on as you work through the chapter. In fact, these activities are called "Focus on Reading."

- Second, as you can see in the example at right, we tell you where to go for more help. The back of the book has a reading handbook with a full-page practice lesson to match the reading skill or strategy in every chapter.

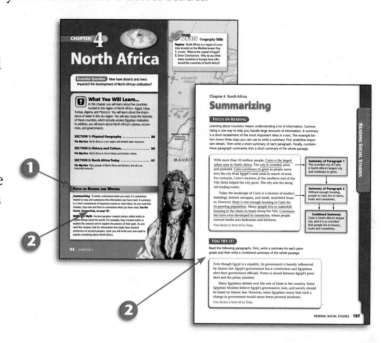

- Third, we give you short practice activities and examples as you read the chapter. These activities and examples show up in the margin of your book. Again, look for the words, "Focus on Reading."

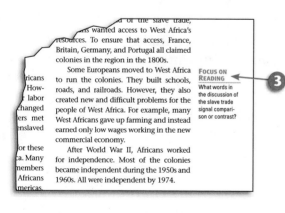

- Finally, we provide another practice activity in the Chapter Review at the end of every chapter. That activity gives you one more chance to make sure you know how to use the reading skill or strategy.

Tip #3

Pay Attention to Vocabulary

It is no fun to read something when you don't know what the words mean, but you can't learn new words if you only use or read the words you already know. In this book, we know we have probably used some words you don't know. But, we have followed a pattern as we have used more difficult words.

- First, at the beginning of each section you will find a list of key terms that you will need to know. Be on the lookout for those words as you read through the section. You will find that we have defined those words right there in the paragraph where they are used. Look for a word that is in boldface with its definition highlighted in yellow.

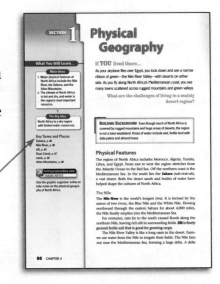

- Second, when we use a word that is important in all classes, not just social studies, we define it in the margin under the heading Academic Vocabulary. You will run into these academic words in other textbooks, so you should learn what they mean while reading this book.

Tip #4

Read Like a Skilled Reader

You won't be able to climb to the top of Mount Everest if you do not train! If you want to make it to the top of Mount Everest then you must start training to climb that huge mountain.

Training is also necessary to become a good reader. You will never get better at reading your social studies book—or any book for that matter—unless you spend some time thinking about how to be a better reader.

Skilled readers do the following:

1. They preview what they are supposed to read before they actually begin reading. When previewing, they look for vocabulary words, titles of sections, information in the margin, or maps or charts they should study.

2. They get ready to take some notes while reading by dividing their notebook paper into two parts. They title one side "Notes from the Chapter" and the other side "Questions or Comments I Have."

3. As they read, they complete their notes.

4. They read like **active readers**. The Active Reading list below shows you what that means.

5. Finally, they use clues in the text to help them figure out where the text is going. The best clues are called signal words. These are words that help you identify chronological order, causes and effects, or comparisons and contrasts.

Chronological Order Signal Words: *first, second, third, before, after, later, next, following that, earlier, subsequently, finally*

Cause and Effect Signal Words: *because of, due to, as a result of, the reason for, therefore, consequently, so, basis for*

Comparison/Contrast Signal Words: *likewise, also, as well as, similarly, on the other hand*

Active Reading

There are three ways to read a book: You can be a turn-the-pages-no-matter-what type of reader. These readers just keep on turning pages whether or not they understand what they are reading. Or, you can be a stop-watch-and-listen kind of reader. These readers know that if they wait long enough, someone will tell them what they need to know. Or, you can be an active reader. These readers know that it is up to them to figure out what the text means. Active readers do the following as they read:

Predict what will happen next based on what has already happened. When your predictions don't match what happens in the text, re-read the confusing parts.

Question what is happening as you read. Constantly ask yourself why things have happened, what things mean, and what caused certain events. Jot down notes about the questions you can't answer.

Summarize what you are reading frequently. Do not try to summarize the entire chapter! Read a bit and then summarize it. Then read on.

Connect what is happening in the section you're reading to what you have already read.

Clarify your understanding. Be sure that you understand what you are reading by stopping occasionally to ask yourself whether you are confused by anything. Sometimes you might need to re-read to clarify. Other times you might need to read further and collect more information before you can understand. Still other times you might need to ask the teacher to help you with what is confusing you.

Visualize what is happening in the text. In other words, try to see the events or places in your mind. It might help you to draw maps, make charts, or jot down notes about what you are reading as you try to visualize the action in the text.

Social Studies Words

As you read this textbook, you will be more successful if you learn the meanings of the words on this page. You will come across these words many times in your social studies classes, like geography and history. Read through these words now to become familiar with them before you begin your studies.

Social Studies Words

WORDS ABOUT TIME

AD	refers to dates after the birth of Jesus
BC	refers to dates before Jesus's birth
BCE	refers to dates before Jesus's birth, stands for "before the common era"
CE	refers to dates after Jesus's birth, stands for "common era"
century	a period of 100 years
decade	a period of 10 years
era	a period of time
millennium	a period of 1,000 years

WORDS ABOUT THE WORLD

climate	the weather conditions in a certain area over a long period of time
geography	the study of the world's people, places, and landscapes
physical features	features on Earth's surface, such as mountains and rivers
region	an area with one or more features that make it different from surrounding areas
resources	materials found on Earth that people need and value

WORDS ABOUT PEOPLE

anthropology	the study of people and cultures
archaeology	the study of the past based on what people left behind
citizen	a person who lives under the control of a government
civilization	the way of life of people in a particular place or time
culture	the knowledge, beliefs, customs, and values of a group of people
custom	a repeated practice or tradition
economics	the study of the production and use of goods and services
economy	any system in which people make and exchange goods and services
government	the body of officials and groups that run an area
history	the study of the past
politics	the process of running a government
religion	a system of beliefs in one or more gods or spirits
society	a group of people who share common traditions
trade	the exchange of goods or services

Academic Words

What are academic words? They are important words used in all of your classes, not just social studies. You will see these words in other textbooks, so you should learn what they mean while reading this book. Review this list now. You will use these words again in the chapters of this book.

Academic Words

acquire	to get	**features**	characteristics
affect	to change or influence	**impact**	effect, result
authority	power, right to rule	**implement**	to put in place
contracts	binding legal agreements	**method**	a way of doing something
distribute	to divide among a group of people	**process**	a series of steps by which a task is accomplished
execute	to perform, carry out		

> Academic Words features provide definitions for important terms that will help you understand social studies content.

ACADEMIC VOCABULARY

process a series of steps by which a task is accomplished

The exchange of gold and salt sometimes followed a process called silent barter. **Silent barter** is a process in which people exchange goods without ever contacting each other directly. The method made sure that the traders did business peacefully. It also kept the exact location of the gold mines secret from the salt traders.

In the silent barter process, salt traders went to a riverbank near gold fields. There they left slabs of salt in rows and beat a drum to tell the gold miners that trading had begun. Then the salt traders moved back several miles from the riverbank.

Soon afterward, the gold miners arrived by boat. They left what they considered a fair amount of gold in exchange for the salt. Then the gold miners also moved

back several miles so the salt traders could return. If they were happy with the amount of gold left there, the salt traders beat the drum again, took the gold, and left. The gold miners then returned and picked up their salt. Trading continued until both sides were happy with the exchange.

Growth of Trade

As the trade in gold and salt increased, Ghana's rulers gained power. Over time, their military strength grew as well. With their armies they began to take control of this trade from the merchants who had once controlled it. Merchants from the north and south met to exchange goods in Ghana. As a result of their control of trade routes, the rulers of Ghana became wealthy.

Additional sources of wealth and trade were developed to add to Ghana's wealth. Wheat came from the north. Sheep, cattle, and honey came from the south. Local products, including leather and cloth, were also traded for wealth. Among the prized special local products were tassels made from golden thread.

As trade increased, Ghana's capital grew as well. The largest city in West Africa, Koumbi Saleh (KOOM-bee SAHL-uh) was an oasis for travelers. These travelers could find all the region's goods for sale in its markets. As a result, Koumbi Saleh gained a reputation as a great trading center.

READING CHECK Generalizing How did trade help Ghana develop?

Ghana Builds an Empire

By 800 Ghana was firmly in control of West Africa's trade routes. Nearly all trade between northern and southern Africa passed through Ghana. Traders were protected by Ghana's army, which kept trade routes free from bandits. As a result, trade became safer. Knowing they would be protected, traders were not scared to travel to Ghana. Trade increased, and Ghana's influence grew as well.

Taxes and Gold

With so many traders passing through their lands, Ghana's rulers looked for ways to make money from them. One way they raised money was by forcing traders to pay taxes. Every trader who entered Ghana had to pay a special tax on the goods he carried. Then he had to pay another tax on any goods he took with him when he left.

Traders were not the only people who had to pay taxes. The people of Ghana also had to pay taxes. In addition, Ghana conquered many small neighboring tribes, then forced them to pay tribute. Rulers used the money from taxes and tribute to support Ghana's growing army.

Not all of Ghana's wealth came from taxes and tribute. Ghana's rich mines produced huge amounts of gold. Some of this gold was carried by traders to lands as far away as England, but not all of Ghana's gold was traded. Ghana's kings kept huge stores of gold for themselves. In fact, all the gold produced in Ghana was officially the property of the king.

Knowing that rare materials are worth far more than common ones, the rulers banned anyone else in Ghana from owning gold nuggets. Common people could own only gold dust, which they used as money. This ensured that the king was richer than his subjects.

Salt and Gold

Ghana's rulers became rich by controlling the trade in salt and gold. Salt came from the north in large slabs like the ones shown at left. Gold, like the woman above is wearing, came from the south.

Making This Book Work for You

Studying geography will be easy for you with this textbook. Take a few minutes now to become familiar with the easy-to-use structure and special features of your book. See how it will make geography come alive for you!

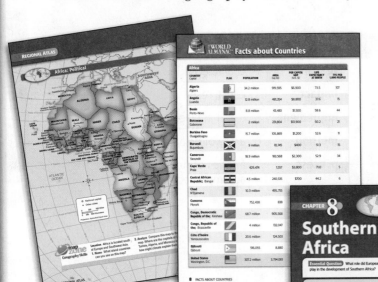

Your book begins with a satellite image, a regional atlas, and a table with facts about each country. Use these pages to get an overview of the region you will study.

Chapter

Each chapter includes an introduction, a Social Studies Skills activity, Chapter Review pages, and a Standardized Test Practice page.

Reading Social Studies Chapter reading lessons give you skills and practice to help you read the textbook. More help with each lesson can be found in the back of the book. Margin notes and questions in the chapter make sure you understand the reading skill.

Social Studies Skills The Social Studies Skills lessons give you an opportunity to learn, practice, and apply an important skill. Chapter Review questions then follow up on what you learned.

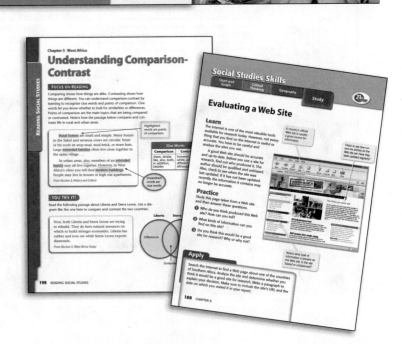

Section

The section opener pages include Main Ideas, an overarching Big Idea, and Key Terms and Places. In addition, each section includes these special features.

If YOU Lived There . . . Each section begins with a situation for you to respond to, placing you in a place that relates to the content you will be studying in the section.

Building Background Building Background connects what will be covered in each section with what you already know.

Short Sections of Content The information in each section is organized into small chunks of text that you can easily understand.

Taking Notes Suggested graphic organizers help you read and take notes on the important ideas in the section.

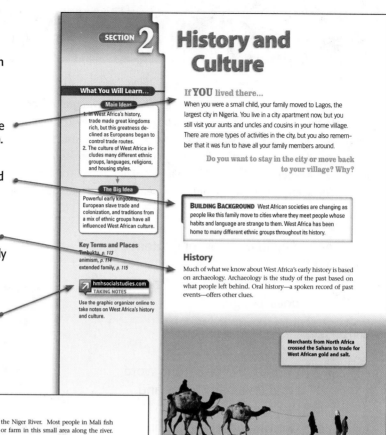

SECTION 2

History and Culture

What You Will Learn...

Main Ideas
1. In West Africa's history, trade made great kingdoms rich, but this greatness declined as Europeans began to control trade routes.
2. The culture of West Africa includes many different ethnic groups, languages, religions, and housing styles.

The Big Idea
Powerful early kingdoms, European slave trade and colonization, and traditions from a mix of ethnic groups have all influenced West African culture.

Key Terms and Places
Timbuktu, p. 113
animism, p. 114
extended family, p. 115

hmhsocialstudies.com
TAKING NOTES

Use the graphic organizer online to take notes on West Africa's history and culture.

If YOU lived there...
When you were a small child, your family moved to Lagos, the largest city in Nigeria. You live in a city apartment now, but you still visit your aunts and uncles and cousins in your home village. There are more types of activities in the city, but you also remember that it was fun to have all your family members around.

Do you want to stay in the city or move back to your village? Why?

BUILDING BACKGROUND West African societies are changing as people like this family move to cities where they meet people whose habits and language are strange to them. West Africa has been home to many different ethnic groups throughout its history.

History
Much of what we know about West Africa's early history is based on archaeology. Archaeology is the study of the past based on what people left behind. Oral history—a spoken record of past events—offers other clues.

Merchants from North Africa crossed the Sahara to trade for West African gold and salt.

---

the Niger River. Most people in Mali fish or farm in this small area along the river. Cotton and gold are Mali's main exports.

Mali's economy does have some bright spots, however. A fairly stable democratic government has begun economic reforms. Also, the ancient cities of Timbuktu and Gao (GOW) continue to attract tourists.

Burkina Faso is also a poor country. It has thin soil and few mineral resources. Few trees remain in or near the capital, Ouagadougou (wah-gah-DOO-goo), because they have been cut for firewood and building material. Jobs in the city are also scarce. To support their families many men try to find work in other countries. Thus, when unrest disrupts work opportunities in other countries, Burkina Faso's economy suffers.

READING CHECK Summarizing What are the challenges facing Chad and Burkina Faso?

SUMMARY AND PREVIEW Countries in West Africa struggle with poor economies. In addition, many have faced political instability since independence. In the next chapter, you will learn about how the countries in East Africa face some similar issues.

Water well

Dry Croplands
This aerial view shows how, with just a little water, people can farm in the dry Sahel.

The future may hold more promise for Chad. A long civil war finally ended in the 1990s. Also, oil was recently discovered there, and Chad began to export this valuable resource in 2004.

Mali and Burkina Faso
The Sahara covers about 40 percent of the land in Mali. The scarce amount of land available for farming makes Mali among the world's poorest countries. The available farmland lies in the southwest, along

---

Section 3 Assessment

hmhsocialstudies.com
ONLINE QUIZ

Reviewing Ideas, Terms, and Places
1. **a. Recall** Why did the Igbo try to **secede**?
   b. Evaluate What do you think were some benefits and drawbacks to Nigeria's leaders moving the capital from **Lagos** to Abuja?
2. **a. Identify** What is West Africa's only island country?
   b. Compare What are some similarities between Togo and Benin?
   c. Elaborate Why do you think countries with poor economies often have unstable governments?
3. **a. Describe** What caused **famine** in Niger?
   b. Evaluate What do you think is the biggest problem facing the Sahel countries? Explain.

Critical Thinking
4. **Compare and Contrast** Review your notes on the coastal countries and the Sahel countries. Then use a diagram like the one here to compare and contrast the two regions.

Coastal   Sahel

FOCUS ON SPEAKING
5. **Describing Countries of West Africa** Think about the countries of West Africa. Which one might be a good location for the person you are going to describe? Take some notes about that place.

122 CHAPTER 5

Reading Check Questions end each section of content so you can check to make sure you understand what you just studied.

Summary and Preview The Summary and Preview connects what you studied in the section to what you will study in the next section.

Section Assessment Finally, the section assessment boxes make sure that you understand the main ideas of the section. We also provide assessment practice online!

Scavenger Hunt

Are you ready to explore the world of geography? *Holt McDougal: Africa* is your ticket to this exciting world. Before you begin your journey, complete this scavenger hunt to get to know your book and discover what's inside.

On a separate sheet of paper, fill in the blanks to complete each sentence below. In each answer, one letter will be in a yellow box. When you have answered every question, copy these letters in order to reveal the answer to the question at the bottom of the page.

1 According to the Table of Contents, the title of Chapter 2 is History of ☐☐☐☐☐☐ Kush. On what page does it begin?

2 On page 97, the second word listed under Key Terms and Places is ☐☐☐☐☐☐☐. On what page will you find this word used?

3 The Case Study that begins on page 154 is called Mapping Central Africa's ☐☐☐☐☐☐☐.

4 Page 225 is the beginning of the ☐☐☐☐☐☐☐ and Spanish Glossary. What is the first term listed?

5 On pages 138–139, there is a Close-up illustration of the ☐☐☐☐☐☐☐☐☐ Plain. What can you see in this illustration?

6 The Literature selection on page 123 is called ☐☐☐ : The Years of Childhood. Who wrote this selection?

7 The Biography on page 28 is about Queen ☐☐☐☐☐☐☐☐☐. When did she live?

Fact!

The world's fastest land animal lives on the plains of southern and eastern Africa. What is it?

☐☐☐☐☐☐☐

Africa

The Sahara

The world's largest desert, the Sahara, dominates land and life in North Africa.

Savannas

Grassy plains called savannas stretch across large parts of the continent and are home to much African wildlife.

Africa

Rift Valleys

In East Africa, Earth's crust is slowly being pulled apart. This causes hills, long lakes, and wide "rift valleys" to form.

Explore the Satellite Image A huge continent, Africa is home to many different kinds of physical features. Based on this satellite image, how would you describe Africa's physical geography?

The Satellite's Path

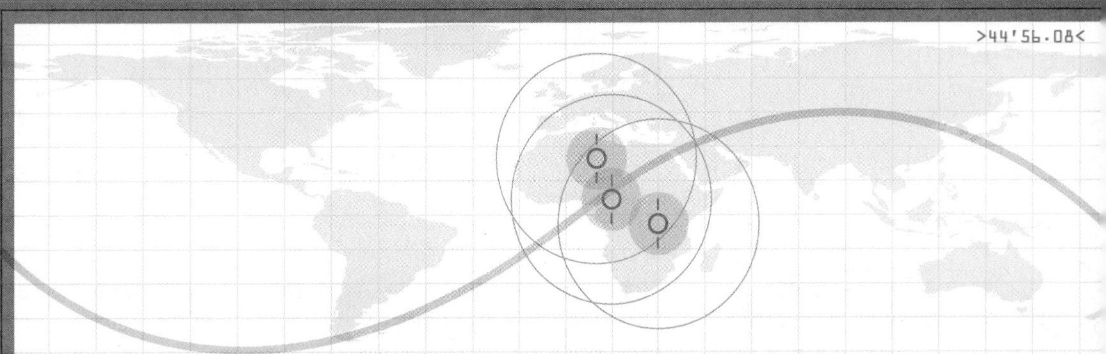

>44'56.08<

>>>>>>>>>665.00'87<

+803
+799

+669

+355

567.476.348

456.094.

Africa: Physical

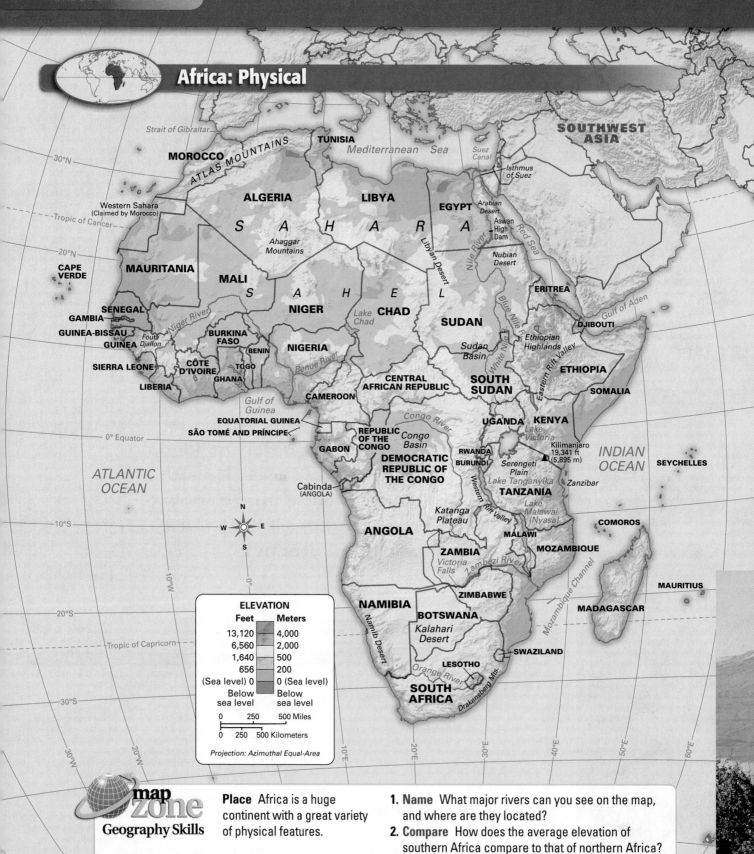

Strait of Gibraltar

SOUTHWEST ASIA

Mediterranean Sea

Suez Canal

Isthmus of Suez

30°N

MOROCCO

ATLAS MOUNTAINS

TUNISIA

ALGERIA

LIBYA

EGYPT

Arabian Desert

Aswan High Dam

Western Sahara (Claimed by Morocco)

Tropic of Cancer

S   A   H   A   R   A

Ahaggar Mountains

Libyan Desert

Nile River

Red Sea

Nubian Desert

20°N

CAPE VERDE

MAURITANIA

MALI

S   A   H   E   L

NIGER

CHAD

Lake Chad

SUDAN

ERITREA

Blue Nile River

Gulf of Aden

DJIBOUTI

SENEGAL

GAMBIA

Niger River

BURKINA FASO

Sudan Basin

White Nile River

Ethiopian Highlands

Eastern Rift Valley

GUINEA-BISSAU

GUINEA

Fouta Djallon

BENIN

NIGERIA

ETHIOPIA

SIERRA LEONE

CÔTE D'IVOIRE

TOGO

Benue River

CENTRAL AFRICAN REPUBLIC

SOUTH SUDAN

SOMALIA

LIBERIA

GHANA

CAMEROON

Gulf of Guinea

Congo River

UGANDA

KENYA

EQUATORIAL GUINEA

SÃO TOMÉ AND PRÍNCIPE

0° Equator

Lake Victoria

REPUBLIC OF THE CONGO

Congo Basin

GABON

Cabinda (ANGOLA)

DEMOCRATIC REPUBLIC OF THE CONGO

RWANDA

BURUNDI

Kilimanjaro 19,341 ft (5,895 m)

INDIAN OCEAN

SEYCHELLES

Serengeti Plain

Lake Tanganyika

Zanzibar

ATLANTIC OCEAN

Western Rift Valley

TANZANIA

Lake Malawi (Nyasa)

COMOROS

10°S

Katanga Plateau

MALAWI

MOZAMBIQUE

ANGOLA

ZAMBIA

MAURITIUS

Victoria Falls

Zambezi River

Mozambique Channel

MADAGASCAR

20°S

NAMIBIA

ZIMBABWE

BOTSWANA

Kalahari Desert

Namib Desert

SWAZILAND

Tropic of Capricorn

LESOTHO

Orange River

Drakensberg Mts.

30°S

SOUTH AFRICA

ELEVATION

Feet	Meters
13,120	4,000
6,560	2,000
1,640	500
656	200
(Sea level) 0	0 (Sea level)
Below sea level	Below sea level

0   250   500 Miles

0   250   500 Kilometers

Projection: Azimuthal Equal-Area

N W E S

map zone
Geography Skills

Place Africa is a huge continent with a great variety of physical features.

1. **Name** What major rivers can you see on the map, and where are they located?

2. **Compare** How does the average elevation of southern Africa compare to that of northern Africa?

THE WORLD ALMANAC®
Facts about the World

Geographical Extremes: Africa

Longest River	Nile River, Egypt: 4,160 miles (6,693 km)	**Driest Place**	Wadi Halfa, Sudan: .1 inches (.3 cm) average precipitation per year
Highest Point	Mount Kilimanjaro, Tanzania: 19,340 feet (5,895 m)	**Largest Country**	Algeria: 919,595 square miles (2,381,740 square km)
Lowest Point	Lake Assal, Djibouti: 512 feet (156 m) below sea level	**Smallest Country**	Seychelles: 176 square miles (455 square km)
Highest Recorded Temperature	El Azizia, Libya: 136°F (57.8°C)	**Largest Desert**	Sahara: 3,500,000 square miles (9,065,000 square km)
Lowest Recorded Temperature	Ifrane, Morocco: -11°F (-23.9°C)	**Largest Island**	Madagascar: 226,658 square miles (587,044 square km)
Wettest Place	Debundscha, Cameroon: 405 inches (1,028.7 cm) average precipitation per year	**Highest Waterfall**	Tugela, South Africa: 2,800 feet (853 m)

↗ hmhsocialstudies.com

Size Comparison: The United States and Africa

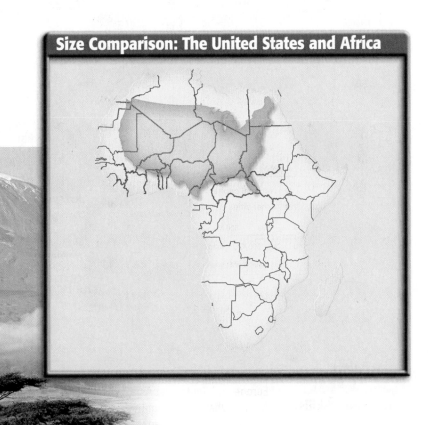

Mount Kilimanjaro, Tanzania

Africa: Political

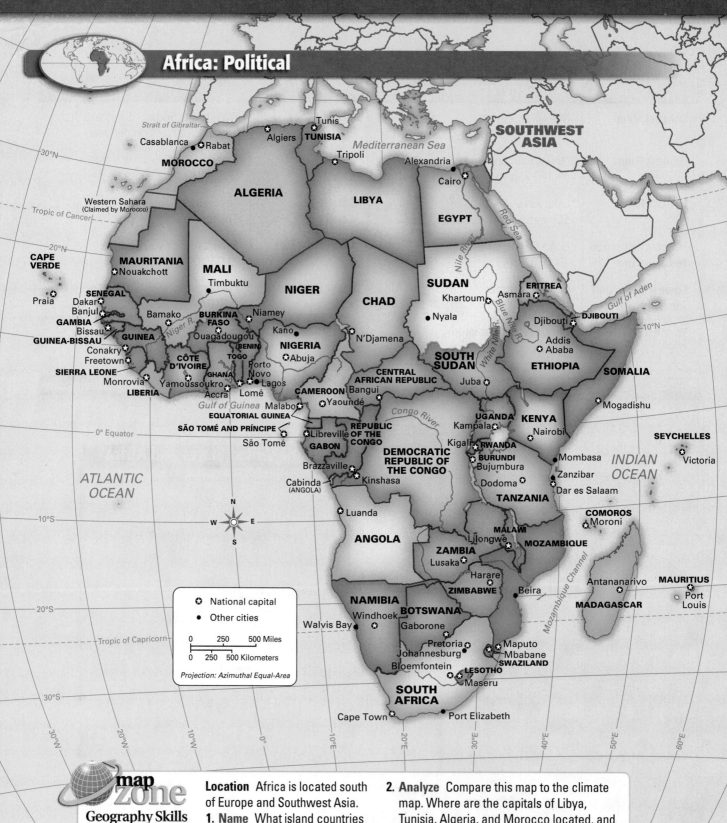

Strait of Gibraltar

Casablanca
Rabat
MOROCCO

Algiers
TUNISIA
Tunis

SOUTHWEST ASIA

Tripoli

Mediterranean Sea

Alexandria
Cairo

30°N

Western Sahara
(Claimed by Morocco)

ALGERIA

LIBYA

EGYPT

Tropic of Cancer

Red Sea

20°N

CAPE VERDE

MAURITANIA
Nouakchott

MALI
Timbuktu

NIGER

CHAD

SUDAN
Khartoum

Nyala

ERITREA
Asmara

Gulf of Aden

Praia

SENEGAL
Dakar
Banjul

Bamako

BURKINA FASO
Niamey

Nile River

DJIBOUTI
Djibouti

10°N

GAMBIA

GUINEA-BISSAU
Bissau

GUINEA
Conakry

Kano

Ouagadougou

BENIN

NIGERIA
Abuja

N'Djamena

Blue Nile R.

Addis Ababa

Niger R.

SOUTH SUDAN

White Nile

ETHIOPIA

SOMALIA

Freetown

CÔTE D'IVOIRE

TOGO
GHANA

Porto Novo

CENTRAL AFRICAN REPUBLIC

Juba

SIERRA LEONE
Monrovia
Yamoussoukro

Lagos
Lomé

Accra
LIBERIA

CAMEROON
Bangui

UGANDA
Kampala

KENYA
Nairobi

Mogadishu

SEYCHELLES

0° Equator

Gulf of Guinea
Malabo

Yaoundé

Congo River

Kigali
RWANDA
BURUNDI
Bujumbura

Mombasa

Victoria

EQUATORIAL GUINEA
SÃO TOMÉ AND PRÍNCIPE
São Tomé

Libreville
REPUBLIC OF THE CONGO

GABON

DEMOCRATIC REPUBLIC OF THE CONGO

Dodoma

Zanzibar

INDIAN OCEAN

ATLANTIC OCEAN

Brazzaville

Kinshasa

Dar es Salaam

TANZANIA

Cabinda
(ANGOLA)

COMOROS
Moroni

10°S

Luanda

ANGOLA

ZAMBIA
Lusaka

MALAWI
Lilongwe

MOZAMBIQUE

MAURITIUS

Harare

Antananarivo

Port Louis

20°S

NAMIBIA
Windhoek

ZIMBABWE

Beira

MADAGASCAR

Mozambique Channel

Walvis Bay

BOTSWANA
Gaborone

National capital
Other cities

Pretoria
Johannesburg
Bloemfontein

Maputo
Mbabane
SWAZILAND

0   250   500 Miles

0   250   500 Kilometers

LESOTHO
Maseru

Projection: Azimuthal Equal-Area

SOUTH AFRICA

30°S

Cape Town

Port Elizabeth

30°W   20°W   10°W   0°   10°E   20°E   30°E   40°E   50°E   60°E

map zone
Geography Skills

Location Africa is located south of Europe and Southwest Asia.
1. Name What island countries can you see on this map?

2. Analyze Compare this map to the climate map. Where are the capitals of Libya, Tunisia, Algeria, and Morocco located, and how might climate explain their locations?

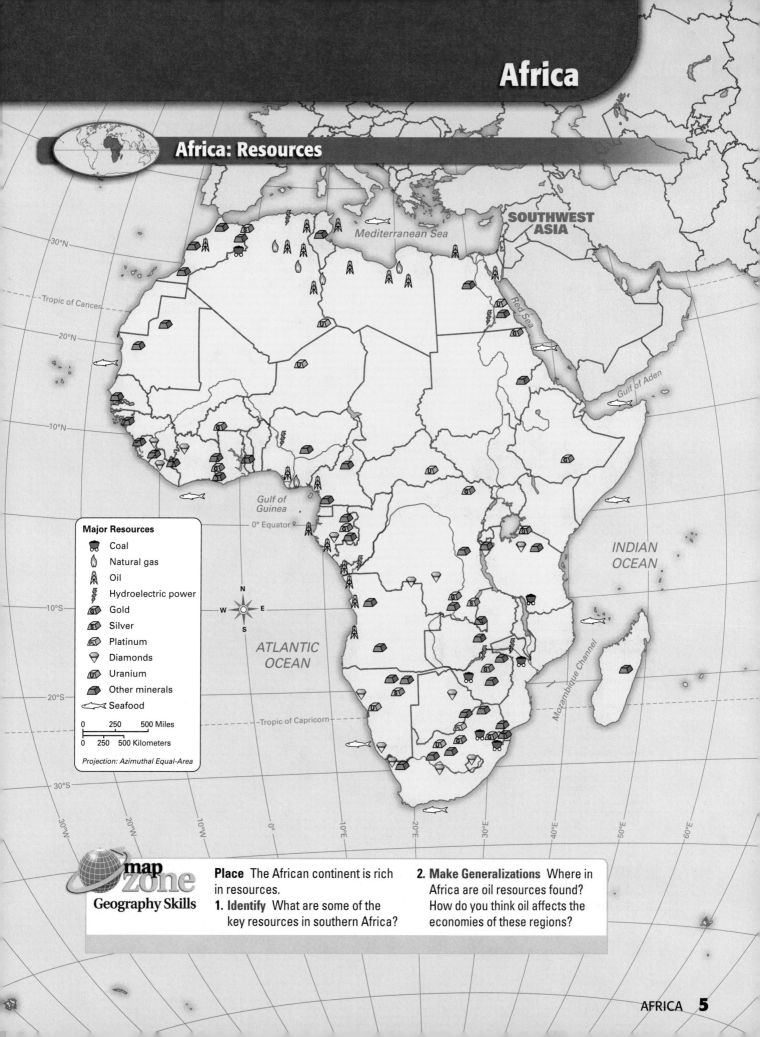

Africa

SOUTHWEST ASIA

Mediterranean Sea

Red Sea

Gulf of Aden

Tropic of Cancer

30°N

20°N

10°N

Gulf of Guinea

0° Equator

INDIAN OCEAN

Major Resources

- Coal
- Natural gas
- Oil
- Hydroelectric power
- Gold
- Silver
- Platinum
- Diamonds
- Uranium
- Other minerals
- Seafood

| 0 | 250 | 500 Miles |
| 0 | 250 | 500 Kilometers |

Projection: Azimuthal Equal-Area

10°S

ATLANTIC OCEAN

Mozambique Channel

20°S

Tropic of Capricorn

30°S

30°W 20°W 10°W 0° 10°E 20°E 30°E 40°E 50°E 60°E

map zone
Geography Skills

Place The African continent is rich in resources.

1. Identify What are some of the key resources in southern Africa?

2. Make Generalizations Where in Africa are oil resources found? How do you think oil affects the economies of these regions?

Africa: Population

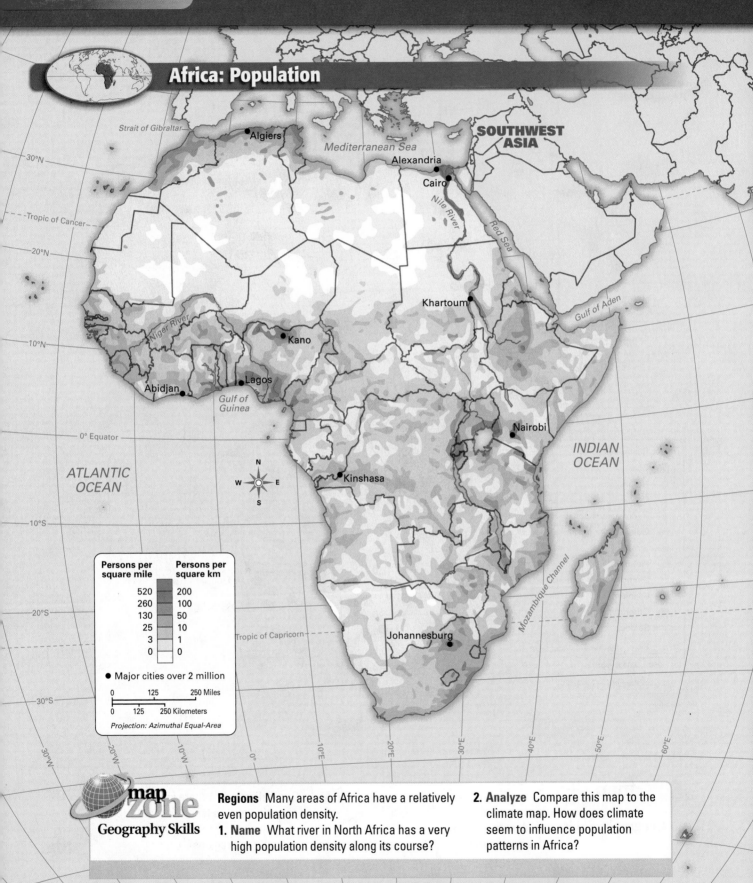

Strait of Gibraltar

Algiers

Mediterranean Sea

Alexandria

Cairo

SOUTHWEST ASIA

Nile River

Red Sea

30°N

Tropic of Cancer

20°N

Khartoum

Gulf of Aden

Niger River

10°N

Kano

Lagos

Abidjan

Gulf of Guinea

Nairobi

INDIAN OCEAN

0° Equator

ATLANTIC OCEAN

N W E S

Kinshasa

10°S

Mozambique Channel

Persons per square mile	**Persons per square km**
520	200
260	100
130	50
25	10
3	1
0	0

20°S

Tropic of Capricorn

Johannesburg

● Major cities over 2 million

0   125   250 Miles
0   125   250 Kilometers

Projection: Azimuthal Equal-Area

30°S

30°W   20°W   10°W   0°   10°E   20°E   30°E   40°E   50°E   60°E

map zone
Geography Skills

Regions Many areas of Africa have a relatively even population density.

1. Name What river in North Africa has a very high population density along its course?

2. Analyze Compare this map to the climate map. How does climate seem to influence population patterns in Africa?

Africa: Climate

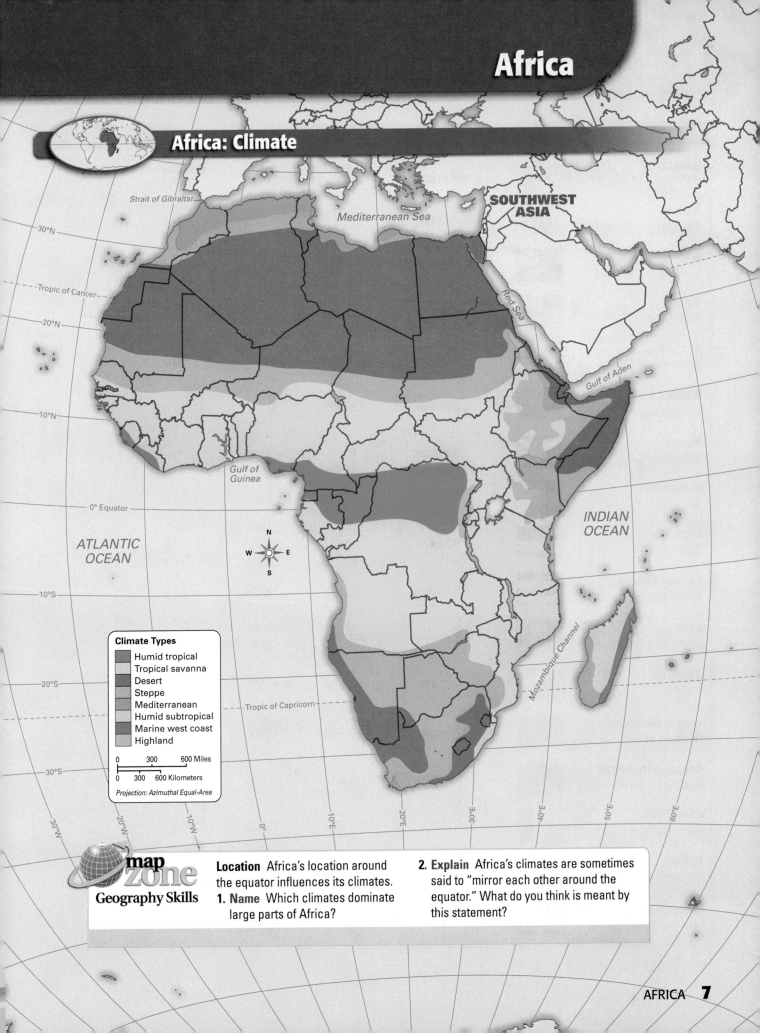

Strait of Gibraltar

Mediterranean Sea

SOUTHWEST ASIA

30°N

Tropic of Cancer

20°N

Red Sea

Gulf of Aden

10°N

Gulf of Guinea

0° Equator

ATLANTIC OCEAN

N
W   E
S

INDIAN OCEAN

10°S

Mozambique Channel

Climate Types
- Humid tropical
- Tropical savanna
- Desert
- Steppe
- Mediterranean
- Humid subtropical
- Marine west coast
- Highland

20°S

0   300   600 Miles
0   300   600 Kilometers

Projection: Azimuthal Equal-Area

Tropic of Capricorn

30°S

30°W   20°W   10°W   0°   10°E   20°E   30°E   40°E   50°E   60°E

map zone
Geography Skills

Location Africa's location around the equator influences its climates.

1. Name Which climates dominate large parts of Africa?

2. Explain Africa's climates are sometimes said to "mirror each other around the equator." What do you think is meant by this statement?

Africa

COUNTRY Capital	FLAG	POPULATION	AREA (sq mi)	PER CAPITA GDP (U.S. $)	LIFE EXPECTANCY AT BIRTH	TVS PER 1,000 PEOPLE
Algeria Algiers		34.2 million	919,595	$6,900	73.5	107
Angola Luanda		12.8 million	481,354	$8,800	37.6	15
Benin Porto-Novo		8.8 million	43,483	$1,500	58.6	44
Botswana Gaborone		2 million	231,804	$13,900	50.2	21
Burkina Faso Ouagadougou		15.7 million	105,869	$1,200	52.6	11
Burundi Bujumbura		9 million	10,745	$400	51.3	15
Cameroon Yaoundé		18.9 million	183,568	$2,300	52.9	34
Cape Verde Praia		429,474	1,557	$3,800	71.0	5
Central African Republic; Bangui		4.5 million	240,535	$700	44.2	6
Chad N'Djamena		10.3 million	495,755	$1,600	47.9	1
Comoros Moroni		752,438	838	$1,000	62.7	4
Congo, Democratic Republic of the; Kinshasa		68.7 million	905,568	$300	54	2
Congo, Republic of the; Brazzaville		4 million	132,047	$3,900	53.3	13
Côte d'Ivoire Yamoussoukro		20.6 million	124,503	$1,700	54.7	65
Djibouti Djibouti		516,055	8,880	$3,700	43.3	48
United States Washington, D.C.		307.2 million	3,794,083	$46,900	78.2	844

COUNTRY Capital	FLAG	POPULATION	AREA (sq mi)	PER CAPITA GDP (U.S. $)	LIFE EXPECTANCY AT BIRTH	TVS PER 1,000 PEOPLE
Egypt Cairo		83.1 million	386,662	$5,400	71.6	170
Equatorial Guinea Malabo		633,441	10,831	$37,200	61.3	116
Eritrea Asmara		5.6 million	46,842	$700	61.5	16
Ethiopia Addis Ababa		85.2 million	435,186	$800	55	5
Gabon Libreville		1.5 million	103,347	$14,200	54.0	251
Gambia, The Banjul		1.8 million	4,363	$1,300	54.5	3
Ghana Accra		23.8 million	92,456	$1,500	59.1	115
Guinea Conakry		10.1 million	94,926	$1,100	56.6	47
Guinea-Bissau Bissau		1.5 million	13,946	$600	47.2	43
Kenya Nairobi		39 million	224,962	$1,600	56.7	22
Lesotho Maseru		2.1 million	11,720	$1,500	40.2	16
Liberia Monrovia		3.4 million	43,000	$500	40.4	26
Libya Tripoli		6.3 million	679,362	$14,400	76.9	139
Madagascar Antananarivo		20.7 million	226,657	$1,000	62.1	23
Malawi Lilongwe		14.3 million	45,745	$800	43.0	3
United States Washington, D.C.		307.2 million	3,794,083	$46,900	78.2	844

COUNTRY Capital	FLAG	POPULATION	AREA (sq mi)	PER CAPITA GDP (U.S. $)	LIFE EXPECTANCY AT BIRTH	TVS PER 1,000 PEOPLE
Mali Bamako		12.7 million	478,767	$1,200	49.5	13
Mauritania Nouakchott		3.1 million	397,955	$2,100	53.5	95
Mauritius Port Louis		1.3 million	788	$12,000	73.9	248
Morocco Rabat		34.9 million	172,414	$4,000	71.2	165
Mozambique Maputo		21.7 million	309,496	$900	40.9	5
Namibia Windhoek		2.1 million	318,696	$6,300	49.9	38
Niger Niamey		15.3 million	489,191	$700	44.3	15
Nigeria Abuja		149.2 million	356,669	$2,300	46.6	69
Rwanda Kigali		10.5 million	10,169	$1,000	49.0	0.09
São Tomé and Príncipe; São Tomé		212,679	387	$1,300	67.6	229
Senegal Dakar		13.7 million	75,749	$1,600	56.7	41
Seychelles Victoria		87,476	176	$19,800	72.3	214
Sierra Leone Freetown		6.4 million	27,699	$700	40.6	13
Somalia Mogadishu		9.8 million	246,201	$600	48.8	14
United States Washington, D.C.		307.2 million	3,794,083	$46,900	78.2	844

COUNTRY Capital	FLAG	POPULATION	AREA (sq mi)	PER CAPITA GDP (U.S. $)	LIFE EXPECTANCY AT BIRTH	TVS PER 1,000 PEOPLE
South Africa; Pretoria, Cape Town, Bloemfontein		49.1 million	471,011	$10,100	48.9	138
South Sudan Juba		8.3 million	248,777	—	—	—
Sudan Khartoum		42.4 million	718,723	$2,200*	50.3*	173*
				* Data for Sudan and South Sudan combined (2011)		
Swaziland Mbabane		1.1 million	6,704	$5,100	32.2	112
Tanzania Dar es Salaam, Dodoma		41 million	364,900	$1,300	51.5	21
Togo Lomé		6 million	21,925	$900	57.9	22
Tunisia Tunis		10.5 million	63,170	$7,900	75.3	190
Uganda Kampala		32.4 million	91,136	$1,300	51.8	28
Zambia Lusaka		11.9 million	290,586	$1,500	38.4	145
Zimbabwe Harare		11.4 million	150,804	$200	44.3	35
United States Washington, D.C.		307.2 million	3,794,083	$46,900	78.2	844

Africa's Growing Population

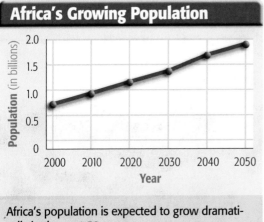

Africa's population is expected to grow dramatically in the next 50 years.

Africa and the World

	Average Age	Life Expec- tancy at Birth	Per Capita GDP (in U.S. $)
Africa	19.3 years	51.9	$2,800
Rest of the World	28.0 years	65.7	$10,000

Compared to the rest of the world, Africa's population is younger, has a shorter life expectancy, and has less money.

ANALYSIS SKILL ANALYZING INFORMATION

1. Based on the information above, what do you think are some key challenges in Africa today?

History of Ancient Egypt

4500–500 BC

Essential Question What were the major accomplishments of ancient Egypt?

What You Will Learn...

In this chapter you will learn about the fascinating civilization of ancient Egypt and how it developed along the Nile River.

FOCUS ON READING AND WRITING

Categorizing A good way to make sense of what you read is to separate facts and details into groups called categories. For example, you could sort facts about ancient Egypt into categories like geography, history, and culture. As you read this chapter, look for ways to categorize the information you are learning. **See the lesson, Categorizing, on page 194.**

Writing a Riddle In this chapter you will read about the civilization of the ancient Egyptians. In ancient times a sphinx, and imaginary creature like the sculpture in Egypt shown on the next page, was suppose to have demanded the answer to a riddle. People died if they did not answer the riddle correctly. After you read this chapter, you will write a riddle. The answer to your riddle should be "Egypt."

— Tropic of Cancer —

— 20°N —

map zone

Geography Skills

Location The civilization of ancient Egypt developed along the fertile Nile River.
1. **Name** What other bodies of water are near Egypt?
2. **Make Inferences** Based on the land around ancient Egypt, why do you think the Nile was so important to life?

| 0 | 75 | 150 Miles |
| 0 | 75 | 150 Kilometers |

Projection: Lambert Equal-Area

The Gift of the Nile The fertile land along the Nile River drew early people to the region. Cities are still found along the Nile today.

Ancient Egypt, 4500–500 BC

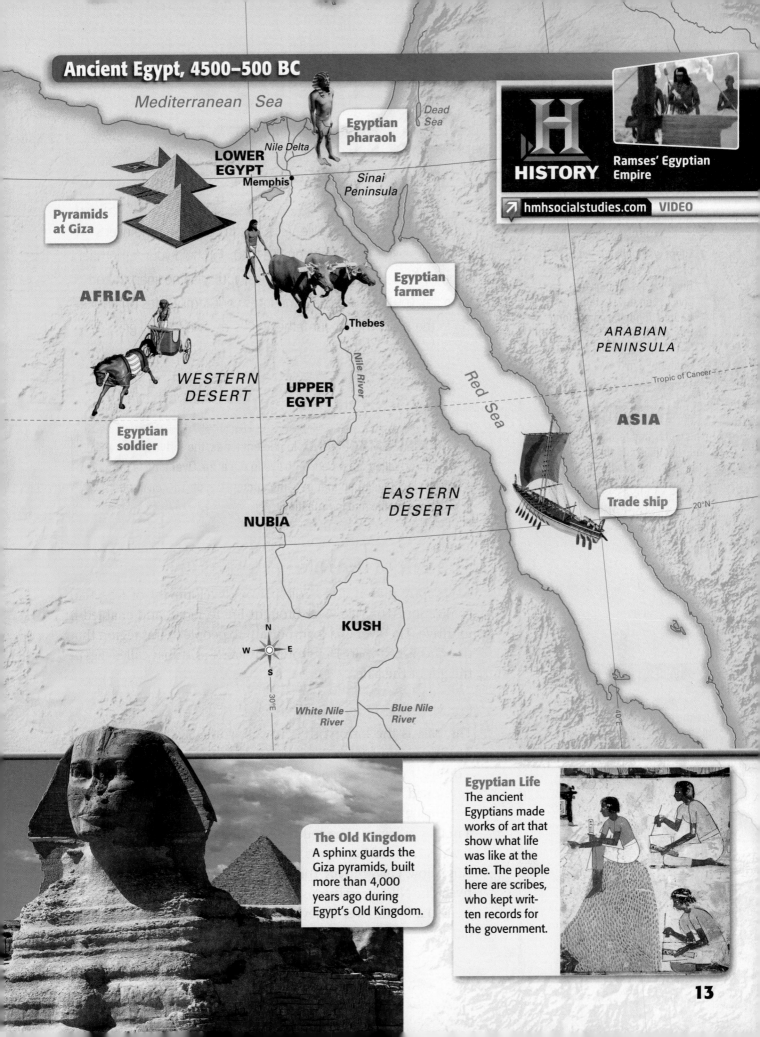

Mediterranean Sea

Egyptian pharaoh

Dead Sea

Nile Delta

LOWER EGYPT

Memphis

Sinai Peninsula

Pyramids at Giza

AFRICA

Egyptian farmer

Thebes

Nile River

WESTERN DESERT

UPPER EGYPT

ARABIAN PENINSULA

Tropic of Cancer

Egyptian soldier

ASIA

Red Sea

EASTERN DESERT

Trade ship

20°N

NUBIA

KUSH

N W E S

30°E

40°E

White Nile River   *Blue Nile River*

HISTORY

Ramses' Egyptian Empire

hmhsocialstudies.com VIDEO

The Old Kingdom
A sphinx guards the Giza pyramids, built more than 4,000 years ago during Egypt's Old Kingdom.

Egyptian Life
The ancient Egyptians made works of art that show what life was like at the time. The people here are scribes, who kept written records for the government.

13

Geography and Early Egypt

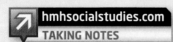
If YOU lived there...

Your family farms in the Nile Valley. Each year when the river's floodwaters spread rich soil on the land, you help your father plant barley. When you are not in the fields, you spin fine linen thread from flax you have grown. Sometimes your family goes on an outing to the river, where your father hunts birds in the tall grasses.

Why do you like living in the Nile Valley?

BUILDING BACKGROUND In ancient times, the fertile land in the Nile River Valley drew people to live in the area. Over time, a farming civilization developed that became ancient Egypt. This civilization would be stable and long-lasting.

The Gift of the Nile

Geography played a key role in the development of Egyptian civilization. The **Nile River** brought life to Egypt and enabled it to thrive. The river was so important to people in this region that the Greek historian Herodotus (hi-RAHD-uh-tuhs) called Egypt the gift of the Nile.

Location and Physical Features

The Nile is the longest river in the world. It begins in central Africa and runs north through Egypt to the Mediterranean Sea, a distance of over 4,000 miles. The civilization of ancient Egypt developed along a 750-mile stretch of the Nile.

Ancient Egypt included two regions, a southern region and a northern region. The southern region was called **Upper Egypt**. It was so named because it was located upriver in relation to the Nile's flow. **Lower Egypt**, the northern region, was located downriver. The Nile sliced through the desert of Upper Egypt. There, it created a fertile river valley about 13 miles wide. On either side of the Nile lay hundreds of miles of bleak desert sands.

As you can see on the map, the Nile flowed through rocky, hilly land to the south of Egypt. At several points, this rough terrain caused **cataracts**, or rapids, to form. The first cataract was located 720 miles south of the Mediterranean Sea. This cataract, shown by a red bar on the map, marked the southern border of Upper Egypt. Five more cataracts lay farther south. These cataracts made sailing on that portion of the Nile very difficult.

In Lower Egypt, the Nile divided into several branches that fanned out and flowed into the Mediterranean Sea. These branches formed a **delta**, a triangle-shaped area of land made from soil deposited by a river. At the time of ancient Egypt, swamps and marshes covered much of the Nile Delta. Some two-thirds of Egypt's fertile farmland was located in the Nile Delta.

The Floods of the Nile

Because little rain fell in the region, most of Egypt was desert. Each year, however, rain fell far to the south of Egypt in the highlands of East Africa. This rainfall caused the Nile River to flood. Almost every year, the Nile flooded Upper Egypt in mid-summer and Lower Egypt in the fall.

The Nile's flooding coated the land around it with a rich silt. This silt made the soil ideal for farming. The silt also made the land a dark color. That is why Egyptians called their country the black land. They called the dry, lifeless desert beyond the river valley the red land.

Each year, Egyptians eagerly awaited the flooding of the Nile River. For them, the river's floods were a life-giving miracle. Without the Nile's regular flooding, people never could have farmed in Egypt. The Nile truly was a gift to Egypt.

READING CHECK **Finding Main Ideas** Why was Egypt called the gift of the Nile?

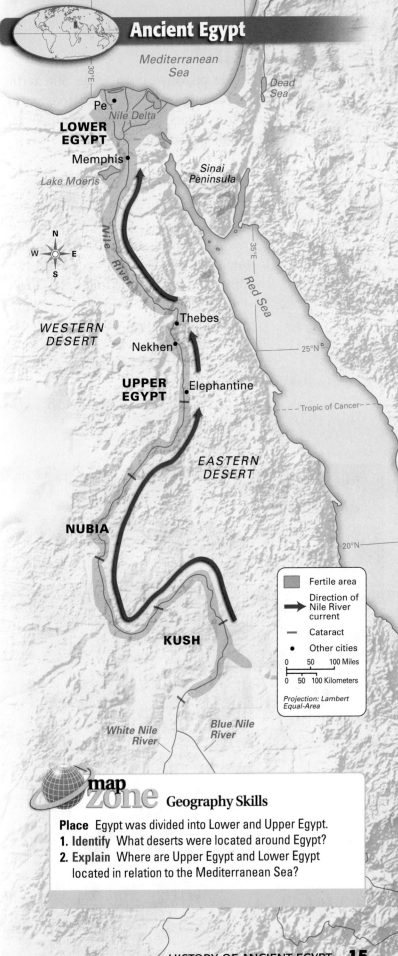

Ancient Egypt

map zone Geography Skills

Place Egypt was divided into Lower and Upper Egypt.
1. **Identify** What deserts were located around Egypt?
2. **Explain** Where are Upper Egypt and Lower Egypt located in relation to the Mediterranean Sea?

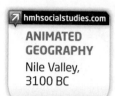
Civilization Develops in Egypt

The Nile provided both water and fertile soil for farming. Over time, scattered farms grew into villages and cities. Eventually, an Egyptian civilization developed.

Increased Food Production

Hunter-gatherers first moved into the Nile Valley more than 12,000 years ago. They found plants, wild animals, and fish there to eat. In time, these people learned how to farm, and they settled along the Nile. By 4500 BC, farmers living in small villages grew wheat and barley.

Over time, farmers in Egypt developed an irrigation system. This system consisted of a series of canals that directed the Nile's flow and carried water to the fields.

The Nile provided Egyptian farmers with an abundance of food. Farmers in Egypt grew wheat, barley, fruits, and vegetables. They also raised cattle and sheep. The river provided many types of fish, and hunters trapped wild geese and ducks along its banks. With these many sources of food, the Egyptians enjoyed a varied diet.

Two Kingdoms

In addition to a stable food supply, Egypt's location offered another advantage. It had natural barriers, which made it hard to invade Egypt. To the west, the desert was too big and harsh to cross. To the north, the Mediterranean Sea kept many enemies away. To the east, more desert and the Red Sea provided protection. Finally, to the south, cataracts in the Nile made it difficult for invaders to sail into Egypt that way.

Farming in Egypt

Protected from invaders, the villages of Egypt grew. Wealthy farmers emerged as village leaders. In time, strong leaders gained control over several villages. By 3200 BC, villages had grown and banded together to create two kingdoms—Lower Egypt and Upper Egypt.

Each kingdom had its own capital city where its ruler was based. The capital city of Lower Egypt was Pe, located in the Nile Delta. There, wearing a red crown, the king of Lower Egypt ruled. The capital city of Upper Egypt was Nekhen, located on the Nile's west bank. In this southern kingdom, the king wore a cone-shaped white crown. For centuries, Egyptians referred to their country as the two lands.

READING CHECK **Summarizing** What attracted early settlers to the Nile Valley?

Farmers in ancient Egypt learned how to grow wheat and barley. The tomb painting at left shows a couple harvesting their crop. As the photo above shows, people in Egypt still farm along the Nile.

ANALYZING VISUALS Based on the above photo, what methods do Egyptian farmers use today?

Kings Unify Egypt

According to tradition, around 3100 BC Menes (MEE-neez) rose to power in Upper Egypt. Some historians think Menes is a myth and that his accomplishments were really those of other ancient kings named Aha, Scorpion, or Narmer.

Menes wanted to unify the kingdoms of Upper and Lower Egypt. He had his armies invade Lower Egypt and take control of it. Menes then married a princess from Lower Egypt to strengthen his control over the newly unified country.

Menes wore both the white crown of Upper Egypt and the red crown of Lower Egypt to symbolize his leadership over the two kingdoms. Later, he combined the two crowns into a double crown, as you can see on the next page.

Many historians consider Menes to be Egypt's first **pharaoh** (FEHR-oh), the title used by the rulers of ancient Egypt. The title *pharaoh* means "great house." Menes also founded Egypt's first **dynasty**, or series of rulers from the same family.

Menes built a new capital city at the southern tip of the Nile Delta. The city was later named Memphis. It was near where Lower Egypt met Upper Egypt, close to what is now Cairo, Egypt. For centuries, Memphis was the political and cultural center of Egypt. Many government offices were located there, and the city bustled with artistic activity.

Egypt's First Dynasty was a theocracy that lasted for about 200 years. A theocracy is a government ruled by religious leaders such as priests or a monarch thought to be divine.

Over time, Egypt's rulers extended Egyptian territory southward along the Nile River and into Southwest Asia. They also improved irrigation and trade, making Egypt wealthier.

FOCUS ON READING

Identify two or three categories that you could use to organize the information under Kings Unify Egypt.

Crown of United Egypt

The pharaoh Menes combined the white crown of Upper Egypt and the red crown of Lower Egypt as a symbol of his rule of a united Egypt.

Eventually, however, rivals arose to challenge Egypt's First Dynasty for power. These challengers took over Egypt and established the Second Dynasty. In time, some 30 dynasties would rule ancient Egypt over a span of more than 2,500 years.

READING CHECK Drawing Inferences Why do you think Menes wanted to rule over both kingdoms of Egypt?

SUMMARY AND PREVIEW As you have read, ancient Egypt began in the fertile Nile River Valley. Two kingdoms developed in this region. The two kingdoms were later united under one ruler, and Egyptian territory grew. In the next section you will learn how Egypt continued to grow and change under later rulers in a period known as the Old Kingdom.

Section 1 Assessment

hmhsocialstudies.com
ONLINE QUIZ

Reviewing Ideas, Terms, and Places

1. **a. Identify** Where was the Egyptian kingdom of **Lower Egypt** located?
   b. Analyze Why was the **delta** of the **Nile River** well suited for settlement?
   c. Predict How might the Nile's **cataracts** have both helped and hurt Egypt?
2. **a. Describe** What foods did the Egyptians eat?
   b. Analyze What role did the Nile play in supplying Egyptians with the foods they ate?
   c. Elaborate How did the desert on both sides of the Nile help ancient Egypt?
3. **a. Identify** Who was the first **pharaoh** of Egypt?
   b. Draw Conclusions Why did the pharaohs of the First Dynasty wear a double crown?

Critical Thinking

4. **Categorizing** Create a chart like the one shown here. Use your notes to provide information for each category in the chart.

Development along Nile	Two Kingdoms	United Kingdoms

FOCUS ON WRITING

5. **Thinking about Geography and Early History** In your riddle, what clues could you include related to Egypt's geography and early history? For example, you might include the Nile River or pharaohs as clues. Add some ideas to your notes.

The Old Kingdom

If YOU lived there...

You are a farmer in ancient Egypt. To you, the pharaoh is the god Horus as well as your ruler. You depend on his strength and wisdom. For part of the year, you are busy planting crops in your fields. But at other times of the year, you work for the pharaoh. You are helping to build a great tomb so that your pharaoh will be comfortable in the afterlife.

How do you feel about working for the pharaoh?

> **BUILDING BACKGROUND** As in other ancient cultures, Egyptian society was based on a strict order of social classes. A small group of royalty and nobles ruled Egypt. They depended on the rest of the population to supply food, crafts, and labor. Few people questioned this arrangement of society.

Life in the Old Kingdom

The First and Second Dynasties ruled ancient Egypt for about four centuries. Around 2700 BC, though, a new dynasty rose to power in Egypt. Called the Third Dynasty, its rule began a period in Egyptian history known as the Old Kingdom.

Early Pharaohs

The **Old Kingdom** was a period in Egyptian history that lasted for about 500 years, from about 2700 to 2200 BC. During this time, the Egyptians continued to develop their political system. The system they developed was based on the belief that Egypt's pharaoh, or ruler, was both a king and a god.

The ancient Egyptians believed that Egypt belonged to the gods. The Egyptians believed the pharaoh had come to Earth in order to manage Egypt for the rest of the gods. As a result, he had absolute power over all the land and people in Egypt.

But the pharaoh's status as both king and god came with many responsibilities. People blamed him if crops did not grow well or if disease struck. They also demanded that the pharaoh make trade profitable and prevent wars.

What You Will Learn...

Main Ideas

1. Life in the Old Kingdom was influenced by pharaohs, roles in society, and trade.
2. Religion shaped Egyptian life.
3. The pyramids were built as tombs for Egypt's pharaohs.

The Big Idea

Egyptian government and religion were closely connected during the Old Kingdom.

Key Terms

Old Kingdom, *p. 19*
nobles, *p. 20*
afterlife, *p. 22*
mummies, *p. 22*
elite, *p. 23*
pyramids, *p. 24*
engineering, *p. 24*

hmhsocialstudies.com
TAKING NOTES

Use the graphic organizer online to take notes on government and religion during Egypt's Old Kingdom.

Egyptian Society

Pharaoh
The pharaoh ruled Egypt as a god.

Nobles
Officials and priests helped run the government and temples.

Scribes and Craftspeople
Scribes and craftspeople wrote and produced goods.

Farmers, Servants, and Slaves
Most Egyptians were farmers, servants, or slaves.

ANALYSIS SKILL ANALYZING VISUALS
Which group helped run the government and temples?

---

hmhsocialstudies.com

ANIMATED GEOGRAPHY
Egyptian Social Roles

The most famous pharaoh of the Old Kingdom was Khufu (KOO-foo), who ruled in the 2500s BC. Even though he is famous, we know relatively little about Khufu's life. Egyptian legend says that he was cruel, but historical records tell us that the people who worked for him were well fed. Khufu is best known for the monuments that were built to him.

Society and Trade

ACADEMIC VOCABULARY

acquire (uh-KWYR) to get

By the end of the Old Kingdom, Egypt had about 2 million people. As the population grew, social classes appeared. The Egyptians believed that a well-ordered society would keep their kingdom strong.

At the top of Egyptian society was the pharaoh. Just below him were the upper classes, which included priests and key government officials. Many of these priests and officials were **nobles**, or people from rich and powerful families.

Next in society was the middle class. This class included lesser government officials, scribes, and a few rich craftspeople.

The people in Egypt's lower class, more than 80 percent of the population, were mostly farmers. During flood season, when they could not work in the fields, farmers worked on the pharaoh's building projects. Servants and slaves also worked hard.

As society developed during the Old Kingdom, Egypt traded with some of its neighbors. Traders traveled south along the Nile to Nubia to **acquire** gold, copper, ivory, slaves, and stone for building. Trade with Syria provided Egypt with wood for building and for fire.

Egyptian society grew more complex during this time. It continued to be organized, disciplined, and highly religious.

READING CHECK **Generalizing** How was society structured in the Old Kingdom?

Religion and Egyptian Life

Worshipping the gods was a part of daily life in Egypt. But the Egyptian focus on religion extended beyond people's lives. Many customs focused on what happened after people died.

The Gods of Egypt

The Egyptians practiced polytheism. Before the First Dynasty, each village worshipped its own gods. During the Old Kingdom, however, Egyptian officials expected everyone to worship the same gods, though how people worshipped the gods might differ from place to place.

The Egyptians built temples to the gods all over the kingdom. Temples collected payments from both worshippers and the government. These payments enabled the temples to grow more influential.

Over time, certain cities became centers for the worship of certain gods. In the city of Memphis, for example, people prayed to Ptah, the creator of the world.

The Egyptians worshipped many gods besides Ptah. They had gods for nearly everything, including the sun, the sky, and Earth. Many gods blended human and animal forms. For example, Anubis, the god of the dead, had a human body but a jackal's head. Other major gods included

- Re, or Amon-Re, the sun god
- Osiris, the god of the underworld
- Isis, the goddess of magic
- Horus, a sky god; god of the pharaohs
- Thoth, the god of wisdom
- Geb, the Earth god

Egyptian families also worshipped household gods at shrines in their homes.

FOCUS ON READING

How is the text under the heading Religion and Egyptian Life categorized?

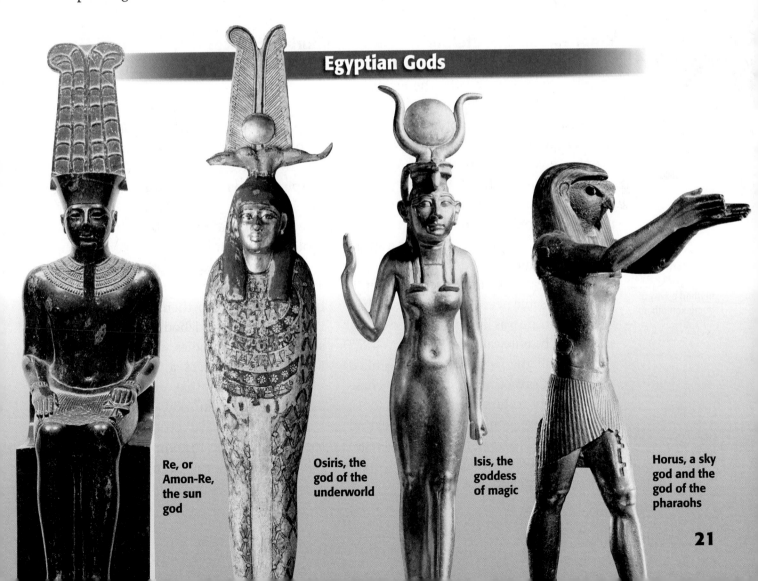

Egyptian Gods

Re, or Amon-Re, the sun god

Osiris, the god of the underworld

Isis, the goddess of magic

Horus, a sky god and the god of the pharaohs

21

Mummies and the Afterlife

Osiris, god of the underworld, waited to judge the dead person's soul.

The god Anubis weighed the dead person's heart against the feather of truth. If they weighed the same amount, the person was allowed into the underworld.

ACADEMIC VOCABULARY

method a way of doing something

Emphasis on the Afterlife

Much of Egyptian religion focused on the **afterlife**, or life after death. The Egyptians believed that the afterlife was a happy place. Paintings from Egyptian tombs show the afterlife as an ideal world where all the people are young and healthy.

The Egyptian belief in the afterlife stemmed from their idea of *ka* (KAH), or a person's life force. When a person died, his or her *ka* left the body and became a spirit. The *ka* remained linked to the body and could not leave its burial site. However, it had all the same needs that the person had when he or she was living. It needed to eat, sleep, and be entertained.

To fulfill the *ka*'s needs, people filled tombs with objects for the afterlife. These objects included furniture, clothing, tools, jewelry, and weapons. Relatives of the dead were expected to bring food and beverages to their loved ones' tombs so the *ka* would not be hungry or thirsty.

Burial Practices

Egyptian ideas about the afterlife shaped their burial practices. For example, the Egyptians believed that a body had to be prepared for the afterlife before it could be placed in a tomb. This meant the body had to be preserved. If the body decayed, its spirit could not recognize it. That would break the link between the body and spirit. The *ka* would then be unable to receive the food and drink it needed.

To help the *ka*, Egyptians developed a **method** called embalming to preserve bodies and to keep them from decaying. Egyptians preserved bodies as **mummies**, specially treated bodies wrapped in cloth. Embalming preserves a body for many, many years. A body that was not embalmed decayed far more quickly.

Embalming was a complex process that took several weeks to complete. In the first step, embalmers cut open the body and removed all organs except for the heart.

1 Only the god Anubis was allowed to perform the first steps in preparing a mummy.

2 The body's organs were preserved in special jars and kept next to the mummy.

Embalmers stored the removed organs in special jars. Next, the embalmers used a special substance to dry out the body. They later applied some special oils. The embalmers then wrapped the dried-out body with linen cloths and bandages, often placing special charms inside the cloth wrappings.

Wrapping the body was the last step in the mummy-making process. Once it was completely wrapped, a mummy was placed in a coffin called a sarcophagus, such as the one shown at right.

Only royalty and other members of Egypt's **elite** (AY-leet), or people of wealth and power, could afford to have mummies made. Peasant families did not need the process. They buried their dead in shallow graves at the edge of the desert. The hot, dry sand preserved the bodies naturally.

3 The body was preserved as a mummy and kept in a case called a sarcophagus.

READING CHECK **Analyzing** How did religious beliefs affect Egyptian burial practices?

ANALYSIS SKILL **ANALYZING VISUALS**

How did gods participate in the afterlife?

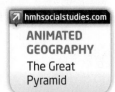

The Pyramids

Egyptians believed that burial sites, especially royal tombs, were very important. For this reason, they built spectacular monuments in which to bury their rulers. The most spectacular were the **pyramids**—huge, stone tombs with four triangle-shaped sides that met in a point on top.

The Egyptians built the first pyramids during the Old Kingdom. Some of the largest pyramids were built during that time.

Many of these huge Egyptian pyramids are still standing. The largest is the Great Pyramid of Khufu near the town of Giza. It covers more than 13 acres at its base and stands 481 feet (146 m) high. This one pyramid took thousands of workers and more than 2 million limestone blocks to build. Like all the pyramids, it is an amazing example of Egyptian **engineering**, the application of scientific knowledge for practical purposes.

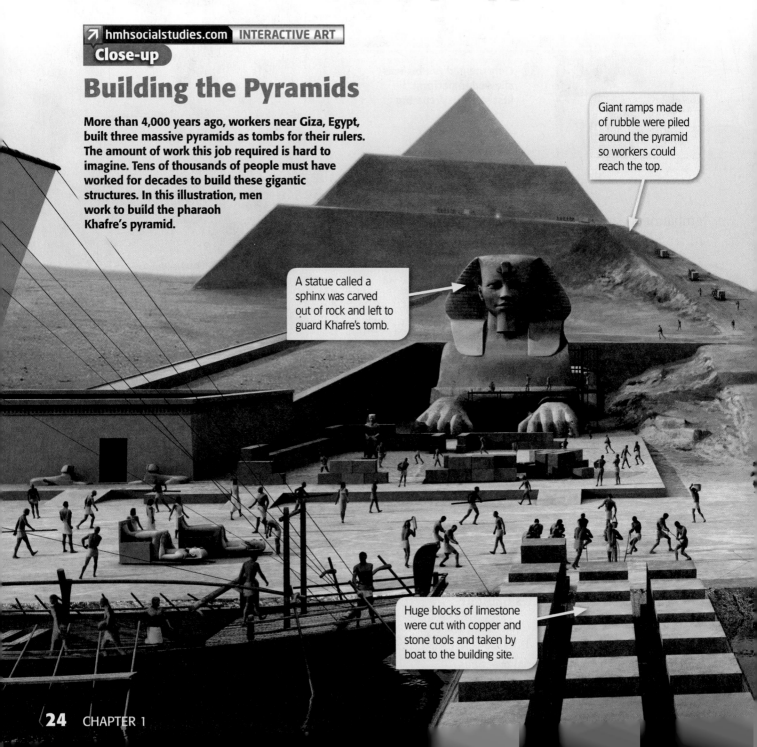

↗ hmhsocialstudies.com INTERACTIVE ART
Close-up

Building the Pyramids

More than 4,000 years ago, workers near Giza, Egypt, built three massive pyramids as tombs for their rulers. The amount of work this job required is hard to imagine. Tens of thousands of people must have worked for decades to build these gigantic structures. In this illustration, men work to build the pharaoh Khafre's pyramid.

Giant ramps made of rubble were piled around the pyramid so workers could reach the top.

A statue called a sphinx was carved out of rock and left to guard Khafre's tomb.

Huge blocks of limestone were cut with copper and stone tools and taken by boat to the building site.

Building the Pyramids

The earliest pyramids did not have the smooth sides we usually imagine when we think of pyramids. The Egyptians began building the smooth-sided pyramids we usually see around 2700 BC. The steps of these pyramids were filled and covered with limestone. The burial chamber was located deep inside the pyramid. After the pharaoh's burial, workers sealed the passages to this room with large blocks.

Historians do not know for certain how the ancient Egyptians built the pyramids. What is certain is that such massive projects required a huge labor force. As many as 100,000 workers may have been needed to build just one pyramid. The government paid the people working on the pyramids.

Inside the Great Pyramid, tunnels led to the pharaoh's burial chamber, which was sealed off with rocks.

Teams of workers dragged the stones on wooden sleds to the pyramid.

ANALYSIS SKILL **ANALYZING VISUALS**

How did workers get their stone blocks to the pyramids?

Wages for working on construction projects were paid in goods such as grain instead of money, however.

For years, scholars have debated how the Egyptians moved the massive stones used to build the pyramids. Some scholars think that during the Nile's flooding, builders floated the stones downstream directly to the construction site. Most historians believe that workers used brick ramps and strong wooden sleds to drag the stones up the pyramid once at the building site.

Significance of the Pyramids

Burial in a pyramid showed a pharaoh's importance. Both the size and shape of the pyramid were symbolic. Pointing to the sky above, the pyramid symbolized the pharaoh's journey to the afterlife. The Egyptians wanted the pyramids to be spectacular because they believed the pharaoh, as their link to the gods, controlled everyone's afterlife. Making the pharaoh's spirit happy was a way of ensuring happiness in one's own afterlife.

To ensure that the pharaohs remained safe after death, the Egyptians sometimes wrote magical spells and hymns on tombs.

Together, these spells and hymns are called Pyramid Texts. The first such text, addressed to Re, the sun god, was carved into the pyramid of King Unas (OO-nuhs). He was a pharaoh of the Old Kingdom.

> " Re, this Unas comes to you,
> A spirit indestructible . . .
> Your son comes to you, this Unas . . .
> May you cross the sky united in the dark,
> May you rise in lightland, [where] you shine! "
>
> –from Pyramid Text, Utterance 217

The builders of Unas's pyramid wanted the god Re to look after their leader's spirit. Even after death, the Egyptians' pharaoh was important to them.

READING CHECK Identifying Points of View
Why were pyramids important to the ancient Egyptians?

SUMMARY AND PREVIEW As you have read, during the Old Kingdom, new political and social orders were created in Egypt. Religion was important, and many pyramids were built for pharaohs. In the next section you will learn about Egypt's Middle and New Kingdoms.

Section 2 Assessment

Reviewing Ideas, Terms, and Places

1. **a. Define** To what Egyptian period does the phrase **Old Kingdom** refer?
   b. Analyze Why did Egyptians never question the pharaoh's authority?
   c. Elaborate Why do you think pharaohs might have wanted the support of **nobles**?
2. **a. Define** What did Egyptians mean by the **afterlife**?
   b. Analyze Why was embalming important to Egyptians?
3. **a. Describe** What is **engineering**?
   b. Elaborate What does the building of the **pyramids** tell us about Egyptian society?

Critical Thinking

4. **Generalizing** Using your notes, complete this graphic organizer by listing three facts about the relationship between government and religion in the Old Kingdom.

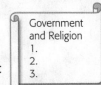

Government and Religion
1.
2.
3.

FOCUS ON WRITING

5. **Noting Characteristics of the Old Kingdom** The Old Kingdom has special characteristics of government, society, and religion. Write down details about any of those characteristics that you might want to include as one of the clues in your Egypt riddle.

The Middle and New Kingdoms

If YOU lived there...

You are a servant to Hatshepsut, the ruler of Egypt. You admire her, but some people think a woman should not rule. She calls herself king and dresses like a pharaoh—even wearing a fake beard. That was your idea! But you want to help more.

What could Hatshepsut do to show her authority?

BUILDING BACKGROUND The power of the pharaohs expanded during the Old Kingdom. Society was orderly, based on great differences between social classes. But rulers and dynasties changed, and Egypt changed with them. In time, these changes led to new eras in Egyptian history, eras called the Middle and New Kingdoms.

The Middle Kingdom

At the end of the Old Kingdom, the wealth and power of the pharaohs declined. Building and maintaining pyramids cost a lot of money. Pharaohs could not collect enough taxes to keep up with their expenses. At the same time, ambitious nobles used their government positions to take power from pharaohs.

In time, nobles gained enough power to challenge Egypt's pharaohs. By about 2200 BC the Old Kingdom had fallen. For the next 160 years, local nobles ruled much of Egypt. During this period, the kingdom had no central ruler.

What You Will Learn...

Main Ideas

1. The Middle Kingdom was a period of stable government between periods of disorder.
2. The New Kingdom was the peak of Egyptian trade and military power, but its greatness did not last.
3. Work and daily life differed among Egypt's social classes.

The Big Idea

During the Middle and New Kingdoms, order and greatness were restored in Egypt.

Key Terms and Places

Middle Kingdom, *p. 28*
New Kingdom, *p. 28*
Kush, *p. 28*
trade routes, *p. 29*

hmhsocialstudies.com
TAKING NOTES

Use the graphic organizer online to take notes on the Middle and New Kingdoms and on work and life in ancient Egypt.

Time Line

Periods of Egyptian History

3000 BC	2000 BC	1000 BC
c. 2700–2200 BC Old Kingdom	**c. 2050–1750 BC** Middle Kingdom	**c. 1550–1050 BC** New Kingdom

hmhsocialstudies.com
ANIMATED
GEOGRAPHY
The Powerful
New Kingdom
1539-1075 B.C.

Finally, around 2050 BC, a powerful pharaoh defeated his rivals. Once again all of Egypt was united. His rule began the **Middle Kingdom**, a period of order and stability that lasted to about 1750 BC. Toward the end of the Middle Kingdom, however, Egypt began to fall into disorder once again.

Around 1750 BC, a group from Southwest Asia called the Hyksos (HIK-sohs) invaded. The Hyksos used horses, chariots, and advanced weapons to conquer Lower Egypt. The Hyksos then ruled the region as pharaohs for 200 years.

The Egyptians eventually fought back. In the mid-1500s BC, Ahmose (AHM-ohs) of Thebes declared himself king and drove the Hyksos out of Egypt. Ahmose then ruled all of Egypt.

READING CHECK **Summarizing** What caused the end of the Middle Kingdom?

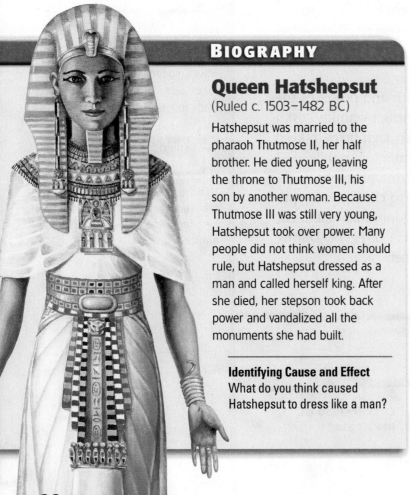

BIOGRAPHY

Queen Hatshepsut
(Ruled c. 1503–1482 BC)

Hatshepsut was married to the pharaoh Thutmose II, her half brother. He died young, leaving the throne to Thutmose III, his son by another woman. Because Thutmose III was still very young, Hatshepsut took over power. Many people did not think women should rule, but Hatshepsut dressed as a man and called herself king. After she died, her stepson took back power and vandalized all the monuments she had built.

Identifying Cause and Effect
What do you think caused Hatshepsut to dress like a man?

The New Kingdom

Ahmose's rise to power marked the start of Egypt's eighteenth dynasty. More importantly, it was the start of the **New Kingdom**, the period during which Egypt reached the height of its power and glory. During the New Kingdom, which lasted from about 1550 to 1050 BC, conquest and trade brought wealth to the pharaohs.

Building an Empire

After battling the Hyksos, Egypt's leaders feared future invasions. To prevent such invasions from occurring, they decided to take control of all possible invasion routes into the kingdom. In the process, these leaders turned Egypt into an empire.

Egypt's first target was the homeland of the Hyksos. After taking over that area, the army continued north and conquered Syria. As you can see from the map, Egypt took over the entire eastern shore of the Mediterranean and the kingdom of **Kush**, south of Egypt. By the 1400s BC, Egypt was the leading military power in the region. Its empire extended from the Euphrates River to southern Nubia.

Military conquests made Egypt rich as well as powerful. The kingdoms that Egypt conquered regularly sent gifts and treasure to their Egyptian conquerors. For example, the kingdom of Kush in Nubia sent yearly payments of gold, precious stones, and leopard skins to the pharaohs. In addition, Assyrian, Babylonian, and Hittite kings sent expensive gifts to Egypt in an effort to maintain good relations.

Growth and Effects of Trade

As Egypt's empire expanded, so did its trade. Conquest brought Egyptian traders into contact with more distant lands. Many of these lands had valuable resources for trade. The Sinai Peninsula is one example.

It had valuable supplies of turquoise and copper. Profitable **trade routes**, or paths followed by traders, developed from Egypt to these lands, as the map shows.

One of Egypt's rulers who worked to increase trade was Queen Hatshepsut. She sent Egyptian traders south to trade with the kingdom of Punt on the Red Sea and north to trade with people in Asia Minor and Greece.

Hatshepsut and later pharaohs used the money they gained from trade to support the arts and architecture. Hatshepsut in particular is remembered for the many impressive monuments and temples built during her reign. The best known of these structures was a magnificent temple built for her near the city of Thebes.

Invasions of Egypt

Despite its military might, Egypt still faced threats to its power. In the 1200s BC the pharaoh Ramses (RAM-seez) II, or Ramses the Great, fought the Hittites, who came from Asia Minor. The two powers fought fiercely for years, but neither one could defeat the other.

Egypt faced threats in other parts of its empire as well. To the west, a people known as the Tehenu invaded the Nile Delta. Ramses fought them off and built a series of forts to strengthen the western frontier. This proved to be a wise decision because the Tehenu invaded again a century later. Faced with Egypt's strengthened defenses, the Tehenu were defeated once again.

Soon after Ramses the Great died, invaders called the Sea Peoples sailed into Southwest Asia. Little is known about these people. Historians are not even sure who they were. All we know is that they were strong warriors who had crushed the Hittites and destroyed cities in Southwest Asia. Only after 50 years of fighting were the Egyptians able to turn them back.

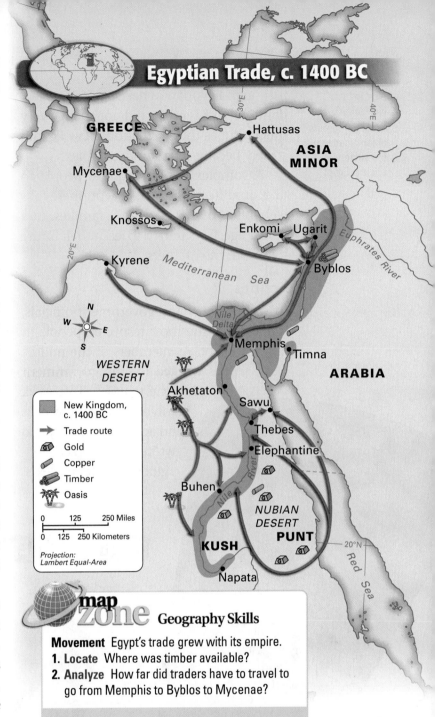

Egyptian Trade, c. 1400 BC

GREECE
Hattusas
ASIA MINOR
Mycenae
Knossos
Enkomi   Ugarit
Euphrates River
Kyrene
Mediterranean   Sea
Byblos
Nile Delta
Memphis
Timna
WESTERN DESERT
Akhetaton
Sawu
ARABIA
Thebes
Elephantine
Buhen
NUBIAN DESERT
PUNT
Nile River
KUSH
Napata
Red Sea

New Kingdom, c. 1400 BC
→ Trade route
Gold
Copper
Timber
Oasis

0   125   250 Miles
0   125   250 Kilometers
Projection: Lambert Equal-Area

map zone **Geography Skills**

Movement Egypt's trade grew with its empire.
1. **Locate** Where was timber available?
2. **Analyze** How far did traders have to travel to go from Memphis to Byblos to Mycenae?

Egypt survived, but its empire in Asia was gone. Shortly after the invasions of the Hittites and the Sea Peoples, the New Kingdom came to an end. Ancient Egypt fell into a period of violence and disorder. Egypt would never regain its power.

READING CHECK **Identifying Cause and Effect** What caused Egypt's growth of trade during the New Kingdom?

Work and Daily Life

FOCUS ON READING
What categories of jobs made up the society of ancient Egypt?

Although Egyptian dynasties rose and fell, daily life for Egyptians did not change very much. But as the population grew, Egypt's society became even more complex.

A complex society requires people to take on different jobs. In Egypt, these jobs were often passed on within families. At a young age, boys started to learn their future jobs from their fathers.

Scribes

After the priests and government officials, scribes were the most respected people in ancient Egypt. As members of the middle class, scribes worked for the government and the temples. This work involved keeping records and accounts. Scribes also wrote and copied religious and literary texts.

Because of their respected position, scribes did not have to pay taxes. For this reason, many scribes became wealthy.

Artisans, Artists, and Architects

Another group in society was made up of artisans whose jobs required advanced skills. Among the artisans who worked in Egypt were sculptors, builders, carpenters, jewelers, metalworkers, and leatherworkers. Artisans made items such as statues, furniture, jewelry, pottery, and shoes. Most artisans worked for the government or for temples. Egypt's artisans were admired and often paid fairly well.

Architects and artists were admired in Egypt as well. Architects designed the temples and royal tombs for which Egypt is famous. Talented architects could rise to become high government officials. Artists often worked for the state or for temples.

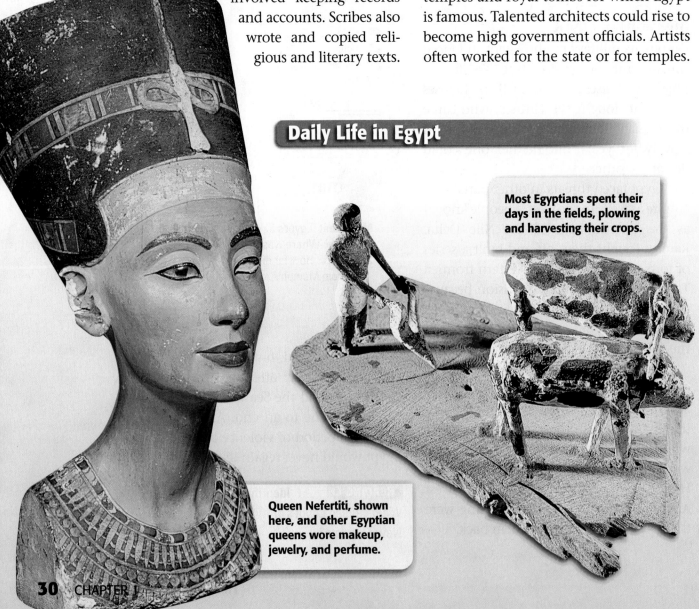

Daily Life in Egypt

Most Egyptians spent their days in the fields, plowing and harvesting their crops.

Queen Nefertiti, shown here, and other Egyptian queens wore makeup, jewelry, and perfume.

Egyptian artists produced many different types of works. Many artists worked in the deep burial chambers of the pharaohs' tombs painting detailed pictures.

Merchants and Traders

Although trade was important to Egypt, only a small group of Egyptians became merchants and traders. Some traveled long distances to buy and sell goods. On their journeys, merchants were usually accompanied by soldiers, scribes, and laborers.

Soldiers

After the wars of the Middle Kingdom, Egypt established a professional army. The military offered people a chance to rise in social status. Soldiers received land as payment and could also keep any treasure they captured in war. Soldiers who excelled could be promoted to officer positions.

Farmers and Other Peasants

As in the society of the Old Kingdom, Egyptian farmers and other peasants were toward the bottom of Egypt's social scale. These hardworking people made up the vast majority of Egypt's population.

Egyptian farmers grew crops to support their families. These farmers depended on the Nile's regular floods to grow their crops. Farmers used wooden hoes or plows pulled by cows to prepare the land before the flood. After the floodwaters had drained away, farmers planted seeds for crops such as wheat and barley. At the end of the growing season, Egypt's farmers worked together to gather the harvest.

Farmers had to give some of their crops to the pharaoh as taxes. These taxes were intended to pay the pharaoh for use of the land. Under Egyptian law, the pharaoh controlled all land in the kingdom.

This jar probably held perfume, a valuable trade item.

Servants worked for Egypt's rulers and nobles and did many jobs, like preparing food.

ANALYSIS SKILL ANALYZING VISUALS
What were some luxury goods used by Egypt's queens and rulers?

All peasants, including farmers, were also subject to special duty. Under Egyptian law, the pharaoh could demand at any time that people work on projects, such as building pyramids, mining gold, or fighting in the army. The government paid the workers in grain.

ACADEMIC VOCABULARY
contracts binding legal agreements

Slaves

The few slaves in Egyptian society were considered lower than farmers. Many slaves were convicted criminals or prisoners captured in war. These slaves worked on farms, on building projects, in workshops, and in private households. Unlike most slaves in history, however, slaves in Egypt had some legal rights. Also, in some cases, they could earn their freedom.

Family Life in Egypt

Family life was very important in Egyptian society. Most Egyptian families lived in their own homes. Sometimes unmarried female relatives lived with them, but men were expected to marry young so that they could start having children.

Most Egyptian women were devoted to their homes and families. Some women, however, did have jobs outside the home.

A few women served as priestesses, and some worked as royal officials, administrators, or artisans. Unlike most women in ancient times, Egyptian women had a number of legal rights. They could own property, make **contracts**, and divorce their husbands. They could even keep their property after a divorce.

Children's lives were not as structured as adults' lives were. Children played with toys such as dolls, tops, and clay animal figurines. Children also played ballgames and hunted. Most children, boys and girls, received some education. At school they learned morals, writing, math, and sports. At age 14 most boys left school to enter their father's profession. At that time, they took their place in Egypt's social structure.

READING CHECK **Categorizing** What types of jobs existed in ancient Egypt?

SUMMARY AND PREVIEW Pharaohs faced many challenges to their rule. After the defeat of the Hyksos, Egypt grew in land and wealth. People in Egypt worked at many jobs. In the next section you will learn about Egyptian achievements.

Section 3 Assessment

hmhsocialstudies.com
ONLINE QUIZ

Reviewing Ideas, Terms, and Places

1. a. **Define** What was the **Middle Kingdom**?
   b. **Analyze** How did Ahmose manage to become king of all Egypt?
2. a. **Recall** What two things brought wealth to the pharaohs during the **New Kingdom**?
   b. **Explain** What did Hatshepsut do as pharaoh of Egypt?
3. a. **Identify** What job employed the majority of the people in Egypt?
   b. **Analyze** What rights did Egyptian women have?
   c. **Elaborate** Why do you think scribes were so honored in Egyptian society?

Critical Thinking

4. **Categorizing** Draw pyramids like the ones shown. Using your notes, fill in the pyramids with the political and military factors that led to the rise and fall of the Middle and New Kingdoms.

Rise Fall Rise Fall
Middle Kingdom   New Kingdom

FOCUS ON WRITING

5. **Developing Ideas from the Middle and New Kingdoms** Your riddle should contain information about these periods. Decide which key ideas you should include and add them to your list.

Ramses the Great

How could a ruler achieve fame that would last 3,000 years?

When did he live? late 1300s and early 1200s BC

Where did he live? As pharaoh, Ramses lived in a city he built on the Nile Delta. The city's name, Pi-Ramesse, means the "house of Ramses."

What did he do? From a young age, Ramses was trained as a ruler and a fighter. Made an army captain at age 10, he began military campaigns even before he became pharaoh. During his reign, Ramses greatly increased the size of his kingdom.

Why is he important? Many people consider Ramses the last great Egyptian pharaoh. He accomplished great things, but the pharaohs who followed could not maintain them. Both a great warrior and a great builder, he is known largely for the massive monuments he built. The temples at Karnak, Luxor, and Abu Simbel stand as 3,000-year-old symbols of the great pharaoh's power.

Drawing Conclusions Why do you think Ramses built monuments all over Egypt?

KEY IDEAS

Ramses had a poem praising him carved into the walls of five temples, including Karnak. One verse of the poem praises Ramses as a great warrior and the defender of Egypt.

" Gracious lord and bravest
        king, savior–guard
Of Egypt in the battle, be our
        ward;
Behold we stand alone, in the
        hostile Hittite ring,
Save for us the breath of life,
Give deliverance from the
        strife,
Oh! protect us Ramses Miamun!
Oh! save us, mighty king! "

–Pen-ta-ur, quoted in *The World's Story*, edited by Eva March Tappan

VIDEO
Ramses'
Egyptian
Empire

hmhsocialstudies.com

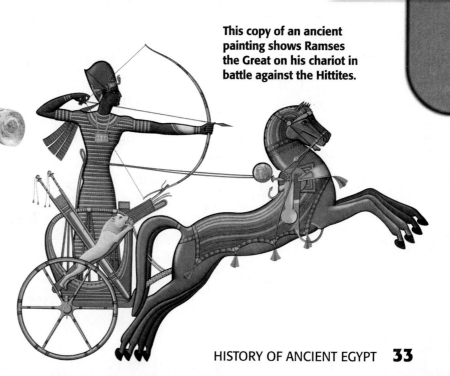

This copy of an ancient painting shows Ramses the Great on his chariot in battle against the Hittites.

Egyptian Achievements

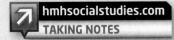
If YOU lived there...

You are an artist in ancient Egypt. A powerful noble has hired you to decorate the walls of his family tomb. You are standing inside the new tomb, studying the bare, stone walls that you will decorate. No light reaches this chamber, but your servant holds a lantern high. You've met the noble only briefly but think that he is someone who loves his family, the gods, and Egypt.

What will you include in your painting?

BUILDING BACKGROUND The ancient Egyptians had a rich and varied history. Today, though, most people remember them for their cultural achievements. Egyptian art, such as the tomb paintings mentioned above, and Egypt's unique writing system are admired by millions of tourists in museums around the world.

Egyptian Writing

If you were reading a book and saw pictures of folded cloth, a leg, a star, a bird, and a man holding a stick, would you know what it meant? You would if you were an ancient Egyptian. In the Egyptian writing system, or **hieroglyphics** (hy-ruh-GLIH-fiks), those five symbols together meant "to teach." Egyptian hieroglyphics were one of the world's first writing systems.

Writing in Ancient Egypt

The earliest known examples of Egyptian writing are from around 3300 BC. These early Egyptian writings were carved in stone or on other hard materials. Later, Egyptians learned how to make **papyrus** (puh-PY-ruhs), a long-lasting, paperlike material made from reeds. The Egyptians made papyrus by pressing layers of reeds together and pounding them into sheets. These sheets were tough and durable, yet could be rolled into scrolls. Scribes wrote on papyrus using brushes and ink.

Egyptian Writing

Egyptian hieroglyphics used picture symbols to represent sounds.

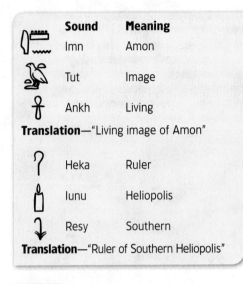

	Sound	Meaning
	Imn	Amon
	Tut	Image
	Ankh	Living

Translation—"Living image of Amon"

	Heka	Ruler
	Iunu	Heliopolis
	Resy	Southern

Translation—"Ruler of Southern Heliopolis"

ANALYSIS SKILL **ANALYZING VISUALS**

What does the symbol for ruler look like?

The hieroglyphic writing system used more than 600 symbols, mostly pictures of objects. Each symbol represented one or more sounds in the Egyptian language. For example, a picture of an owl represented the same sound as our letter M.

Hieroglyphics could be written either horizontally or vertically. They could be written from right to left or from left to right. These options made hieroglyphics flexible to write but difficult to read. The only way to tell which way a text is written is to look at individual symbols.

The Rosetta Stone

Historians and archaeologists have known about hieroglyphics for centuries. For a long time, though, historians did not know how to read them. In fact, it was not until 1799 that a lucky discovery by a French soldier gave historians the key they needed to read ancient Egyptian writing.

That key was the **Rosetta Stone**, a huge, stone slab inscribed with hieroglyphics. In addition to the hieroglyphics, the Rosetta Stone had text in Greek and a later form of Egyptian. Because the message in all three languages was the same, scholars who knew Greek were able to figure out what the hieroglyphics said.

Egyptian Texts

Because papyrus did not decay in Egypt's dry climate, many ancient Egyptian texts still survive. These texts include government records, historical records, science texts, and medical manuals. In addition, many literary works have survived. Some of them, such as *The Book of the Dead,* tell about the afterlife. Others tell stories about gods and kings.

READING CHECK **Comparing** How is our writing system similar to hieroglyphics?

THE IMPACT TODAY

An object that helps solve a difficult mystery is sometimes now called a Rosetta Stone.

Egypt's Great Temples

In addition to their writing system, the ancient Egyptians are famous for their magnificent architecture. You have already read about the Egyptians' most famous structures, the pyramids. But the Egyptians also built massive temples. Those that survive are among the most spectacular sites in Egypt today.

The Egyptians believed that temples were the homes of the gods. People visited the temples to worship, offer the gods gifts, and ask for favors.

Many Egyptian temples shared some similar features. Rows of stone **sphinxes**—imaginary creatures with the bodies of lions and the heads of other animals or humans—lined the path leading to the entrance. That entrance itself was a huge, thick gate. On either side of the gate might stand an **obelisk** (AH-buh-lisk), a tall, four-sided pillar that is pointed on top.

Inside, Egyptian temples were lavishly decorated, as you can see in the drawing of the Temple of Karnak. Huge columns supported the temple's roof. These columns were often covered with paintings and hieroglyphics, as were the temple walls. Statues of gods and pharaohs often stood along the walls as well. The sanctuary, the most sacred part of the building, was at the far end of the temple.

The Temple of Karnak is only one of Egypt's great temples. Other temples were built by Ramses the Great at Abu Simbel and Luxor. The temple at Abu Simbel is especially known for the huge statues that stand next to its entrance. The 66-foot-tall statues are carved out of sandstone cliffs and show Ramses the Great as pharaoh. Nearby are smaller statues of his family.

READING CHECK **Generalizing** What were some features of ancient Egyptian temples?

THE IMPACT TODAY

The Washington Monument, in Washington, D.C., is an obelisk.

Close-up

The Temple of Karnak

The Temple of Karnak was Egypt's largest temple. Built mainly to honor Amon-Re, the sun god, Karnak was one of Egypt's major religious centers for centuries. Over the years, pharaohs added to the temple's many buildings. This illustration shows how Karnak's great hall might have looked during an ancient festival.

Karnak's interior columns and walls were painted brilliant colors.

ANALYSIS SKILL **ANALYZING VISUALS**

What features of Egyptian architecture can you see in this illustration?

Treasures of King Tut's Tomb

In 1922 the archaeologist Howard Carter discovered the tomb of King Tut. Unlike most Egyptian tombs, it had never been robbed and was still filled with treasures, some of which are shown here.

Howard Carter examining King Tut's coffin in 1922

Egyptian Art

FOCUS ON READING

What categories could you use to organize the information under Egyptian Art?

One reason Egypt's temples are so popular with tourists is the art they contain. The ancient Egyptians were masterful artists. Many of their greatest works were created to fill the tombs of pharaohs and other nobles. The Egyptians took great care in making these items because they believed the dead could enjoy them in the afterlife.

Paintings

Egyptian art was filled with lively, colorful scenes. Detailed works covered the walls of temples and tombs. Artists also painted on canvas, papyrus, pottery, plaster, and wood. Most Egyptians never saw these paintings, however. Only kings, priests, and important people could enter temples and tombs, and even they rarely entered the tombs.

The subjects of Egyptian paintings vary widely. Some of the paintings show important historical events, such as the crowning of a new king or the founding of a temple.

Others show major religious rituals. Still other paintings show scenes from everyday life, such as farming or hunting.

Egyptian painting has a distinctive style. People, for example, are drawn in a certain way. In Egyptian paintings, people's heads and legs are always seen from the side, but their upper bodies and shoulders are shown straight on. In addition, people do not all appear the same size. Important figures such as pharaohs appear huge in comparison to others, especially servants or conquered people. In contrast, Egyptian animals were usually drawn realistically.

Carvings and Jewelry

Painting was not the only art form Egyptians practiced. The Egyptians were also skilled stoneworkers. Many tombs included huge statues and detailed carvings.

In addition, the Egyptians made lovely objects out of gold and precious stones. They made jewelry for both men and women.

The back of King Tut's chair was decorated with this image of the pharaoh and his wife.

Gold mask

ANALYSIS
SKILL ANALYZING VISUALS

What might archaeologists learn about ancient Egypt from these artifacts?

This jewelry included necklaces, bracelets, and collars. The Egyptians also used gold to make burial items for their pharaohs.

Over the years, treasure hunters emptied many pharaohs' tombs. At least one tomb, however, was not disturbed. In 1922 some archaeologists found the tomb of King Tutankhamen (too-tang-KAHM-uhn), or King Tut. The tomb was filled with many treasures, including boxes of jewelry, robes, a burial mask, and ivory statues. King Tut's treasures have taught us much about Egyptian burial practices and beliefs.

READING CHECK Summarizing What types of artwork were contained in Egyptian tombs?

SUMMARY AND PREVIEW The Egyptians developed one of the best-known cultures of the ancient world. Next, you will learn about a culture that developed in the shadow of Egypt—Kush.

Section 4 Assessment

hmhsocialstudies.com
ONLINE QUIZ

Reviewing Ideas, Terms, and Places

1. **a. Define** What are **hieroglyphics**?
   b. Contrast How was hieroglyphic writing different from our writing today?
   c. Evaluate Why was the **Rosetta Stone** important?
2. **a. Describe** What were two ways the Egyptians decorated their temples?
   b. Evaluate Why do you think pharaohs like Ramses the Great built huge temples?
3. **Recall** Why did Egyptians fill tombs with art, jewelry, and other treasures?

Critical Thinking

4. **Summarizing** Draw a chart like the one below. In each column, write a statement that summarizes Egyptian achievements in the listed category.

Writing	Architecture	Art

FOCUS ON WRITING

5. **Considering Egyptian Achievements** For your riddle, note some Egyptian achievements in writing, architecture, and art that make Egypt different from other places.

Analyzing Primary and Secondary Sources

Learn

Primary sources are materials created by people who lived during the times they describe. Examples include letters, diaries, and photographs. *Secondary sources* are accounts written later by someone who was not present. They often teach about or discuss a historical topic. This chapter is an example of a secondary source.

By studying both types, you can get a better picture of a historical period or event. However, not all sources are accurate or reliable. Use these checklists to judge which sources are reliable.

Checklist for Primary Sources

• Who is the author? Is he or she trustworthy?

• Was the author present at the event described in the source? Might the author have based his or her writing on rumor, gossip, or hearsay?

• How soon after the event occurred was the source written? The more time that passed, the greater the chance for error.

• What is the purpose? Authors can have reasons to exaggerate—or even lie—to suit their own purposes. Look for evidence of emotion, opinion, or bias in the source. They can affect the accuracy.

• Can the information in the source be verified in other primary or secondary sources?

Checklist for Secondary Sources

• Who is the author? What are his or her qualifications? Is he or she an authority on the subject?

• Where did the author get his or her information? Good historians always tell you where they got their information.

• Has the author drawn valid conclusions?

Practice

"The Egyptians quickly extended their military and commercial influence over an extensive [wide] region that included the rich provinces of Syria ... and the numbers of Egyptian slaves grew swiftly."

–C. Warren Hollister, from *Roots of the Western Tradition*

"Let me tell you how the soldier fares ... how he goes to Syria, and how he marches over the mountains. His bread and water are borne [carried] upon his shoulders like the load of [a donkey]; ... and the joints of his back are bowed [bent] ... When he reaches the enemy, ... he has no strength in his limbs."

–from *Wings of the Falcon: Life and Thought of Ancient Egypt*, translated by Joseph Kaster

1 Which of the above passages is a primary source, and which is a secondary source?

2 Is there evidence of opinion, emotion, or bias in the second passage? Why, or why not?

3 Which passage would be better for learning about what life was like for Egyptian soldiers, and why?

Apply

Refer to the Ramses the Great biography in this chapter to answer the following questions.

1. Identify the primary source in the biography.

2. What biases or other issues might affect the reliability or accuracy of this primary source?

Chapter Review

Geography's Impact
video series
Review the video to answer the closing question:
What do the pyramids of ancient Egypt tell you about the people of that civilization?

Visual Summary

Use the visual summary below to help you review the main ideas of the chapter.

QUICK FACTS

Egyptian civilization developed along the Nile River, which provided water and fertile soil for farming.

Egypt's kings were considered gods, and Egyptians made golden burial masks and pyramids in their honor.

Egyptian cultural achievements included beautiful art and the development of a hieroglyphic writing system.

Reviewing Vocabulary, Terms, and Places

Imagine these terms are answers to items in a crossword puzzle. Write the clues for the answers. Then make the puzzle with answers down and across.

1. cataract
2. Nile River
3. pharaoh
4. nobles
5. mummy
6. acquire
7. contract
8. pyramids
9. hieroglyphics
10. sphinxes

Comprehension and Critical Thinking

SECTION 1 *(Pages 14–18)*

11. **a. Identify** Where was most of Egypt's fertile land located?

    b. Make Inferences Why did Memphis become a political and social center of Egypt?

    c. Predict How might history have been different if the Nile had not flooded every year?

SECTION 2 *(Pages 19–26)*

12. **a. Describe** Who were the pharaohs, and what responsibilities did they have?

    b. Analyze How were beliefs about the afterlife linked to items placed in tombs?

    c. Elaborate What challenges, in addition to moving stone blocks, do you think the pyramid builders faced?

SECTION 3 *(Pages 27–32)*

13. **a. Describe** What did a scribe do, and what benefits did a scribe receive?

    b. Analyze When was the period of the New Kingdom, and what two factors contributed to Egypt's wealth during that period?

    c. Evaluate Ramses the Great was a powerful pharaoh. Do you think his military successes or his building projects are more important to evaluating his greatness? Why?

SECTION 4 *(Pages 34–39)*

14. a. Describe For what was papyrus used?

b. Contrast How are the symbols in Egyptian hieroglyphics different from the symbols used in our writing system?

c. Elaborate How does the Egyptian style of painting people reflect their society?

Social Studies Skills

Analyzing Primary and Secondary Sources *Each of the questions below lists two sources that a historian might consult to answer a question about ancient Egypt. For each question, decide which source is likely to be more accurate or reliable and why. Then indicate whether that source is a primary or secondary source.*

15. What were Egyptian beliefs about the afterlife?

a. Egyptian tomb inscriptions

b. writings by a priest who visited Egypt in 1934

16. Why did the Nile flood every year?

a. songs of praise to the Nile River written by Egyptian priests

b. a book about the rivers of Africa written by a modern geographer

17. What kinds of goods did the Egyptians trade?

a. ancient Egyptian trade records

b. an ancient Egyptian story about a trader

18. What kind of warrior was Ramses the Great?

a. a poem in praise of Ramses

b. a description of a battle in which Ramses fought, written by an impartial observer

Using the Internet

19. Activity: Creating Egyptian Art The Egyptians excelled in the arts. Egyptian artwork included beautiful paintings, carvings, and jewelry. Egyptian architecture included huge pyramids and temples. Through the online book, research Egyptian art and architecture. Then imagine you are an Egyptian. Create a work of art for the pharaoh's tomb. Provide hieroglyphics telling the pharaoh about your art.

Map Activity

20. Ancient Egypt On a separate sheet of paper, match the letters on the map with their correct labels.

Lower Egypt	Red Sea
Mediterranean Sea	Sinai Peninsula
Nile River	Upper Egypt

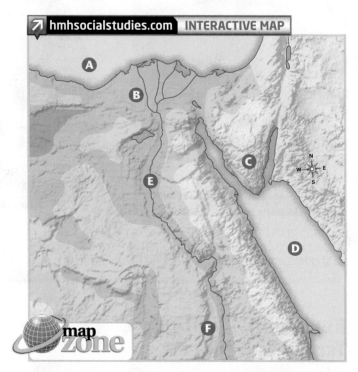

FOCUS ON READING AND WRITING

21. Categorizing Create a chart with three columns. Title the chart "Egyptian Pharaohs." Label the three chart columns "Positions of power," "Responsibilities," and "Famous Pharaohs." Then list facts and details from the chapter under each category in the chart.

22. Writing a Riddle Choose five details about Egypt. Then write a sentence about each detail. Each sentence of your riddle should be a statement ending with "me." For example, if you were writing about the United States, you might say, "People come from all over the world to join me." After you have written your five sentences, end your riddle with "Who am I?" The answer to your riddle must be "Egypt."

Standardized Test Prep

DIRECTIONS: Read questions 1 through 8 and write the letter of the best response. Then read question 9 and write your own well-constructed response.

1 **Which statement about how the Nile helped civilization develop in Egypt is false?**

A It provided a source of food and water.

B It enabled farming in the area.

C Its flooding enriched the soil along its banks.

D It protected against invasion from the west.

2 **The most fertile soil in Egypt was located in the**

A Nile Delta.

B deserts.

C cataracts.

D far south.

3 **The high position that priests held in Egyptian society shows that**

A the pharaoh was a descendant of a god.

B government was large and powerful.

C religion was important in Egyptian life.

D the early Egyptians worshipped many gods.

4 **The Egyptians are probably *best* known for building**

A pyramids.

B irrigation canals.

C cataracts.

D deltas.

5 **During which period did ancient Egypt reach the height of its power and glory?**

A First Dynasty

B Old Kingdom

C Middle Kingdom

D New Kingdom

> Oh great god and ruler, the gift of Amon-Re, god of the Sun.
> Oh great protector of Egypt and its people.
> Great one who saved us from the Tehenu.
> You, who have fortified our western border to protect us from our enemies.
> You, who honored the gods with mighty temples at Abu Simbel and Luxor.
> We bless you, oh great one.
> We worship and honor you, oh great and mighty pharaoh.

6 **A tribute such as the one above might have been written in honor of which Egyptian ruler?**

A Menes

B Ramses the Great

C King Tutankhamen

D Queen Hatshepsut

7 **What discovery gave historians the key they needed to read Egyptian hieroglyphics?**

A obelisk

B papyrus

C Rosetta Stone

D sphinx

8 **Which of the following groups made up the majority of people in ancient Egypt?**

A artisans and artists

B farmers and other peasants

C merchants and traders

D scribes

9 **Extended Response** Examine the diagram titled Egyptian Society in Section 2. Based on the information in the diagram and in the text, explain the role that religion and government played in the organization of Egyptian society.

History of Ancient Kush

2300 BC–AD 350

Essential Question How did Kush progress from being controlled by Egypt to being its own separate kingdom?

Trade caravan in the Sahara

What You Will Learn...

In this chapter you will learn about the geography and history of ancient Kush. You will also discover the connections between Egypt and Kush. Finally, you will study the culture of ancient Kush and the reasons for its decline.

map zone

Geography Skills

Location The kingdom of Kush was located on the Upper Nile.
1. **Locate** What powerful civilization was located to the north of Kush?
2. **Make Inferences** What do the icons on the map indicate to you about Kush?

FOCUS ON READING AND WRITING

Asking Questions As you read new information, asking questions can help you learn and remember. After you read a paragraph or section, ask yourself who or what the passage is about, when and where the events took place, and why the information is important. **See the lesson, Asking Questions, on p. 195.**

Writing a Fictional Narrative In this chapter you will read about events surrounding the rise and fall of Kush. Then you will write a short story about fictional characters who lived through these events. The main character in your story will be from Kush. Other characters could be from Egypt, Assyria, and Aksum.

Kushite Pyramids Egyptian culture greatly influenced the people of Kush. Kush's leaders built pyramids like these as tombs.

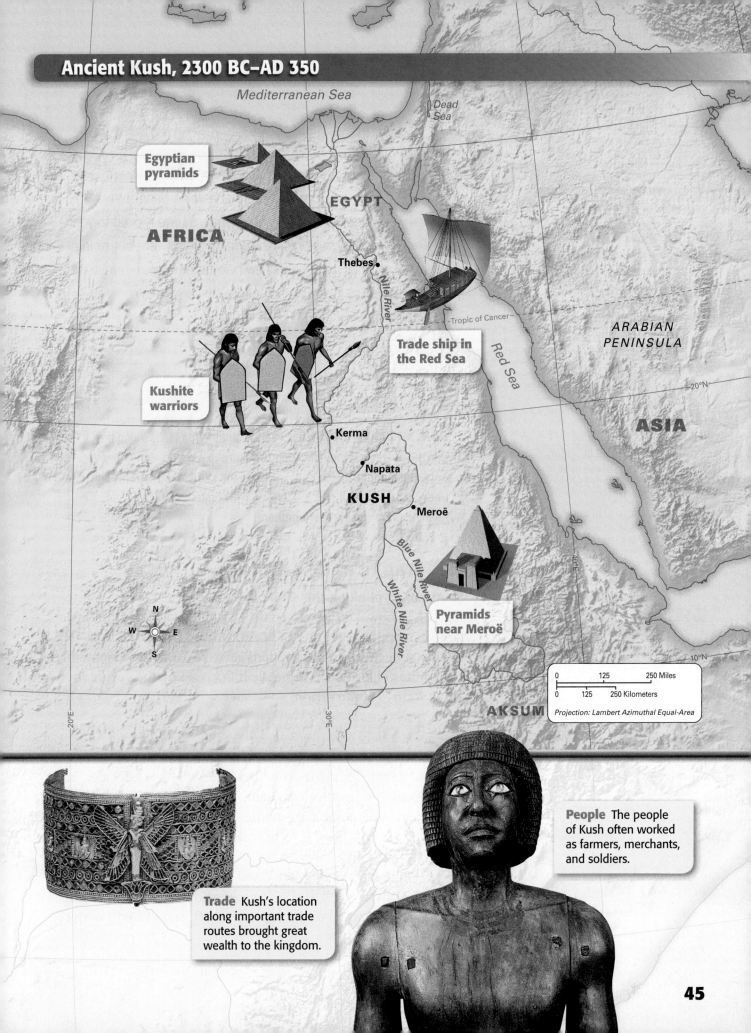

Mediterranean Sea

Dead Sea

Egyptian pyramids

EGYPT

AFRICA

Thebes

Nile River

Trade ship in the Red Sea

Tropic of Cancer

ARABIAN PENINSULA

Red Sea

20°N

Kushite warriors

ASIA

Kerma

Napata

KUSH

Meroë

Blue Nile River

White Nile River

Pyramids near Meroë

40°E

10°N

0   125   250 Miles

0   125   250 Kilometers

Projection: Lambert Azimuthal Equal-Area

N
W   E
S

20°E

30°E

AKSUM

People The people of Kush often worked as farmers, merchants, and soldiers.

Trade Kush's location along important trade routes brought great wealth to the kingdom.

Kush and Egypt

If **YOU** lived there...

You live along the Nile River, where it moves quickly through rapids. A few years ago, armies from the powerful kingdom of Egypt took over your country. Some Egyptians have moved to your town. They bring new customs, which many people are beginning to imitate. Now your sister has a new baby and wants to give it an Egyptian name! This upsets many people in your family.

How do you feel about following Egyptian customs?

BUILDING BACKGROUND Egypt dominated the lands along the Nile, but it was not the only ancient culture to develop along the river. Another kingdom, called Kush, arose to the south of Egypt. Through trade, conquest, and political dealings, the histories of Egypt and Kush became closely tied together.

Geography and Early Kush

South of Egypt along the Nile, a group of people settled in the region we now call Nubia. These Africans established the first large kingdom in the interior of Africa. We know this kingdom by the name the ancient Egyptians gave it—Kush. Development of Kushite civilization was greatly influenced by the geography and resources of the region.

The Land of Nubia

Nubia is a region in northeast Africa. It lies on the Nile River south of Egypt. Today desert covers much of Nubia, located in the present-day country of Sudan. In ancient times, however, the region was much more fertile. Heavy rainfall flooded the Nile every year. These floods provided a rich layer of fertile soil to nearby lands. The kingdom of Kush developed in this area.

In addition to having fertile soil, ancient Nubia was rich in valuable minerals such as gold, copper, and stone. These natural resources contributed to the region's wealth and played a major role in its history.

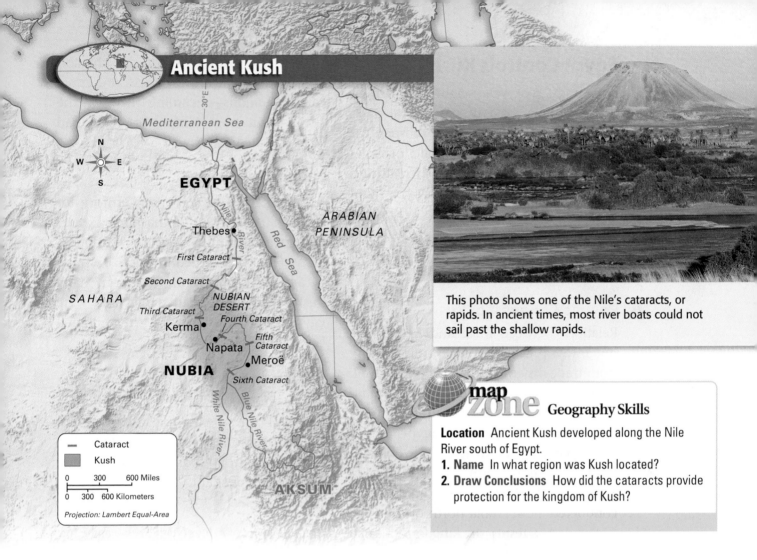

Ancient Kush

Mediterranean Sea

EGYPT

Thebes

First Cataract

Second Cataract

SAHARA

NUBIAN DESERT

Third Cataract

Kerma

Fourth Cataract

Napata

Fifth Cataract

NUBIA

Meroë

Sixth Cataract

Red Sea

ARABIAN PENINSULA

White Nile River

Blue Nile River

AKSUM

Cataract

Kush

0   300   600 Miles

0   300   600 Kilometers

Projection: Lambert Equal-Area

This photo shows one of the Nile's cataracts, or rapids. In ancient times, most river boats could not sail past the shallow rapids.

map zone Geography Skills

Location Ancient Kush developed along the Nile River south of Egypt.
1. **Name** In what region was Kush located?
2. **Draw Conclusions** How did the cataracts provide protection for the kingdom of Kush?

Early Civilization in Nubia

Like all early civilizations, the people of Nubia depended on agriculture for their food. Fortunately for them, the Nile's floods allowed the Nubians to plant both summer and winter crops. Among the crops they grew were wheat, barley, and other grains. In addition to farmland, the banks of the river provided grazing land for cattle and other livestock. As a result, farming villages thrived all along the Nile by about 3500 BC.

Over time some farmers became richer and more successful than others. These farmers became leaders of their villages. Sometime around 2000 BC, one of these leaders took control of other villages and made himself king of the region. His new kingdom was called Kush.

The early kings of Kush ruled from their capital at Kerma (KAR-muh). This city was located on the Nile just south of a cataract, or stretch of rapids. Cataracts made travel through some parts of the Nile extremely difficult. As a result, the cataracts were natural barriers against invaders. For many years the cataracts kept Kush safe from the powerful Egyptian kingdom to the north.

As time passed, Kushite society grew more complex. In addition to farmers and herders, some people of Kush became priests or artisans. Early on, civilizations to the south greatly influenced the kingdom of Kush. Later, however, Egypt played a greater role in the kingdom's history.

READING CHECK **Finding Main Ideas** How did geography help civilization grow in Nubia?

FOCUS ON READING
What is this paragraph about? Why is it important?

Egypt Controls Kush

Kush and Egypt were neighbors. At times the neighbors lived in peace with each other and helped each other prosper. For example, Kush became a supplier of slaves and raw materials to Egypt. The Kushites sent materials such as gold, copper, and stone to Egypt. The Kushites also sent the Egyptians **ebony**, a type of dark, heavy wood, and **ivory**, a white material taken from elephant tusks.

Egypt's Conquest of Kush

Relations between Kush and Egypt were not always peaceful. As Kush grew wealthy from trade, its army grew stronger as well. Egypt's rulers soon feared that Kush would grow even stronger. They were afraid that a powerful Kush might attack Egypt.

To prevent such an attack, the pharaoh Thutmose I sent an army to take control of Kush around 1500 BC. The pharaoh's army conquered all of Nubia north of the Fifth Cataract. As a result, the kingdom of Kush became part of Egypt.

After his army's victory, the pharaoh destroyed the Kushite palace at Kerma. Later pharaohs—including Ramses the Great—built huge temples in what had been Kushite territory.

Effects of the Conquest

Kush remained an Egyptian territory for about 450 years. During that time, Egypt's influence over Kush grew tremendously. Many Egyptians settled in Kush. Egyptian became the language of the region. Many Kushites used Egyptian names and wore Egyptian-style clothing. They also adopted Egyptian religious practices.

A Change in Power

In the mid-1000s BC the New Kingdom in Egypt was ending. As the power of Egypt's pharaohs declined, Kushite leaders regained control of Kush. Kush once again became independent.

READING CHECK Identifying Cause and Effect
How did Egyptian rule change Kush?

Kush and Egypt

Early in its history, Egypt dominated Kush, forcing Kushites to give tribute to Egypt.

Kush Rules Egypt

We know almost nothing about the history of the Kushites for about 200 years after they regained independence from Egypt. Kush is not mentioned in any historical records until the 700s BC, when armies from Kush swept into Egypt and conquered it.

The Conquest of Egypt

By around 850 BC, Kush had regained its strength. It was once again as strong as it had been before it was conquered by Egypt. Because the Egyptians had captured the old capital at Kerma, the kings of Kush ruled from the city of Napata. Napata was located on the Nile, about 100 miles southeast of Kerma.

As Kush was growing stronger, Egypt was losing power. A series of weak pharaohs left Egypt open to attack. In the 700s BC a Kushite king, Kashta, took advantage of Egypt's weakness. Kashta attacked Egypt. By about 751 BC he had conquered Upper Egypt. He then established relations with Lower Egypt.

After Kashta died, his son Piankhi (PYANG-kee) continued to attack Egypt. The armies of Kush captured many cities, including Egypt's ancient capital. Piankhi fought the Egyptians because he believed that the gods wanted him to rule all of Egypt. By the time he died in about 716 BC, Piankhi had accomplished this task. His kingdom extended north from Napata all the way to the Nile Delta.

Later, as Kush's power increased, its warriors invaded and conquered Egypt. This photo shows Kushite and Egyptian warriors.

After conquering Egypt, Kush established a new dynasty. This sculpture shows one of Kush's pharaohs kneeling before an Egyptian god.

ANALYSIS SKILL **ANALYZING VISUALS**

What did Kushites give to Egypt as tribute?

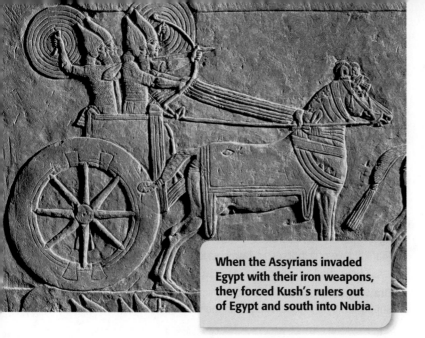

When the Assyrians invaded Egypt with their iron weapons, they forced Kush's rulers out of Egypt and south into Nubia.

The Kushite Dynasty

After Piankhi died, his brother Shabaka (SHAB-uh-kuh) took control of the kingdom and declared himself pharaoh. His declaration marked the beginning of Egypt's Twenty-fifth, or Kushite, Dynasty.

Shabaka and later rulers of his dynasty tried to restore many old Egyptian cultural practices. Some of these practices had died out during Egypt's period of weakness. For example, Shabaka was buried in a pyramid. The Egyptians had stopped building pyramids for their rulers centuries earlier.

The Kushite rulers of Egypt built new temples to Egyptian gods and restored old ones. They also worked to preserve many Egyptian writings. As a result, Egyptian culture thrived during the Kushite dynasty.

The End of Kushite Rule in Egypt

The Kushite dynasty remained strong in Egypt for about 40 years. In the 670s BC, however, the powerful army of the Assyrians from Mesopotamia invaded Egypt. The Assyrians' iron weapons were better than the Kushites' bronze weapons, and the Kushites were slowly pushed out of Egypt. In just 10 years the Assyrians had driven the Kushite forces completely out of Egypt.

READING CHECK **Sequencing** How did the leaders of Kush gain control over Egypt?

SUMMARY AND PREVIEW Kush was conquered by Egypt, but later the Kushites controlled Egypt. In the next section, you will learn how the civilization of Kush developed after the Kushites were forced out of Egypt by the Assyrians.

Section 1 Assessment

hmhsocialstudies.com
ONLINE QUIZ

Reviewing Ideas, Terms, and Places

1. **a. Identify** On which river did Kush develop?
   b. Analyze How did **Nubia**'s natural resources influence the early history of Kush?
2. **a. Describe** What is **ivory**?
   b. Explain How did Egypt's conquest of Kush affect the people of Kush?
   c. Evaluate Why do you think Thutmose I destroyed the Kushite palace at Kerma?
3. **a. Describe** What territory did Piankhi conquer?
   b. Make Inferences Why is the Twenty-fifth Dynasty significant in the history of Egypt?
   c. Predict What might have happened in Kush and Egypt if Kush had developed iron weapons earlier?

Critical Thinking

4. **Sequencing** Use a time line like the one below to show the sequence and dates of important events in the early history of the kingdom of Kush.

2000 BC   680 BC

FOCUS ON WRITING

5. **Planning Characters and Plot** Make a chart with two columns. Label one "Characters," and take notes on the characters and their interactions. Label the other "Plot," and note major events and sources of conflict among the characters.

Later Kush

If **YOU** lived there...

You live in Meroë, the capital of Kush, in 250 BC. Your father is a skilled ironworker. From him you've learned to shape iron tools and weapons. Everyone expects that you will carry on his work. If you do become an ironworker, you will likely make a good living. But you are restless. You'd like to travel down the Nile to see Egypt and the great sea beyond it. Now a neighbor who is a trader has asked you to join his next trading voyage.

Will you leave Meroë to travel? Why or why not?

BUILDING BACKGROUND The Assyrians drove the Kushites out of Egypt in the 600s BC, partly through their use of iron weapons. Although the Kushites lost control of Egypt, their kingdom did not disappear. In fact, they built up another empire in the African interior, based on trade and their own iron industry.

Kush's Economy Grows

After they lost control of Egypt, the people of Kush devoted themselves to improving agriculture and trade. They hoped to make their country rich again. Within a few centuries, Kush had indeed become a rich and powerful kingdom once more.

What You Will Learn...

Main Ideas

1. Kush's economy grew because of its iron industry and trade network.
2. Some elements of Kushite society and culture were borrowed from other cultures while others were unique to Kush.
3. The decline and defeat of Kush was caused by both internal and external factors.

The Big Idea

Although Kush developed an advanced civilization, it eventually declined.

Key Terms and Places

Meroë, *p. 52*
trade network, *p. 52*
merchants, *p. 52*
exports, *p. 52*
imports, *p. 52*

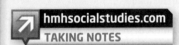
hmhsocialstudies.com
TAKING NOTES

Use the graphic organizer online to take notes about the civilization of Kush and how it finally declined.

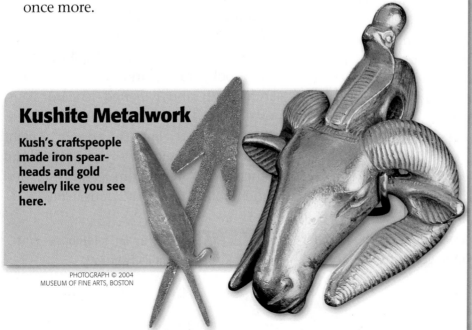

Kushite Metalwork

Kush's craftspeople made iron spearheads and gold jewelry like you see here.

PHOTOGRAPH © 2004
MUSEUM OF FINE ARTS, BOSTON

Close-up

Kush's Trade Network

Ancient Kush was at the center of a large trading network with connections to Europe, Africa, and Asia. Kush's location and production of iron goods helped make it a rich trading center.

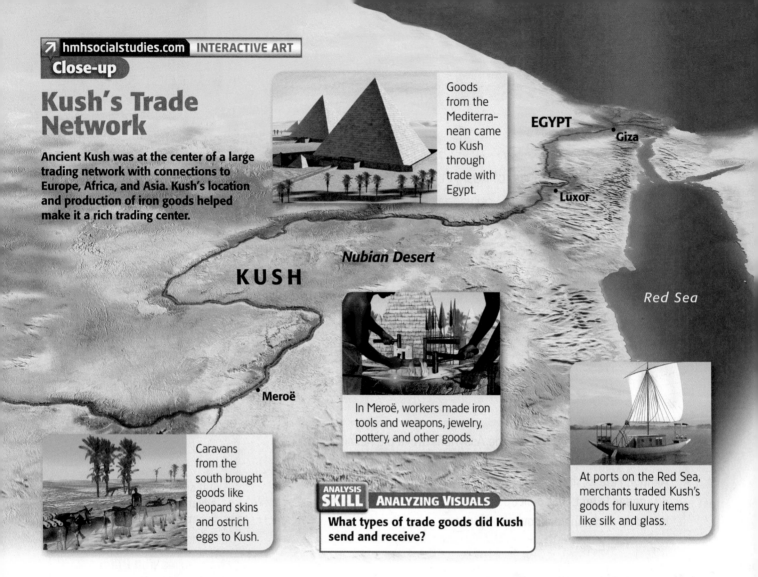

Goods from the Mediterranean came to Kush through trade with Egypt.

EGYPT

• Giza

• Luxor

Nubian Desert

KUSH

Red Sea

• Meroë

In Meroë, workers made iron tools and weapons, jewelry, pottery, and other goods.

Caravans from the south brought goods like leopard skins and ostrich eggs to Kush.

At ports on the Red Sea, merchants traded Kush's goods for luxury items like silk and glass.

ANALYSIS SKILL | **ANALYZING VISUALS**

What types of trade goods did Kush send and receive?

Kush's Iron Industry

FOCUS ON READING

As you read, ask yourself these questions: Where was Meroë? Why was it important?

During this period, the economic center of Kush was **Meroë** (MER-oh-wee), the new Kushite capital. Meroë's location on the east bank of the Nile helped Kush's economy. Gold could be found nearby, as could forests of ebony and other wood. More importantly, the area around Meroë was rich in deposits of iron ore.

In this location the Kushites developed an iron industry. Because resources such as iron ore and wood for furnaces were easily available, the industry grew quickly.

Expansion of Trade

In time, Meroë became the center of a large **trade network**, a system of people in different lands who trade goods back and forth.

The Kushites sent goods down the Nile to Egypt. From there, Egyptian and Greek **merchants**, or traders, carried goods to ports on the Mediterranean and Red seas and to southern Africa. These goods may have eventually reached India and China.

Kush's **exports**—items sent to other regions for trade—included gold, pottery, iron tools, slaves, and ivory. Merchants from Kush also exported leopard skins, ostrich feathers, and elephants. In return, Kushites received **imports**—goods brought in from other regions—such as jewelry and other luxury items from Egypt, Asia, and lands around the Mediterranean Sea.

READING CHECK **Drawing Inferences** What helped Kush's iron industry grow?

Society and Culture

As Kushite trade grew, merchants came into contact with people from many other cultures. As a result, the people of Kush combined customs from other cultures with their own unique culture.

Kushite Culture

The most obvious influence on the culture of Kush was Egypt. Many buildings in Meroë, especially temples, resembled those in Egypt. Many people in Kush worshipped Egyptian gods and wore Egyptian clothing. Like Egyptian rulers, Kush's rulers used the title *pharaoh* and were buried in pyramids.

Many elements of Kushite culture were unique and not borrowed from anywhere else. For example, Kushite daily life and houses were different from those in other places. One Greek geographer noted some of these differences.

"The houses in the cities are formed by inter-weaving split pieces of palm wood or of bricks . . . They hunt elephants, lions, and panthers. There are also serpents, which encounter elephants, and there are many other kinds of wild animals."

–Strabo, from *Geography*

In addition to Egyptian gods, Kushites worshipped their own gods. For example, their most important god was the lion-headed god Apedemek. The people of Kush also developed their own written language, known today as Meroitic. Unfortunately, historians have not yet been able to interpret the Meroitic language.

Women in Kushite Society

Unlike women in other early societies, Kushite women were expected to be active in their society. Like Kushite men, women worked long hours in the fields. They also raised children, cooked, and performed other household tasks. During times of war, many women fought alongside men.

Some Kushite women rose to positions of **authority**, especially religious authority. For example, King Piankhi made his sister a powerful priestess. Later rulers followed his example and made other princesses priestesses as well. Other women from royal families led the ceremonies in which new kings were crowned.

Some Kushite women had even more power. These women served as co-rulers with their husbands or sons. A few Kushite women, such as Queen Shanakhdakheto (shah-nahk-dah-KEE-toh), even ruled the empire alone. Several other queens ruled Kush later, helping increase the strength and wealth of the kingdom. Throughout most of its history, however, Kush was ruled by kings.

READING CHECK **Analyzing** In what ways were the society and culture of Kush unique?

ACADEMIC VOCABULARY

authority power or influence

THE IMPACT TODAY

More than 50 ancient Kushite pyramids still stand near the ruins of Meroë in present-day Sudan.

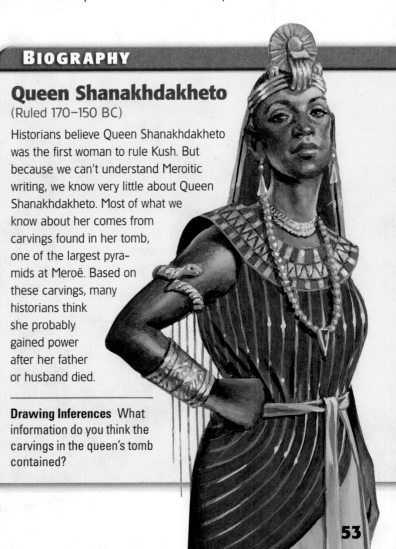

BIOGRAPHY

Queen Shanakhdakheto
(Ruled 170–150 BC)

Historians believe Queen Shanakhdakheto was the first woman to rule Kush. But because we can't understand Meroitic writing, we know very little about Queen Shanakhdakheto. Most of what we know about her comes from carvings found in her tomb, one of the largest pyramids at Meroë. Based on these carvings, many historians think she probably gained power after her father or husband died.

Drawing Inferences What information do you think the carvings in the queen's tomb contained?

53

Rulers of Kush

Like the Egyptians, the people of Kush considered their rulers to be gods. Kush's culture was similar to Egypt's, but there were also important differences.

Like the Egyptians, Kush's rulers built pyramids. Kushite pyramids, however, were much smaller and the style was different.

Kush was at times ruled by powerful queens. Queens seem to have been more important in Kush than in Egypt.

Stone carvings were made to commemorate important buildings and events, just like in Egypt. Kush's writing system was similar to Egyptian hieroglyphics, but scholars have been unable to understand most of it.

ANALYSIS SKILL **ANALYZING VISUALS**

What can you see in the illustration that is similar to Egyptian culture?

Decline and Defeat

The Kushite kingdom centered at Meroë reached its height in the first century BC. Four centuries later, Kush had collapsed. Developments both inside and outside the empire led to its downfall.

Loss of Resources

A series of problems within Kush weakened its economic power. One possible problem was that farmers allowed their cattle to overgraze the land. When the cows ate all the grass, there was nothing to hold the soil down. As a result, wind blew the soil away. Without this soil, farmers could not produce enough food for Kush's people.

In addition, ironmakers probably used up the forests near Meroë. As wood became scarce, furnaces shut down. Kush could no longer produce enough weapons or trade goods. As a result, Kush's military and economic power declined.

Trade Rivals

Kush was also weakened by a loss of trade. Foreign merchants set up new trade routes that went around Kush. For example, a new trade route bypassed Kush in favor of a nearby kingdom, Aksum (AHK-soom).

Rise of Aksum

Aksum was located southeast of Kush on the Red Sea, in present-day Ethiopia and Eritrea. In the first two centuries AD, Aksum grew wealthy from trade. But Aksum's wealth and power came at the expense of Kush. As Kush's power declined, Aksum became the most powerful state in the region.

By the AD 300s, Kush had lost much of its wealth and military might. Seeing that the Kushites were weak, the king of Aksum sent an army to conquer his former trade rival. In about AD 350, the army of Aksum's King Ezana (AY-zah-nah) destroyed Meroë and took over the kingdom of Kush.

In the late 300s, the rulers of Aksum became Christian. Their new religion reshaped culture throughout Nubia, and the last influences of Kush disappeared.

READING CHECK **Summarizing** What internal problems caused Kush's power to decline?

THE IMPACT TODAY

Much of the population of Ethiopia, which includes what used to be Aksum, is still Christian.

SUMMARY AND PREVIEW In this section you learned about the rise and fall of a powerful Kushite kingdom centered in Meroë. Next, you will learn about the rise of strong empires in West Africa.

Section 2 Assessment

hmhsocialstudies.com
ONLINE QUIZ

Reviewing Ideas, Terms, and Places

1. **a. Recall** What were some of Kush's **exports**?
   b. Analyze Why was **Meroë** in a good location?
2. **a. Identify** Who was Queen Shanakhdakheto?
   b. Compare How were Kushite and Egyptian cultures similar?
   c. Elaborate How does our inability to understand Meroitic affect our knowledge of Kush's culture?
3. **a. Identify** What kingdom conquered Kush in about AD 350?
   b. Summarize What was the impact of new trade routes on Kush?

Critical Thinking

4. **Identifying Causes** Review your notes to identify causes of the rise and the fall of the Kushite kingdom centered at Meroë. Use a chart like this one to record the causes.

Causes of rise	Causes of fall

FOCUS ON WRITING

5. **Adding Details** Add details to your chart. What were your characters' lives like? What events caused Kush to change over time? Note events that your characters might take part in during your story.

Social Studies Skills

Identifying Bias

Learn

Occasionally when you read you may come across bias. Bias is a one-sided idea about someone or something. It is based solely on opinion, not facts. An opinion is a personal belief or judgment.

Bias can be either favorable or unfavorable. For example, when voting for a cheerleader, you might have a favorable bias toward your best friend. Identifying bias is an important part of understanding the issues, events, and people in our world. Read the tips below for information on how to identify bias.

• Look for information about the author. What is the author's background? How might that affect his or her attitude?

• Look at the language the author uses. Is the information fact or opinion? Does the author present only one side or point of view?

• Look at the author's sources. Do they favor one side over another?

Practice

As you read the text in this passage, look for possible bias. Then answer the following questions.

❶ What facts are presented in the passage? What opinions are presented?

❷ The author was a famous Greek historian. Why might he be biased regarding the Kushites?

❸ What words or phrases indicate that the author is biased? Do those words indicate a favorable or unfavorable bias?

> "The mode of life of the [Kushites] is wretched; they are for the most part naked, and wander from place to place with their flocks. Their flocks and herds are small in size . . . They [the Kushites] live on millet and barley . . . Some feed even upon grass, the tender twigs of trees, the lotus, or the roots of reeds."
>
> –Strabo, from *Geography*

Apply

Practice identifying bias. Locate a news article that you feel has favorable or unfavorable bias. Then answer the questions below.

1. What issue, event, or person is the article about?

2. What is the author's bias? What words or phrases indicate that?

3. What is the author's background? What opinions does the author give? What sources does he or she cite?

Geography's Impact
video series
Review the video to answer the closing question:
How might the manufacture of iron have led to Meroë's downfall?

Visual Summary

Use the visual summary below to help you review the main ideas of the chapter.

QUICK FACTS

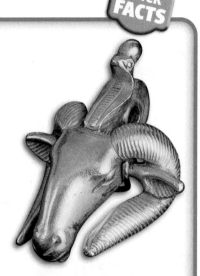

Egypt dominated early Kush and forced the Kushites to pay tribute.

After Kush conquered Egypt, invaders forced the Kushites to move south to their ancient homeland.

Kush's advanced civilization blended unique Kushite traits with culture traits from Egypt and other parts of Africa.

Reviewing Terms and Places

Match the words in the columns with the correct definitions listed below.

1. authority
2. ebony
3. export
4. import
5. merchant
6. Meroë
7. Nubia
8. trade network

a. an item sent to other regions for trade

b. a region along the Nile River in present-day Sudan

c. a trader

d. dark, heavy wood

e. groups of people in different lands who trade goods back and forth

f. the capital and economic center of the kingdom of Kush

g. item brought in for purchase from other regions

h. power or influence

Comprehension and Critical Thinking

SECTION 1 *(Pages 46–50)*

9. a. Describe How did the physical geography of Nubia affect civilization in the region?

b. Analyze Why did the relationship between Kush and Egypt change more than once over the centuries?

c. Predict If an archaeologist found an artifact near the Fourth Cataract, why might he or she have difficulty deciding how to display it in a museum?

SECTION 2 *(Pages 51–55)*

10. a. Identify Who was Queen Shanakhdakheto? Why don't we know more about her?

b. Compare and Contrast What are some features that Kushite and Egyptian cultures had in common? How were they different?

c. Evaluate What do you think was the most important cause of Kush's decline? Why?

Social Studies Skills

Identifying Bias *Read the passage below, then answer the questions that follow.*

> According to inscriptions found at Napata, Piankhi led his army to Egypt to stop a rebellion. As Piankhi approached, his enemies were gripped by fear. His finest troops conquered the cities of the Nile Valley one by one. In victory, the great Pianhki was merciful.

11. What issue, event, or person is this passage about?

12. What sources does the author cite?

13. What words from the passage indicate that the author is biased? Is the author's bias favorable or unfavorable?

Map Activity

14. **Ancient Kush** On a separate sheet of paper, match the letters on the map with their correct labels.

Aksum	Meroë
Blue Nile	Napata
Egypt	Red Sea
Mediterranean Sea	Sahara

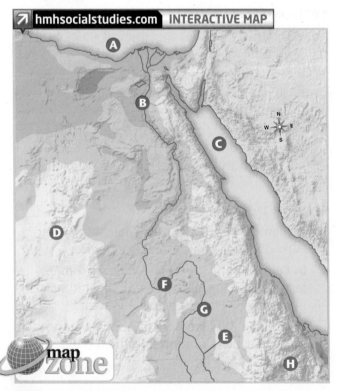

hmhsocialstudies.com INTERACTIVE MAP

map zone

Using the Internet

15. **Activity: Researching Life in Ancient Nubia**
Would you like to travel back in time to ancient Nubia and explore the wonders of that era? Through the online book, find out about the people, their customs, and their homes. Finally, imagine that you are a person living in ancient Kush. Take notes about the home, activities, and religion you might have experienced. Write a journal entry to show what you have learned. In your journal entry, specify which parts of your life have Egyptian influences.

hmhsocialstudies.com

FOCUS ON READING AND WRITING

Asking Questions Read the passage below. As you read, ask yourself questions to help you learn and remember the information. On a separate sheet of paper, write down the questions you created and the answers to those questions.

> After Egypt attacked Napata in the 500s BC, Kush's rulers moved their capital to Meroë. Located about 150 miles (240 km) southeast of Napata, Meroë served as the center for trade and government in Kush.

16. **Writing a Fictional Narrative** Use the notes you have taken to write your short story about a character from Kush. First, identify the setting, or where the story takes place. Then, tell about the problem, or conflict, your main character is facing. Relate the series of events that occur from the beginning of the conflict until it ends. Introduce the other characters as they become involved in the plot of the story.

You can help bring the story to life by adding dialogue as your characters deal with events in the story. At the end of the story, resolve the central problem or conflict. Make sure the ending is believable and satisfies your readers' curiosity about what happened.

Standardized Test Prep

DIRECTIONS: Read questions 1 through 7 and write the letter of the best response. Then read question 8 and write your own well-constructed response.

1 Which of the following statements regarding women in ancient Kush is *true*?

   A Some Kushite women served as religious and political leaders.

   B Kushite women had more rights and opportunities than Kushite men.

   C Kushite women were forbidden to leave their homes.

   D Many Kushite women were wealthy merchants.

2 Around 1500 BC, Egyptian rulers conquered Kush because

   A they wanted to expand their territory.

   B they wanted revenge for a Kushite attack on Thebes.

   C they feared Kush's growing military power.

   D they hoped to gain valuable resources.

3 Which of the following was an advantage of the Kushite capital of Meroë?

   A It had rich deposits of iron ore and gold nearby.

   B It was close to Mediterranean trade routes.

   C It was the religious center of Kush.

   D It was protected from invasion by the Sahara.

4 How did cataracts on the Nile River benefit Kush?

   A They allowed Kushite farmers to plant both summer and winter crops.

   B Because they were highly prized by Egyptians, Kush gained wealth from trade.

   C Because they were difficult to pass through, they provided protection against invaders.

   D They allowed the Kushites to build a powerful army.

" It is surrounded on the side of Libya by great hills of sand, and on that of Arabia by continuous precipices. In the higher parts on the south, it is bounded by . . . Astapa [the White Nile], and Astasobas [the Blue Nile]. On the north is the continuous course of the Nile to Egypt . . ."

–Strabo, from *Geography*

5 What region is the author describing in the quote above?

   A Assyria

   B Egypt

   C Mesopotamia

   D Nubia

6 How did Egyptian culture influence Kush?

   A Egyptians taught Kushites how to raise cattle.

   B Kushites adopted Christianity.

   C Egyptians taught Kushites how to make iron.

   D Kushites modeled their pyramids after Egyptian pyramids.

7 Which of the following is a cause of the decline of Kush?

   A Egypt conquered Kush hoping to steal the technology for making iron.

   B Piankhi's armies were crushed when they attempted to invade Aksum.

   C Invaders from West Africa defeated the Kushites in about 350 BC.

   D The loss of trade severely damaged Kush's economy.

8 **Extended Response** Using the information in the Close-up illustration, Rulers of Kush, in Section 2, write a short paragraph describing the culture of Kush.

CHAPTER 3

History of West Africa

500 BC–AD 1650

Essential Question How did trade influence the rise and fall of early West African empires?

? What You Will Learn...

In this chapter you will learn about the great empires of West Africa, which grew rich from trade. You will also learn about the traditions of West Africa, which include storytelling, art, music, and dance.

FOCUS ON READING AND WRITING

Understanding Cause and Effect When you read about history, it is important to recognize causes and effects. A cause is an action or event that makes something else happen. An effect is the result of a cause. For example, when you read this chapter you could identify the causes that led to great empires in West Africa. Then you can identify the empires' effects. **See the lesson, Understanding Cause and Effect, on page 196.**

A Journal Entry Many people feel that recording their lives in journals helps them to understand their own experiences. Writing a journal entry from someone else's point of view can help you understand what that person's life is, or would have been, like. In this chapter, you will read about the land, people, and culture of early Africa. Then you will imagine a character and write a journal entry from his or her point of view.

ATLANTIC OCEAN

Trade West Africa's salt mines were a great source of wealth. Camels carried salt from the mines of the Sahara to the south to trade for gold.

West Africa, 500 BC–AD 1650

Moroccan gold coins

S A H A R A

20°N

Mosque

Timbuktu

Koumbi Saleh

Djenné

Niger River

Trading caravan

Clay sculpture

Gulf of Guinea

map zone

Place Great empires in West Africa grew rich from trade.
1. **Identify** On what river were major cities located?
2. **Make Inferences** What might the icons on the map tell you about West Africa during this period of history?

Traditions Storytellers, or griots, kept the cultures of West Africa alive with their stories.

Religion During the Mali Empire, Islam spread throughout West Africa. Muslim architects built hundreds of mud-walled mosques throughout the empire.

61

Empire of Ghana

What You Will Learn...

Main Ideas

1. Ghana controlled trade and became wealthy.
2. Through its control of trade, Ghana built an empire.
3. Attacking invaders, overgrazing, and the loss of trade caused Ghana's decline.

The Big Idea

The rulers of Ghana built an empire by controlling the salt and gold trade.

Key Terms

silent barter, *p. 64*

hmhsocialstudies.com
TAKING NOTES

Use the graphic organizer online to make a list of important events from the beginning to the end of the empire of Ghana.

If **YOU** lived there...

You are a trader, traveling in a caravan from the north into West Africa in about 1000. The caravan carries many goods, but the most precious is salt. Salt is so valuable that people trade gold for it! You have never met the mysterious men who trade you the gold. You wish you could talk to them to find out where they get it.

Why do you think the traders are so secretive?

BUILDING BACKGROUND The various regions of Africa provide people with different resources. West Africa, for example, was rich in both fertile soils and minerals, especially gold and iron. Other regions had plentiful supplies of other resources, such as salt. Over time, trade developed between regions with different resources. This trade led to the growth of the first great empire in West Africa.

Ghana Controls Trade

For hundreds of years, trade routes crisscrossed West Africa. For most of that time, West Africans did not profit much from the Saharan trade because the routes were run by Berbers from northern Africa. Eventually, that situation changed. Ghana (GAH-nuh), an empire in West Africa, gained control of the valuable routes. As a result, Ghana became a powerful state.

As you can see on the map on the following page, the empire of Ghana lay between the Niger and Senegal rivers. This location was north and west of the location of the modern nation that bears the name Ghana.

Ghana's Beginnings

Archaeology provides some clues to Ghana's early history, but we do not know much about its earliest days. Historians think the first people in Ghana were farmers. Sometime after 300 these farmers, the Soninke (soh-NING-kee), were threatened by nomadic herders. The herders wanted to take the farmers' water and pastures. For protection, groups of Soninke families began to band together. This banding together was the beginning of Ghana.

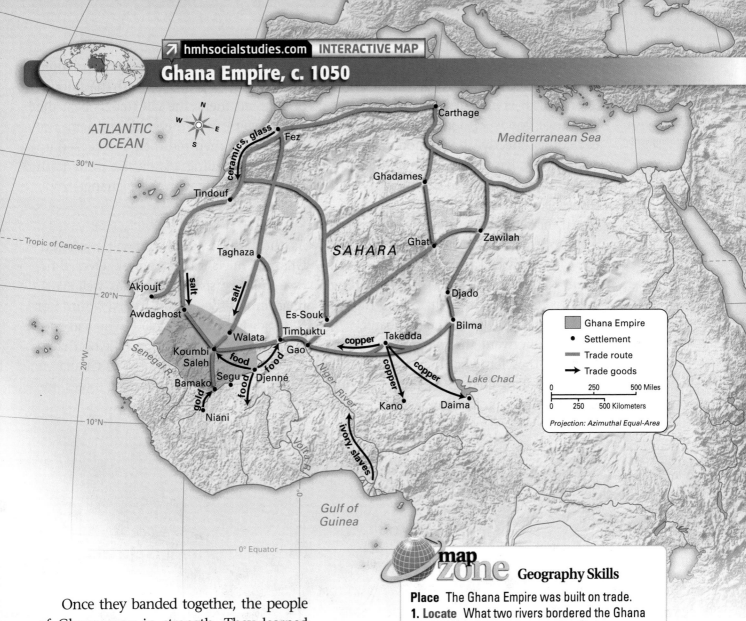

Ghana Empire, c. 1050

ATLANTIC OCEAN

Mediterranean Sea

SAHARA

Carthage

Fez

ceramics, glass

Tindouf

Ghadames

Ghat

Zawilah

Taghaza

salt

salt

Akjoujt

Awdaghost

Es-Souk

Timbuktu

Djado

Bilma

copper

Takedda

Walata

Koumbi Saleh

food

Gao

food

copper

copper

Lake Chad

Segu

Djenné

food

Bamako

gold

Kano

Daima

Niani

ivory, slaves

Senegal R.

Niger River

Volta R.

Gulf of Guinea

	Ghana Empire
•	Settlement
	Trade route
→	Trade goods

0 250 500 Miles
0 250 500 Kilometers
Projection: Azimuthal Equal-Area

map zone Geography Skills

Place The Ghana Empire was built on trade.
1. **Locate** What two rivers bordered the Ghana Empire?
2. **Analyze** What goods came to Ghana from the north?

↗ hmhsocialstudies.com
ANIMATED GEOGRAPHY
West African Trading Empires

Once they banded together, the people of Ghana grew in strength. They learned how to work with iron and used iron tools to farm the land along the Niger River. They also herded cattle for meat and milk. Because these farmers and herders could produce plenty of food, the population of Ghana increased. Towns and villages grew.

Besides farm tools, iron was also useful for making weapons. Other armies in the area had weapons made of bone, wood, and stone. These were no match for the iron spear points and blades used by Ghana's army.

Trade in Valuable Goods

Ghana lay between the vast Sahara Desert and deep forests. In this location, they were in a good position to trade in the region's most valuable resources—gold and salt. Gold came from the south, from mines near the Gulf of Guinea and along the Niger. Salt came from the Sahara in the north.

People wanted gold for its beauty. But they needed salt in their diets to survive. Salt, which could be used to preserve food, also made bland food tasty. These qualities made salt very valuable. In fact, Africans sometimes cut up slabs of salt and used the pieces as money.

ACADEMIC
VOCABULARY

process a
series of steps
by which a task
is accomplished

The exchange of gold and salt sometimes followed a **process** called silent barter. **Silent barter** is a process in which people exchange goods without ever contacting each other directly. The method made sure that the traders did business peacefully. It also kept the exact location of the gold mines secret from the salt traders.

In the silent barter process, salt traders went to a riverbank near gold fields. There they left slabs of salt in rows and beat a drum to tell the gold miners that trading had begun. Then the salt traders moved back several miles from the riverbank.

Soon afterward, the gold miners arrived by boat. They left what they considered a fair amount of gold in exchange for the salt. Then the gold miners also moved back several miles so the salt traders could return. If they were happy with the amount of gold left there, the salt traders beat the drum again, took the gold, and left. The gold miners then returned and picked up their salt. Trading continued until both sides were happy with the exchange.

Growth of Trade

As the trade in gold and salt increased, Ghana's rulers gained power. Over time, their military strength grew as well. With their armies they began to take control of this trade from the merchants who had once controlled it. Merchants from the north and south met to exchange goods in Ghana. As a result of their control of trade routes, the rulers of Ghana became wealthy.

Salt and Gold

Additional sources of wealth and trade were developed to add to Ghana's wealth. Wheat came from the north. Sheep, cattle, and honey came from the south. Local products, including leather and cloth, were also traded for wealth. Among the prized special local products were tassels made from golden thread.

As trade increased, Ghana's capital grew as well. The largest city in West Africa, Koumbi Saleh (KOOM-bee SAHL-uh) was an oasis for travelers. These travelers could find all the region's goods for sale in its markets. As a result, Koumbi Saleh gained a reputation as a great trading center.

READING CHECK **Generalizing** How did trade help Ghana develop?

Ghana's rulers became rich by controlling the trade in salt and gold. Salt came from the north in large slabs like the ones shown at left. Gold, like the woman above is wearing, came from the south.

Ghana Builds an Empire

By 800 Ghana was firmly in control of West Africa's trade routes. Nearly all trade between northern and southern Africa passed through Ghana. Traders were protected by Ghana's army, which kept trade routes free from bandits. As a result, trade became safer. Knowing they would be protected, traders were not scared to travel to Ghana. Trade increased, and Ghana's influence grew as well.

Taxes and Gold

With so many traders passing through their lands, Ghana's rulers looked for ways to make money from them. One way they raised money was by forcing traders to pay taxes. Every trader who entered Ghana had to pay a special tax on the goods he carried. Then he had to pay another tax on any goods he took with him when he left.

Traders were not the only people who had to pay taxes. The people of Ghana also had to pay taxes. In addition, Ghana conquered many small neighboring tribes, then forced them to pay tribute. Rulers used the money from taxes and tribute to support Ghana's growing army.

Not all of Ghana's wealth came from taxes and tribute. Ghana's rich mines produced huge amounts of gold. Some of this gold was carried by traders to lands as far away as England, but not all of Ghana's gold was traded. Ghana's kings kept huge stores of gold for themselves. In fact, all the gold produced in Ghana was officially the property of the king.

Knowing that rare materials are worth far more than common ones, the rulers banned anyone else in Ghana from owning gold nuggets. Common people could own only gold dust, which they used as money. This ensured that the king was richer than his subjects.

Expansion of the Empire

Ghana's kings used their great wealth to build a powerful army. With this army the kings of Ghana conquered many of their neighbors. Many of these conquered areas were centers of trade. Taking over these areas made Ghana's kings even richer.

Ghana's kings didn't think that they could rule all the territory they conquered by themselves. Their empire was quite large, and travel and communication in West Africa could be difficult. To keep order in their empire, they allowed conquered kings to retain much of their power. These kings acted as governors of their territories, answering only to the king.

The empire of Ghana reached its peak under Tunka Manin (TOOHN-kah MAH-nin). This king had a splendid court where he displayed the vast wealth of the empire. A Spanish writer noted the court's splendor.

FOCUS ON READING

How is this quotation an example of the effects of the king's wealth?

"The king adorns himself . . . round his neck and his forearms, and he puts on a high cap decorated with gold and wrapped in a turban of fine cotton. Behind the king stand ten pages holding shields and swords decorated with gold."

–al-Bakri, from *The Book of Routes and Kingdoms*

READING CHECK **Summarizing** How did the rulers of Ghana control trade?

BIOGRAPHY

Tunka Manin
(Ruled around 1068)

All we know about Tunka Manin comes from the writings of a Muslim geographer who wrote about Ghana. From his writings, we know that Tunka Manin was the nephew of the previous king, a man named Basi. Kingship and property in Ghana did not pass from father to son, but from uncle to nephew. Only the king's sister's son could inherit the throne. Once he did become king, Tunka Manin surrounded himself with finery and many luxuries.

Contrasting How was inheritance in Ghana different from inheritance in other societies you have studied?

Ghana's Decline

In the mid-1000s Ghana was rich and powerful, but by the end of the 1200s, the empire had collapsed. Three major factors contributed to its end.

Invasion

The first factor that helped bring about Ghana's end was invasion. A Muslim group called the Almoravids (al-moh-RAH-vidz) attacked Ghana in the 1060s in an effort to force its leaders to convert to Islam.

The people of Ghana fought hard against the Almoravid army. For 14 years they kept the invaders at bay. In the end, however, the Almoravids won. They destroyed the city of Koumbi Saleh.

The Almoravids didn't control Ghana for long, but they certainly weakened the empire. They cut off many trade routes through Ghana and formed new trading partnerships with Muslim leaders instead. Without this trade Ghana could no longer support its empire.

Overgrazing

A second factor in Ghana's decline was a result of the Almoravid conquest. When the Almoravids moved into Ghana, they brought herds of animals with them. These animals ate all the grass in many pastures, leaving the soil exposed to hot desert winds. These winds blew away the soil, leaving the land worthless for farming or herding. Unable to grow crops, many farmers had to leave in search of new homes.

Internal Rebellion

A third factor also helped bring about the decline of Ghana's empire. In about 1200 the people of a country that Ghana had conquered rose up in rebellion. Within a few years the rebels had taken over the entire empire of Ghana.

Overgrazing

Too many animals grazing in one area can lead to problems, such as the loss of farmland that occurred in West Africa.

1 Animals are allowed to graze in areas with lots of grass.

2 With too many animals grazing, however, the grass disappears, leaving the soil below exposed to the wind.

3 The wind blows the soil away, turning what was once grassland into desert.

Once in control, however, the rebels found that they could not keep order in Ghana. Weakened, Ghana was attacked and defeated by one of its neighbors. The empire fell apart.

READING CHECK **Identifying Cause and Effect** Why did Ghana decline in the 1000s?

SUMMARY AND PREVIEW The empire of Ghana in West Africa grew rich and powerful through its control of trade routes. The empire lasted for centuries, but eventually Ghana fell. In the next section you will learn that it was replaced by a new empire, Mali.

Section 1 Assessment

Reviewing Ideas, Terms, and Places

1. a. **Identify** What were the two most valuable resources traded in Ghana?
   b. **Explain** How did the **silent barter** system work?
2. a. **Identify** Who was Tunka Manin?
   b. **Generalize** What did Ghana's kings do with the money they raised from taxes?
   c. **Elaborate** Why did the rulers of Ghana not want everyone to have gold?
3. a. **Identify** What group invaded Ghana in the late 1000s?
   b. **Summarize** How did overgrazing help cause the fall of Ghana?

Critical Thinking

4. **Identifying Causes** Draw a diagram like the one shown here. Use it to identify factors that caused Ghana's trade growth and those that caused its decline.

Growth → Ghana's Trade → Decline

FOCUS ON WRITING

5. **Gathering Information** Think about what it would have been like to live in Ghana. Whose journal would you create? Would you choose the powerful Tunka Manin? a trader? Jot down some ideas.

Crossing the Sahara

Crossing the Sahara has never been easy. Bigger than the entire continent of Australia, the Sahara is one of the hottest, driest, and most barren places on earth. Yet for centuries, people have crossed the Sahara's gravel-covered plains and vast seas of sand. Long ago, West Africans crossed the desert regularly to carry on a rich trade.

Salt, used to preserve and flavor food, was available in the Sahara. Traders from the north took salt south. Camel caravans carried huge slabs of salt weighing hundreds of pounds.

In exchange for salt, people in West Africa offered other valuable trade goods, especially gold. Gold dust was measured with special spoons and stored in boxes. Ivory, from the tusks of elephants, was carved into jewelry.

Tindouf

Akjoujt

Taghaza

Walata

Koumbi Saleh

Timbuktu

Es-Souk

Gao

Taked

A F R I C A

Gulf of Guinea

Hogback Mtn

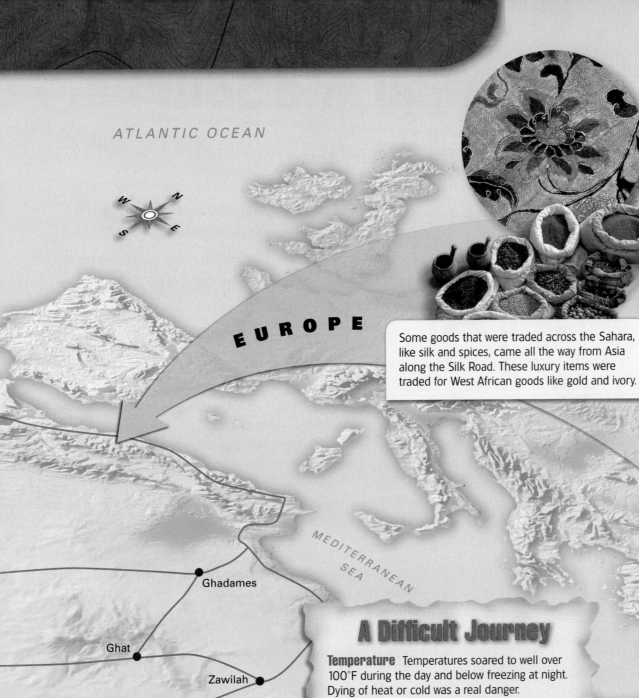

ATLANTIC OCEAN

EUROPE

Some goods that were traded across the Sahara, like silk and spices, came all the way from Asia along the Silk Road. These luxury items were traded for West African goods like gold and ivory.

MEDITERRANEAN SEA

Ghadames

Ghat

Zawilah

S A H A R A

Bilma

Daima

Trade route
Settlement
Scale varies on this map.

RED SEA

A Difficult Journey

Temperature Temperatures soared to well over 100°F during the day and below freezing at night. Dying of heat or cold was a real danger.

Water Most areas of the Sahara get less than one inch of rain per year. Travelers had to bring lots of water or they could die of thirst.

Distance The Sahara is huge, and the trade routes were not well marked. Travelers could easily get lost.

Bandits Valuable trade goods were a tempting target for bandits. For protection, merchants traveled in caravans.

ANALYSIS
SKILL **ANALYZING VISUALS**

1. What were some goods traded across the Sahara?
2. Why was salt a valued trade good?

Mali and Songhai

What You Will Learn...

Main Ideas

1. The empire of Mali reached its height under the ruler Mansa Musa, but the empire fell to invaders in the 1400s.
2. The Songhai built a new Islamic empire in West Africa, conquering many of the lands that were once part of Mali.

The Big Idea

Between 1000 and 1500 the empires of Mali and Songhai developed in West Africa.

Key Terms and Places

Niger River, *p. 70*
Timbuktu, *p. 71*
mosque, *p. 73*
Gao, *p. 73*
Djenné, *p. 74*

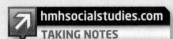
hmhsocialstudies.com
TAKING NOTES

Use the graphic organizer online to take notes about life in the cultures that developed in West Africa—Mali and Songhai.

If YOU lived there...

You are a servant of the great Mansa Musa, ruler of Mali. You've been chosen as one of the servants who will travel with him on a pilgrimage to Mecca. The king has given you all fine new clothes of silk for the trip. He will carry much gold with him. You've never left your home before. But now you will see the great city of Cairo, Egypt, and many other new places.

How do you feel about going on this journey?

BUILDING BACKGROUND Mansa Musa was one of Africa's greatest rulers, and his empire, Mali, was one of the largest in African history. Rising from the ruins of Ghana, Mali took over the trade routes of West Africa and grew into a powerful state.

Mali

Like Ghana, Mali (MAH-lee) lay along the upper **Niger River**. This area's fertile soil helped Mali grow. Mali's location on the Niger also allowed its people to control trade on the river. As a result, the empire grew rich and powerful. According to legend, Mali's rise to power began under a ruler named Sundiata (soohn-JAHT-ah).

Sundiata Makes Mali an Empire

When Sundiata was a boy, a harsh ruler conquered Mali. But as an adult, Sundiata built up an army and won back his country's independence. He then conquered nearby kingdoms, including Ghana, in the 1230s.

After Sundiata conquered Ghana, he took over the salt and gold trades. He also worked to improve agriculture in Mali. Sundiata had new farmlands cleared for beans, onions, rice, and other crops. Sundiata even introduced a new crop—cotton. People made clothing from the cotton fibers that was comfortable in the warm climate. They also sold cotton to other people.

To keep order in his prosperous kingdom, Sundiata took power away from local leaders. Each of these local leaders had the title mansa (MAHN-sah), a title Sundiata now took

Mali and Songhai

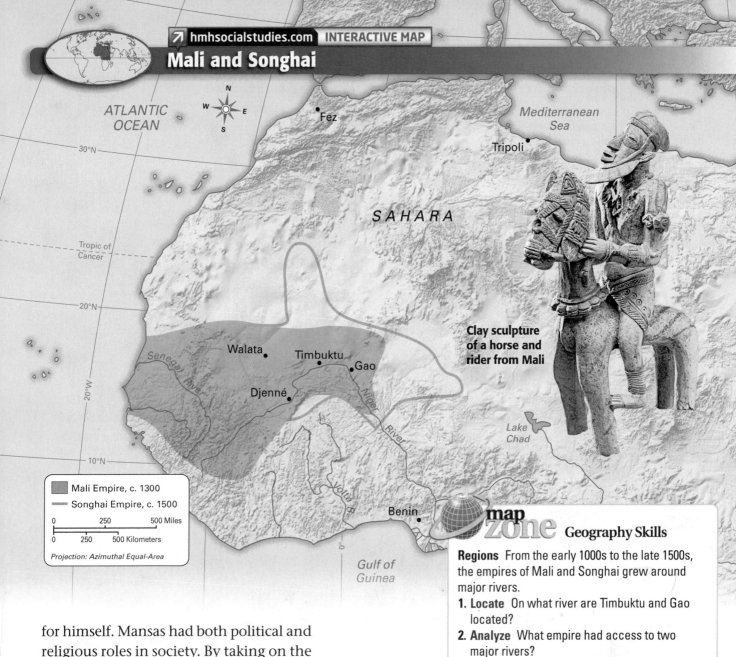

ATLANTIC OCEAN

30°N

Tropic of Cancer

20°N

20°W

10°N

Fez

Tripoli

Mediterranean Sea

S A H A R A

Walata

Timbuktu

Gao

Djenné

Senegal River

Niger River

Volta R.

Benin

Lake Chad

Gulf of Guinea

Clay sculpture of a horse and rider from Mali

Mali Empire, c. 1300
Songhai Empire, c. 1500

0   250   500 Miles
0   250   500 Kilometers

Projection: Azimuthal Equal-Area

map zone **Geography Skills**

Regions From the early 1000s to the late 1500s, the empires of Mali and Songhai grew around major rivers.
1. **Locate** On what river are Timbuktu and Gao located?
2. **Analyze** What empire had access to two major rivers?

for himself. Mansas had both political and religious roles in society. By taking on the religious authority of the mansas, Sundiata gained even more power in Mali.

Sundiata died in 1255. Later rulers of Mali took the title of mansa. Unlike Sundiata, most of these rulers were Muslims.

Mansa Musa

Mali's most famous ruler was a Muslim named Mansa Musa (MAHN-sah moo-SAH). Under his skillful leadership, Mali reached the height of its wealth, power, and fame in the 1300s. Because of Mansa Musa's influence, Islam spread through a large part of West Africa, gaining many new believers.

Mansa Musa ruled Mali for about 25 years, from 1312 to 1337. During that time, Mali added many important trade cities to its empire, including **Timbuktu** (tim-buhk-TOO).

Religion was very important to Mansa Musa. In 1324 he left Mali on a pilgrimage to Mecca. Through his journey, Mansa Musa introduced his empire to the Islamic world. He spread Mali's fame far and wide.

Mansa Musa also supported education. He sent many scholars to study in Morocco.

Timbuktu

Timbuktu became a major trading city at the height of Mali's power under Mansa Musa. Traders came to Timbuktu from the north and south to trade for salt, gold, metals, shells, and many other goods.

Mansa Musa and later rulers built several large mosques in the city, which became a center of Islamic learning.

Winter floods allowed boats to reach Timbuktu from the Niger River.

Timbuktu's walls and buildings were mostly built with bricks made of dried mud. Heavy rains can soften the bricks and destroy buildings.

At crowded market stalls, people traded for goods like sugar, kola nuts, and glass beads.

Camel caravans from the north brought goods like salt, cloth, books, and slaves to trade at Timbuktu.

ANALYSIS SKILL **ANALYZING VISUALS**

How did traders from the north bring their goods to Timbuktu?

These scholars later set up schools in Mali. Mansa Musa stressed the importance of learning to read the Arabic language so that Muslims in his empire could read the Qur'an. To spread Islam in West Africa, Mansa Musa hired Muslim architects to build mosques. A **mosque** (mahsk) is a building for Muslim prayer.

The Fall of Mali

When Mansa Musa died, his son Maghan (MAH-gan) took the throne. Maghan was a weak ruler. When raiders from the southeast poured into Mali, he couldn't stop them. The raiders set fire to Timbuktu's great schools and mosques. Mali never fully recovered from this terrible blow. The empire continued to weaken and decline.

In 1431 the Tuareg (TWAH-reg), nomads from the Sahara, seized Timbuktu. By 1500 nearly all of the lands the empire had once ruled were lost. Only a small area of Mali remained.

 **READING CHECK Sequencing** What steps did Sundiata take to turn Mali into an empire?

Songhai

Even as the empire of Mali was reaching its height, a rival power was growing in the area. That rival was the Songhai (SAHNG-hy) kingdom. From their capital at **Gao**, the Songhai participated in the same trade that had made Ghana and Mali so rich.

The Building of an Empire

In the 1300s Mansa Musa conquered the Songhai, adding their lands to his empire. But as the Mali Empire weakened in the 1400s, the people of Songhai rebelled and regained their freedom.

The Songhai leaders were Muslims. So too were many of the North African Berbers who traded in West Africa. Because of this shared religion, the Berbers were willing to trade with the Songhai, who grew richer.

As the Songhai gained in wealth, they expanded their territory and built an empire. Songhai's expansion was led by Sunni Ali (SOOH-nee ah-LEE), who became ruler of the Songhai in 1464. Before he took over, the Songhai state had been disorganized and poorly run. As ruler, Sunni Ali worked to unify, strengthen, and enlarge his empire. Much of the land that he added to Songhai had been part of Mali.

As king, Sunni Ali encouraged everyone in his empire to work together. To build religious harmony, he participated in both Muslim and local religions. As a result, he brought stability to Songhai.

Askia the Great

Sunni Ali died in 1492. He was followed as king by his son Sunni Baru, who was not a Muslim. The Songhai people feared that if Sunni Baru didn't support Islam, they

THE IMPACT TODAY

Some of the mosques built by Mansa Musa can still be seen in West Africa today.

BIOGRAPHY

Askia the Great
(c. 1443–1538)

Askia the Great became the ruler of Songhai when he was nearly 50 years old. He ruled Songhai for about 35 years. During his reign the cities of Songhai gained power over the countryside.

When he was in his 80s, Askia went blind. His son Musa forced him to leave the throne. Askia was sent to live on an island. He lived there for nine years until another of his sons brought him back to the capital, where he died. His tomb is still one of the most honored places in all of West Africa.

Drawing Inferences Why do you think Askia the Great's tomb is still considered an honored place?

FOCUS ON READING

As you read Songhai Falls to Morocco, identify two causes of Songhai's fall.

would lose their trade with Muslim lands. They rebelled against the king.

The leader of that rebellion was a general named Muhammad Ture (moo-HAH-muhd too-RAY). After overthrowing Sunni Baru, Muhammad Ture chose the title *askia*, a title of high military rank. Eventually, he became known as Askia the Great.

Askia supported education and learning. Under his rule, Timbuktu flourished, drawing thousands to its universities, schools, libraries, and mosques. The city was especially known for the University of Sankore (san-KOH-rah). People arrived there from North Africa and other places to study math, science, medicine, grammar, and law. **Djenné** was another city that became a center of learning.

Most of Songhai's traders were Muslim, and as they gained influence in the empire so did Islam. Askia, himself a devout Muslim, encouraged the growth of Islamic influence. He made many laws similar to those in other Muslim nations.

To help maintain order, Askia set up five provinces within Songhai. He appointed governors who were loyal to him. Askia also created a professional army and specialized departments to oversee tasks.

Songhai Falls to Morocco

A northern rival of Songhai, Morocco, wanted to gain control of Songhai's salt mines. So the Moroccan army set out for the heart of Songhai in 1591. Moroccan soldiers carried advanced weapons, including the terrible arquebus (AHR-kwih-buhs). The arquebus was an early form of a gun.

The swords, spears, and bows used by Songhai's warriors were no match for the Moroccans' guns and cannons. The invaders destroyed Timbuktu and Gao.

Changes in trade patterns completed Songhai's fall. Overland trade declined as port cities on the Atlantic coast became more important. Africans south of Songhai and European merchants both preferred trading at Atlantic ports to dealing with Muslim traders. Slowly, the period of great West African empires came to an end.

READING CHECK **Evaluating** What do you think was Askia's greatest accomplishment?

SUMMARY AND PREVIEW Mali was a large empire famous for its wealth and centers of learning. Songhai similarly thrived. Next, you will learn about historical and artistic traditions of West Africa.

Section 2 Assessment

hmhsocialstudies.com
ONLINE QUIZ

Reviewing Ideas, Terms, and Places

1. **a. Identify** Who was Sundiata?
   b. Explain What major river was important to the people of Mali? Why?
   c. Elaborate What effects did the rule of Mansa Musa have on Mali and West Africa?
2. **a. Identify** Who led the expansion of Songhai in the 1400s?
   b. Explain How did Askia the Great's support of education affect **Timbuktu**?
   c. Elaborate What were two reasons why Songhai fell to the Moroccans?

Critical Thinking

3. **Finding Main Ideas** Use your notes to help you list three major accomplishments of Sundiata and Askia.

Sundiata	Askia

FOCUS ON WRITING

4. **Comparing and Contrasting** Whose journal could you write from the empires of Mali and Songhai? Would you create a journal for an important person, like Mansa Musa or Askia the Great? Or would you create a journal for someone who has a different role in one of the empires? List your ideas.

Mansa Musa

How could one man's travels become a major historic event?

When did he live? the late 1200s and early 1300s

Where did he live? Mali

What did he do? Mansa Musa, the ruler of Mali, was one of the Muslim kings of West Africa. He became a major figure in African and world history largely because of a pilgrimage he made to the city of Mecca.

Why is he important? Mansa Musa's spectacular journey attracted the attention of the Muslim world and of Europe. For the first time, other people's eyes turned to West Africa. During his travels, Mansa Musa gave out huge amounts of gold. His spending made people eager to find the source of such wealth. Within 200 years, European explorers would arrive on the shores of western Africa.

Identifying Points of View How do you think Mansa Musa changed people's views of West Africa?

KEY FACTS

According to chroniclers of the time, Mansa Musa was accompanied on his journey to Mecca by some 60,000 people. Of those people

- **12,000** were servants to attend to the king.

- **500** were servants to attend to his wife.

- **14,000** more were slaves wearing rich fabrics such as silk.

- **500** carried staffs heavily decorated with gold. Historians have estimated that the gold Mansa Musa gave away on his trip would be worth more than $100 million today.

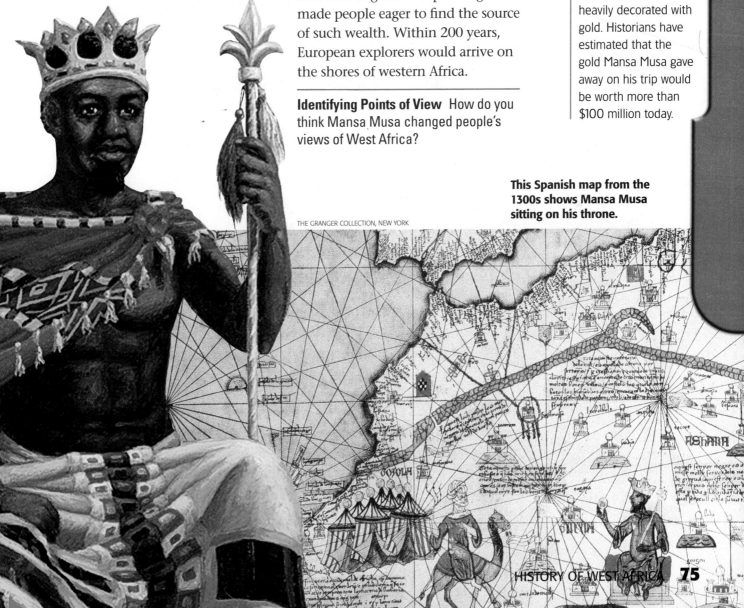

THE GRANGER COLLECTION, NEW YORK

This Spanish map from the 1300s shows Mansa Musa sitting on his throne.

Historical and Artistic Traditions

What You Will Learn...

Main Ideas

1. West Africans have preserved their history through storytelling and the written accounts of visitors.
2. Through art, music, and dance, West Africans have expressed their creativity and kept alive their cultural traditions.

The Big Idea

West African culture has been passed down through oral history, writings by other people, and the arts.

Key Terms

oral history, *p. 76*
griots, *p. 76*
proverbs, *p. 77*
kente, *p. 79*

hmhsocialstudies.com
TAKING NOTES

Use the graphic organizer online to take notes on West African historical and artistic traditions.

If YOU lived there...

You are the youngest and smallest in your family. People often tease you about not being very strong. In the evenings, when work is done, your village gathers to listen to storytellers. One of your favorite stories is about the hero Sundiata. As a boy he was small and weak, but he grew to be a great warrior and hero.

How does the story of Sundiata make you feel?

BUILDING BACKGROUND Although trading empires rose and fell in West Africa, many traditions continued through the centuries. In every town and village, storytellers passed on the people's histories, legends, and wise sayings. These were at the heart of West Africa's arts and cultural traditions.

Preserving History

Writing was never very common in West Africa. In fact, none of the major early civilizations of West Africa developed a written language. Arabic was the only written language they used. The lack of a native written language does not mean that the people of West Africa didn't know their history, though. They passed along information through oral histories. An **oral history** is a spoken record of past events. The task of remembering and telling West Africa's history was entrusted to storytellers.

The Griots

The storytellers of early West Africa were called **griots** (GREE-ohz). They were highly respected in their communities because the people of West Africa were very interested in the deeds of their ancestors. Griots helped keep this history alive for each new generation.

The griots' stories were both entertaining and informative. They told of important past events and of the accomplishments of distant ancestors. For example, some stories explained the rise and fall of the West African empires. Other stories described the actions of powerful kings and warriors. Some griots made their stories more lively by acting out the events like scenes in a play.

In addition to stories, the griots recited **proverbs**, or short sayings of wisdom or truth. They used proverbs to teach lessons to the people. For example, one West African proverb warns, "Talking doesn't fill the basket in the farm." This proverb reminds people that they must work to accomplish things. It is not enough for people just to talk about what they want to do.

In order to tell their stories and proverbs, the griots memorized hundreds of names and events. Through this process the griots passed on West African history from generation to generation. However, some griots confused names and events in their heads. When this happened, the facts of some historical events became distorted. Still, the griots' stories tell us a great deal about life in the West African empires.

West African Epics

Some of the griot poems are epics—long poems about kingdoms and heroes. Many of these epic poems are collected in the *Dausi* (DAW-zee) and the *Sundiata*.

The *Dausi* tells the history of Ghana. Intertwined with historical events, though, are myths and legends. One story is about a seven-headed snake god named Bida. This god promised that Ghana would prosper if the people sacrificed a young woman to him every year. One year a mighty warrior killed Bida. As the god died, he cursed Ghana. The griots say that this curse caused the empire of Ghana to fall.

The *Sundiata* is about Mali's great ruler. According to the epic, when Sundiata was still a boy, a conqueror captured Mali and killed Sundiata's father and 11 brothers.

↗ hmhsocialstudies.com
ANIMATED GEOGRAPHY
Modern Griots

Oral Traditions

West African storytellers called griots had the job of remembering and passing on their people's history. Here, people gather to perform traditional dances and to listen to the stories of a griot.

Music from Mali to Memphis

Did you know that the music you listen to today may have begun with the griots? From the 1600s to the 1800s, many people from West Africa were brought to America as slaves. In America, these slaves continued to sing the way they had in Africa. They also continued to play traditional instruments such as the *kora* played by Senegalese musician Soriba Kouyaté (right), the son of a griot. Over time, this music developed into a style called the blues, made popular by such artists as B. B. King (left). In turn, the blues shaped other styles of music, including jazz and rock. So, the next time you hear a Memphis blues track or a cool jazz tune, listen for its ancient African roots!

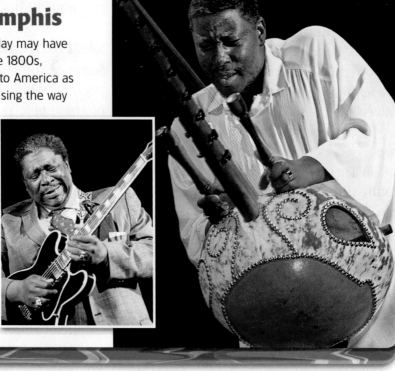

He didn't kill Sundiata, however, because the boy was sick and didn't seem like a threat. But Sundiata grew up to be an expert warrior. Eventually he overthrew the conqueror and became king.

Visitors' Written Accounts

FOCUS ON
READING

What is one effect of visitors' written accounts of West Africa?

In addition to the oral histories told about West Africa, visitors wrote about the region. In fact, much of what we know about early West Africa comes from the writings of travelers and scholars from Muslim lands such as Spain and Arabia.

Ibn Battutah was the most famous Muslim visitor to write about West Africa. From 1353 to 1354 he traveled through the region. Ibn Battutah's account of this journey describes the political and cultural lives of West Africans in great detail.

READING CHECK **Drawing Conclusions** Why were oral traditions important in West Africa?

Art, Music, and Dance

Like most peoples, West Africans valued the arts. They expressed themselves creatively through sculpture, mask-making, cloth-making, music, and dance.

Sculpture

Of all the visual art forms, the sculpture of West Africa is probably the best known. West Africans made ornate statues and carvings out of wood, brass, clay, ivory, stone, and other materials.

Most statues from West Africa are of people—often the sculptor's ancestors. Usually these statues were made for religious rituals, to ask for the ancestors' blessings. Sculptors made other statues as gifts for the gods. These sculptures were kept in holy places. They were never meant to be seen by people.

Because their statues were used in religious rituals, many African artists were deeply respected. People thought artists had been blessed by the gods.

Long after the decline of Ghana, Mali, and Songhai, West African art is still admired. Museums around the world display African art. In addition, African sculpture inspired some European artists of the 1900s, including Henri Matisse and Pablo Picasso.

Masks and Clothing

In addition to statues, the artists of West Africa carved elaborate masks. Made of wood, these masks bore the faces of animals such as hyenas, lions, monkeys, and antelopes. Artists often painted the masks after carving them. People wore the masks during rituals as they danced around fires. The way firelight reflected off the masks made them look fierce and lifelike.

Many African societies were famous for the cloth they wove. The most famous of these cloths is called kente (ken-TAY). **Kente is a hand-woven, brightly colored fabric.** The cloth was woven in narrow strips that were then sewn together. Kings and queens in West Africa wore garments made of kente for special occasions.

Music and Dance

In many West African societies, music and dance were as important as the visual arts. Singing, drumming, and dancing were great entertainment, but they also helped people honor their history and mark special occasions. For example, music was played when a ruler entered a room.

Dance has long been a central part of African society. Many West African cultures used dance to celebrate specific events or ceremonies. For example, they may have performed one dance for weddings and another for funerals. In some parts of West Africa, people still perform dances similar to those performed hundreds of years ago.

READING CHECK **Summarizing** Summarize how traditions were preserved in West Africa.

SUMMARY AND PREVIEW The societies of West Africa did not have written languages, but they preserved their histories and cultures through storytelling and the arts. Next you will read about the modern region of North Africa.

Section 3 Assessment

hmhsocialstudies.com
ONLINE QUIZ

Reviewing Ideas, Terms, and Places

1. **a. Define** What is **oral history**?
   b. Make Generalizations Why were **griots** and their stories important in West African society?
   c. Evaluate Why may an oral history provide different information than a written account of the same event?
2. **a. Identify** What were two forms of visual art popular in West Africa?
   b. Make Inferences Why do you think that the sculptures made as gifts for the gods were not meant to be seen by people?
   c. Elaborate What role did music and dance play in West African society?

Critical Thinking

3. **Summarizing** Use a chart like this one and your notes to summarize the importance of each tradition in West Africa.

Tradition	Importance
Storytelling	
Epics	
Sculpture	

FOCUS ON WRITING

4. **Identifying West African Traditions** Think about the arts and how they affected people who lived in the West African empires. Would you create a journal of one of these artists? Or would you create a journal of someone who is affected by the arts or artists?

Social Studies Skills

Making Decisions

Learn

You make decisions every day. Some decisions are very easy to make and take little time. Others are much harder. Regardless of how easy or hard a decision is, it will have consequences, or results. These consequences can be either positive or negative.

Before you make a decision, consider all your possible options. Think about the possible consequences of each option and decide which will be best for you. Thinking about the consequences of your decision beforehand will allow you to make a better, more thoughtful decision.

Practice

Imagine your parents have given you the option of getting a new pet. Use a graphic organizer like the one on this page to help you decide whether to get one.

❶ What are the consequences of getting a pet? Which of these consequences are positive? Which are negative?

❷ What are the consequences of not getting a pet? Which of them are positive? Which are negative?

❸ Compare your two options. Look at the positive and negative consequences of each option. Based on these consequences, do you think you should get a pet?

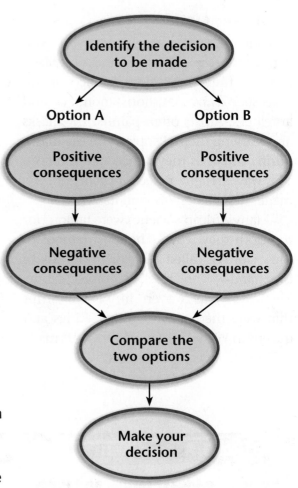

Apply

Imagine that your school has just received money to build either a new art studio or a new track. School officials have asked students to vote on which of these new facilities they would prefer, and you have to decide which option you think would be better for the school. Use a graphic organizer like the one above to consider the consequences of each option. Compare your lists, and then make your decision. Write a short paragraph to explain your decision.

Geography's Impact
video series
Review the video to answer the closing question:
Why was the salt trade important to African civilizations before the 1600s?

Visual Summary

Use the visual summary below to help you review the main ideas of the chapter.

QUICK FACTS

 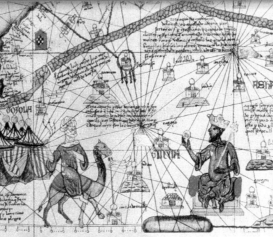 

The Ghana Empire developed in West Africa and controlled the trade of salt and gold.

The empires of Mali and Songhai both grew powerful through trade in salt, gold, and other goods.

The history of West Africa has been preserved through storytelling, visitors' accounts, art, music, and dance.

Reviewing Vocabulary, Terms, and Places

Choose the letter of the answer that best completes each statement below.

1. The Songhai ruled their kingdom from their capital at
  a. Gao.
  b. Djenné.
  c. Kano.
  d. Timbuktu.

2. Mali's rise to power began under a ruler named
  a. Tunka Manin.
  b. Sunni Ali.
  c. Ibn Battutah.
  d. Sundiata.

3. A spoken record of the past is
  a. a Soninke.
  b. an oral history.
  c. a Gao.
  d. an age-set proverb.

4. A West African storyteller is
  a. an Almoravid.
  b. a griot.
  c. an arquebus.
  d. a rift.

5. The Muslim leader of Mali who spread Islam and made a famous pilgrimage to Mecca was
  a. Sunni Baru.
  b. Askia the Great.
  c. Mansa Musa.
  d. Muhammad Ture.

6. A brightly colored African fabric is a
  a. kente.
  b. mansa.
  c. Timbuktu.
  d. Tuareg.

Comprehension and Critical Thinking

SECTION 1 *(pages 62–67)*

7. a. Identify What were the two major trade goods that made Ghana rich?

  b. Make Inferences Why did merchants in Ghana not want other traders to know where their gold came from?

  c. Evaluate Who do you think was more responsible for the collapse of Ghana, the people of Ghana or outsiders? Why?

SECTION 2 *(pages 70–74)*

8. a. Describe How did Islam influence society in Mali?

b. Compare and Contrast How were Sundiata and Mansa Musa similar? How were they different?

c. Evaluate Which group do you think played a larger role in Songhai, warriors or traders?

SECTION 3 *(pages 76–79)*

9. a. Recall What different types of information did griots pass on to their listeners?

b. Analyze Why are the writings of visitors to West Africa so important to our understanding of the region?

c. Evaluate Which of the various arts of West Africa do you think is most important? Why?

Social Studies Skills

10. Making Decisions Imagine that you are a young trader in the Ghana Empire. You have to decide which good you would prefer to trade, salt or gold. Make a list of the consequences that might result from trading each of them. Compare your lists of consequences and make a decision as to which good you will trade. You may wish to conduct research to help make your decision.

Using the Internet

11. Activity: Writing a Proverb Does the early bird get the worm? If you go outside at sunrise to check, you missed the fact that this is a proverb that means "The one that gets there first can earn something good." Griots created many proverbs that expressed wisdom or truth. Through the online book, use Internet resources to write three proverbs that might have been said by griots during the time of the great West African empires. Make sure your proverbs are written from the point of view of a West African person living during those centuries.

↗ **hmhsocialstudies.com**

Map Activity

12. West Africa On a separate sheet of paper, match the letters on the map with their correct labels.

Senegal River   Timbuktu

Lake Chad   Niger River

Gulf of Guinea

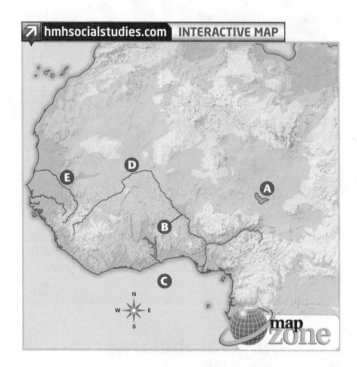

FOCUS ON WRITING

Understanding Cause and Effect *Answer the following questions about causes and effects.*

13. What caused the empire of Ghana to grow?

14. What were some effects of Mansa Musa's rule?

Writing Your Journal *Use your notes and the instructions below to help you create your journal entry.*

15. Review your notes on possible characters for your journal entry. Choose one, and think about an experience that person, or character, might write about in his or her journal. What other people might the journal entry mention? What event or scene might you describe in your journal? What details or information would your character want to include? Write a journal entry of a paragraph or two from the point of view of your character.

Standardized Test Prep

DIRECTIONS: Read questions 1 through 6 and write the letter of the best response. Then read question 7 and write your own well-constructed response.

1 **The wealth of Ghana, Mali, and Songhai was based on**

A raiding other tribes.

B the gold and salt trade.

C trade in ostriches and elephant tusks.

D making iron tools and weapons.

2 **The two rulers who were most responsible for spreading Islam in West Africa were**

A Sunni Ali and Mansa Musa.

B Sundiata and Sunni Ali.

C Ibn Battutah and Tunka Manin.

D Mansa Musa and Askia the Great.

3 **Which of the following rivers helped the development of the West African empires?**

A Niger

B Congo

C Nile

D Zambezi

4 **Griots contributed to West African societies by**

A fighting battles.

B collecting taxes.

C preserving oral history.

D trading with the Berbers.

"Well placed for the caravan trade, it was badly situated to defend itself from the Tuareg raiders of the Sahara. These restless nomads were repeatedly hammering at the gates of Timbuktu, and often enough they burst them open with disastrous results for the inhabitants. Life here was never quite safe enough to recommend it as the centre [center] of a big state."

—Basil Davidson, from *A History of West Africa*

5 **In this quote, the author is discussing why Timbuktu was**

A a good place for universities.

B not a good place for a capital city.

C a good location for trade.

D not a good location for the center of the Tuareg state.

6 **In the second sentence of the passage above, what does the phrase "hammering at the gates of Timbuktu" mean?**

A driving nails into Timbuktu's gates

B knocking on the door to get in the city

C trying to get into and conquer the city

D making noise to anger the inhabitants

7 **Extended Response** Look at the map of Ghana in Section 1. Using information from the map, explain how trade helped build a strong empire.

North Africa

map zone Geography Skills

Regions North Africa is a region of countries located on the Mediterranean Sea.
1. **Locate** What is the capital of Egypt?
2. **Draw Conclusions** Why do you think many countries in Europe have influenced the countries of North Africa?

Essential Question How have deserts and rivers impacted the development of North African civilization?

? What You Will Learn...

In this chapter you will learn about five countries located in the region of North Africa—Egypt, Libya, Tunisia, Algeria, and Morocco. You will learn about the importance of water in this dry region. You will also study the histories of these countries, which include ancient Egyptian civilization. In addition, you will learn about North Africa's cultures, economies, and governments.

FOCUS ON READING AND WRITING

Summarizing To better understand what you read, it is sometimes helpful to stop and summarize the information you have read. A summary is a short restatement of important events or main ideas. As you read this chapter, stop now and then to summarize what you have read. **See the lesson, Summarizing, on page 197.**

Writing a Myth Ancient peoples created stories called myths to explain things about the world. For example, they created myths to explain the seasons and to explain the powers of their gods. As you read this chapter, look for information that might have seemed mysterious to ancient peoples. Later you will write your own myth to explain something about North Africa.

ATLANTIC OCEAN

Strait of Gibraltar

Rabat
Casablanca

MOROCCO

30°N

Canary Islands (SPAIN)

Western Sahara (Claimed by MOROCCO)

Tropic of Cancer

20°N

MAURITANIA

Culture Most North Africans are Muslims and speak Arabic.

North Africa: Political

↗ hmhsocialstudies.com VIDEO

H HISTORY. How Does the Nile Measure Up?

EUROPE

SOUTHWEST ASIA

● Algiers

● Tunis

TUNISIA

Mediterranean Sea

● Tripoli

30°E

Alexandria ●

30°N

● Cairo

ALGERIA

LIBYA

EGYPT

Nile River

Red Sea

Lake Nasser

20°N

MALI

NIGER

CHAD

SUDAN

☉ National capital

● Other cities

0	150	300 Miles
0	150	300 Kilometers

Projection: Azimuthal Equal-Area

0°

10°E

20°E

Geography Most of North Africa is covered by the world's largest desert—the Sahara.

History Artifacts like this one from King Tutankhamen's tomb have revealed clues about the daily lives of ancient Egyptians.

85

Physical Geography

What You Will Learn...

Main Ideas

1. Major physical features of North Africa include the Nile River, the Sahara, and the Atlas Mountains.
2. The climate of North Africa is hot and dry, and water is the region's most important resource.

The Big Idea

North Africa is a dry region with limited water resources.

Key Terms and Places

Sahara, *p. 86*
Nile River, *p. 86*
silt, *p. 86*
Suez Canal, *p. 87*
oasis, *p. 88*
Atlas Mountains, *p. 88*

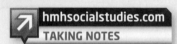
hmhsocialstudies.com
TAKING NOTES

Use the graphic organizer online to take notes on the physical geography of North Africa.

If **YOU** lived there...

As your airplane flies over Egypt, you look down and see a narrow ribbon of green—the Nile River Valley—with deserts on either side. As you fly along North Africa's Mediterranean coast, you see many towns scattered across rugged mountains and green valleys.

What are the challenges of living in a mainly desert region?

BUILDING BACKGROUND Even though much of North Africa is covered by rugged mountains and huge areas of deserts, the region is not a bare wasteland. Areas of water include wet, fertile land with date palms and almond trees.

Physical Features

The region of North Africa includes Morocco, Algeria, Tunisia, Libya, and Egypt. From east to west the region stretches from the Atlantic Ocean to the Red Sea. Off the northern coast is the Mediterranean Sea. In the south lies the **Sahara** (suh-HAR-uh), a vast desert. Both the desert sands and bodies of water have helped shape the cultures of North Africa.

The Nile

The **Nile River** is the world's longest river. It is formed by the union of two rivers, the Blue Nile and the White Nile. Flowing northward through the eastern Sahara for about 4,000 miles, the Nile finally empties into the Mediterranean Sea.

For centuries, rain far to the south caused floods along the northern Nile, leaving rich silt in surrounding fields. **Silt** is finely ground fertile soil that is good for growing crops.

The Nile River Valley is like a long oasis in the desert. Farmers use water from the Nile to irrigate their fields. The Nile fans out near the Mediterranean Sea, forming a large delta. A delta

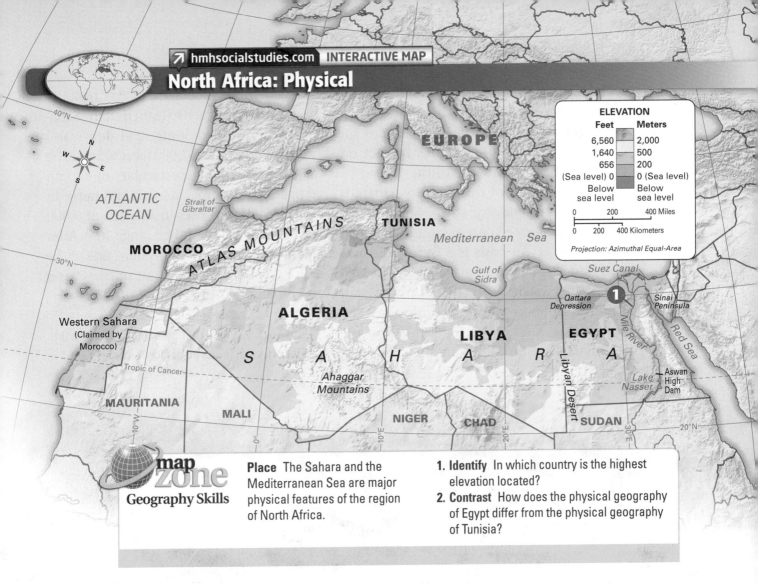

ELEVATION

	Feet	Meters	
	6,560	2,000	
	1,640	500	
	656	200	
	(Sea level) 0	0 (Sea level)	
	Below sea level	Below sea level	

0   200   400 Miles

0   200   400 Kilometers

Projection: Azimuthal Equal-Area

ATLANTIC OCEAN

EUROPE

MOROCCO

ATLAS MOUNTAINS

TUNISIA

Mediterranean Sea

Gulf of Sidra

Suez Canal

Strait of Gibraltar

ALGERIA

LIBYA

EGYPT

Qattara Depression

Sinai Peninsula

Nile River

Red Sea

Western Sahara (Claimed by Morocco)

S A H A R A

Libyan Desert

Tropic of Cancer

Ahaggar Mountains

Lake Nasser

Aswan High Dam

MAURITANIA

MALI

NIGER

CHAD

SUDAN

map zone
Geography Skills

Place The Sahara and the Mediterranean Sea are major physical features of the region of North Africa.

1. **Identify** In which country is the highest elevation located?
2. **Contrast** How does the physical geography of Egypt differ from the physical geography of Tunisia?

is a landform at the mouth of a river that is created by the deposit of sediment. The sediment in the Nile delta makes the area extremely fertile.

The Aswan High Dam controls flooding along the Nile. However, the dam also traps silt, preventing it from being carried downriver. Today some of Egypt's farmers must use fertilizers to enrich the soil.

The Sinai and the Suez Canal

East of the Nile is the triangular Sinai Peninsula. Barren, rocky mountains and desert cover the Sinai. Between the Sinai and the rest of Egypt is the **Suez Canal**. The French built the canal in the 1860s. It is a narrow waterway that connects the Mediterranean Sea with the Red Sea. Large cargo ships carry oil and goods through the canal.

↗ hmhsocialstudies.com

ANIMATED GEOGRAPHY
The Physical Geography of Africa

① Flowing for 4,132 miles, the Nile is the longest river in the world.

The Sahara

The Sahara, the largest desert in the world, covers most of North Africa. The name Sahara comes from the Arabic word for "desert." It has an enormous **impact** on the landscapes of North Africa.

ACADEMIC VOCABULARY
impact effect, result

One impact of the very dry Sahara is that few people live there. Small settlements are located near a water source such as an oasis. An **oasis** is a wet, fertile area in a desert where a natural spring or well provides water.

In addition to broad, windswept gravel plains, sand dunes cover much of the Sahara. Dry streambeds are also common.

Mountains

Do you think of deserts as flat regions? You may be surprised to learn that the Sahara is far from flat. Some sand dunes and ridges rise as high as 1,000 feet (305 m). The Sahara also has spectacular mountain ranges. For example, a mountain range in southern Algeria rises to a height of 9,800 feet (3,000 m). Another range, the **Atlas Mountains** on the northwestern side of the Sahara near the Mediterranean coast, rises even higher, to 13,600 feet (4,160 m).

READING CHECK **Summarizing** What are the major physical features of North Africa?

Close-up

A Sahara Oasis

The largest desert in the world, the Sahara, spans almost 4 million square miles across North Africa. From ancient times to today, traders crossing the Sahara have relied on the desert's oases. These oases provide water and shade.

Date palms thrive on the banks of this natural spring, which provides water to travelers and irrigated fields.

By carrying supplies, camels help the nomadic Tuareg people travel from oasis to oasis.

Climate and Resources

North Africa is very dry. However, rare storms can cause flooding. In some areas these floods as well as high winds have carved bare rock surfaces out of the land.

North Africa has three main climates. A desert climate covers most of the region. Temperatures range from mild to very hot. How hot can it get? Temperatures as high as 136°F (58°C) have been recorded in Libya. However, the humidity is very low. As a result, temperatures can drop quickly after sunset. In winter temperatures can fall below freezing at night.

The second climate type in the region is a Mediterranean climate. Much of the northern coast west of Egypt has this type of climate. Winters there are mild and moist. Summers are hot and dry. Areas between the coast and the Sahara have a steppe climate.

Oil and gas are important resources, particularly for Libya, Algeria, and Egypt. Morocco mines iron ore and minerals used to make fertilizers. The Sahara has natural resources such as coal, oil, and natural gas.

READING CHECK **Generalizing** What are North Africa's major resources?

FOCUS ON READING

Summarize the details of what you just read about North Africa's climate.

Shelters like this one provide a place for travelers to rest.

ANALYSIS SKILL **ANALYZING VISUALS**

Why do you think an oasis would be important to people traveling through the Sahara?

SUMMARY AND PREVIEW In this section, you learned about the physical geography of North Africa. Next, you will learn about the history and cultures of the countries of North Africa.

Section 1 Assessment

hmhsocialstudies.com
ONLINE QUIZ

Reviewing Ideas, Terms, and Places

1. a. **Define** What is an **oasis**?
   b. **Explain** Why is the **Suez Canal** an important waterway?
   c. **Elaborate** Would it be possible to farm in Egypt if the **Nile River** did not exist? Explain your answer.
2. a. **Recall** What is the climate of most of North Africa?
   b. **Draw Conclusions** What resources of North Africa are the most valuable?

Critical Thinking

3. **Categorizing** Draw a diagram like the one shown here. Use your notes to list two facts about each physical feature of North Africa.

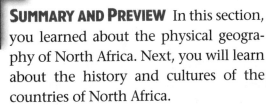

FOCUS ON WRITING

4. **Writing About Physical Geography** What physical feature will you choose as the subject of your myth? How will you describe this feature? Note your ideas.

History and Culture

What You Will Learn...

Main Ideas

1. North Africa's history includes ancient Egyptian civilization.
2. Islam influences the cultures of North Africa and most people speak Arabic.

The Big Idea

North Africa is rich in history and Islamic culture.

Key Terms and Places

Alexandria, *p. 91*
Berbers, *p. 93*

hmhsocialstudies.com
TAKING NOTES

Use the graphic organizer online to take notes on the history and culture of North Africa.

If YOU lived there...

You live in a village in ancient Egypt in about 800 BC. Your family grows wheat and date palms along the banks of the Nile River, which brings water for your crops. You and your friends like to explore the marshy areas along the banks of the river, where many kinds of birds live in the tall reeds.

How is the Nile River important in your life?

BUILDING BACKGROUND Some of the world's earliest civilizations began in river valleys in Asia and Africa. One of these civilizations was the Nile Valley in Egypt. Egypt was called the "gift of the Nile," because the river's floods brought rich soil to the valley. The soil built up a fertile delta where the Nile emptied into the sea.

Egypt's Nile River Valley was home to some of the world's oldest civilizations. These ancient Egyptians built large monuments, participated in trade, and developed a writing system.

The Great Sphinx at Giza is one of the many monuments built by the ancient Egyptians.

North Africa's History

Sometime after 3200 BC people along the northern Nile united into one Egyptian kingdom. The ancient Egyptians built large stone monuments and developed a written system. Later Greeks and Arabs, who wanted to expand their empires, invaded North Africa.

The Ancient Egyptians

What is the first thing that comes to mind when we think of the ancient Egyptians? Most of us think of the great stone pyramids. The Egyptians built these huge monuments as tombs, or burial places, for pharaohs, or kings.

How did the Egyptians build these huge monuments? Scholars believe thousands of workers cut large blocks of stone far away and rolled them on logs to the Nile. From there the blocks were moved on barges. At the building site, the Egyptians finished carving the blocks. They built dirt and brick ramps alongside the pyramids. Then they hauled the blocks up the ramps.

One of the largest pyramids, the Great Pyramid, contains 2.3 million blocks of stone. Each stone averages 2.5 tons (2.25 metric tons) in weight. Building the Great Pyramid probably required from 10,000 to 30,000 workers. They finished the job in about 20 years, and the pyramid still stands thousands of years later.

Egyptian Writing

The ancient Egyptians developed a sophisticated writing system, or hieroglyphics (hy-ruh-GLIH-fiks). This writing system used pictures and symbols that stood for ideas or words. Each symbol represented one or more sounds in the Egyptian language. The Egyptians carved hieroglyphics on their temples and stone monuments. Many of these writings recorded the words and achievements of the pharaohs.

Greek and Arab Civilizations

Because of North Africa's long Mediterranean coastline, the region was open to invaders over the centuries. Those invaders included people from the eastern Mediterranean, Greeks, and Romans. For example, one invader was the Macedonian king Alexander the Great. Alexander founded the city of **Alexandria** in Egypt in 332 BC.

BIOGRAPHY

Cleopatra
(69–30 BC)

After the death of the Egyptian king Ptolemy XII in 51 BC, his daughter, Cleopatra, and her brother became co-rulers of Egypt. From the age of 17, Cleopatra ruled ancient Egypt for more than 20 years. Her reign was during a period of Egyptian history when Egypt was dominated by Rome. Even though she was of Greek descent, Cleopatra was worshipped by ancient Egyptians.

Cleopatra tried to drive out the Romans from Egypt. She feared the Romans would arrest her and take over Egypt. Rather than see them ruling her kingdom, Cleopatra chose to commit suicide. According to tradition, she poisoned herself at the age of 39 with the venom of a deadly snake.

Analyzing What did Cleopatra fear?

FOCUS ON READING

What details would you use to summarize the ancient Egyptians and their writing?

Ancient Egypt's King Tut

More than 3,300 years ago a 19-year-old named King Tutankhamen ruled ancient Egypt. Since the discovery of Tut's mummy in 1922, many have wondered how he died. Scientists have used modern technology to help find possible clues to King Tut's cause of death.

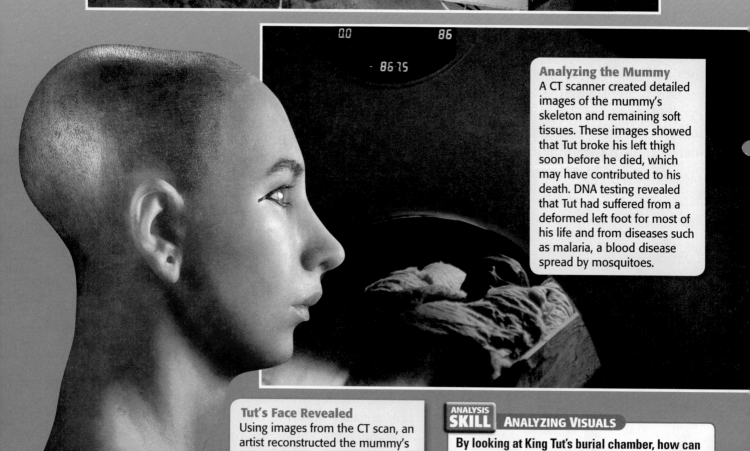

Mummy Unveiled
Inside King Tut's burial chamber, Egyptian archaeologist Zahi Hawass sees the mummy's face for the first time.

Analyzing the Mummy
A CT scanner created detailed images of the mummy's skeleton and remaining soft tissues. These images showed that Tut broke his left thigh soon before he died, which may have contributed to his death. DNA testing revealed that Tut had suffered from a deformed left foot for most of his life and from diseases such as malaria, a blood disease spread by mosquitoes.

Tut's Face Revealed
Using images from the CT scan, an artist reconstructed the mummy's face with clay and plastic.

ANALYSIS SKILL **ANALYZING VISUALS**
By looking at King Tut's burial chamber, how can you tell that King Tut was an important person?

Alexandria became an important seaport and trading center. The city was also a great center of learning.

Beginning in the AD 600s, Arab armies from Southwest Asia swept across North Africa. They brought the Arabic language and Islam to the region. Under Muslim rule, North African cities became major centers of learning, trade, and craft making. These cities included Cairo in Egypt and Fès in Morocco.

European Influence

In the 1800s European countries began to take over the region. By 1912 they had authority over all of North Africa. In that year Italy captured Libya. Spain already controlled northern Morocco. France ruled the rest of Morocco as well as Tunisia and Algeria. The British controlled Egypt.

The countries of North Africa gradually gained independence. Egypt gained limited independence in 1922. The British kept military bases there and maintained control of the Suez Canal until 1956. During World War II the region was a major battleground. Libya, Morocco, and Tunisia each won independence in the 1950s.

Algeria was the last North African country to win independence. Many French citizens had moved to the country, and they considered Algeria part of France. Algeria finally won independence in 1962.

Modern North Africa

Since independence, the countries of North Africa have tried to build stronger ties with other Arab countries. Before signing a peace treaty in 1979, Egypt led other Arab countries in several wars against Israel. In 1976 Morocco took over the former Spanish colony of Western Sahara.

READING CHECK **Evaluating** What was one significant event in North Africa's history?

Cultures of North Africa

As you have just read, many of the countries of North Africa share a common history. Likewise, the people of North Africa share many aspects of culture—language, religion, foods, holidays, customs, and arts and literature.

People and Language

Egyptians, Berbers, and Bedouins make up nearly all of Egypt's population. Bedouins are nomadic herders who travel throughout the deserts of Egypt.

Most people in the other countries of North Africa are of mixed Arab and Berber ancestry. The **Berbers** are an ethnic group who are native to North Africa and speak Berber languages. The majority of North Africans speak Arabic.

Most ethnic Europeans left North Africa after the region's countries became independent. However, because of the European influence in the region, some North Africans also speak French, Italian, and English.

Religion

Most North Africans are Muslims who practice the religion of Islam. Islam plays a major role in North African life. For example, North African Muslims stop to pray five times a day. In addition, Fridays are special days when Muslims meet in mosques for prayer. About 10 percent of Egyptians are Christians or practice other religions.

Foods

What kinds of food would you eat on a trip to North Africa? Grains, vegetables, fruits, and nuts are common foods.

You would also notice that most meals in North Africa include couscous (KOOS-koos). This dish is made from wheat and looks like small pellets of pasta.

Couscous is usually steamed over boiling water or soup. Often it is served with vegetables or meat, butter, and olive oil.

Egyptians also enjoy a dish called *fuul*. It is made with fava beans mashed with olive oil, salt, pepper, garlic, and lemons. It is often served with hard-boiled eggs and bread. Many Egyptians eat these foods on holidays and at family gatherings.

FOCUS ON CULTURE

The Berbers

Before the AD 600s when Arabs settled in North Africa, a people called the Berbers lived in the region. The descendants of these ancient peoples live throughout North Africa today—mostly in Morocco and Algeria. Some Berbers are nomadic and live in goat-hair tents. Other Berbers farm crops that include wheat, barley, fruits, and olives. Some also raise cattle, sheep, or goats.

Berber culture is centered on a community made up of different tribes. Once a year, Berber tribes gather at large festivals. At these gatherings Berbers trade goods, and many couples get married in elaborate ceremonies.

Drawing Conclusions How have Berbers kept their culture alive?

Holidays and Customs

Important holidays in North Africa include the birthday of Muhammad, the prophet of Islam. This holiday is marked with lights, parades, and special sweets of honey, nuts, and sugar. During the holy month of Ramadan, Muslims abstain from food and drink during the day.

Gathering at cafes is a custom practiced by many men in North Africa. The cafes are a place where they go to play chess or dominoes. Most women in North Africa socialize only in their homes.

A certain way of greeting each other on the street is another North African custom. People greet each other by shaking hands and then touching their hand to their heart. If they are family or friends, they will kiss each other on the cheek. The number of kisses varies from country to country.

Many North Africans wear traditional clothes, which are long and loosely fitted. Such styles are ideal for the region's hot climate. Many North African women dress according to Muslim tradition. Their clothing covers all of the body except the face and hands.

The Arts and Literature

North Africa has a rich and varied tradition in the arts and literature. Traditional arts include wood carving and weaving. The region is famous for beautiful hand-woven carpets. The women who weave these carpets use bright colors to create complex geometric patterns. Beautifully detailed handpainted tilework is also a major art form in the region.

Other arts in Egypt include its growing movie industry. Egyptian films in Arabic have become popular throughout Southwest Asia and North Africa.

Many North Africans also enjoy popular music based on singing and poetry. The musical scale there has many more notes

Fès, Morocco

At a tannery in the city of Fès, men dye sheepskins in large vats of dyes. The city's craftspeople use yellow-dyed leather to make distinctive leather shoes.

ANALYZING VISUALS What other colors are the sheepskins dyed?

Vats of different colored dyes

Yellow-dyed sheepskins are laid out to dry.

than are common in Western music. As a result of this difference, North African tunes seem to wail or waver. Musicians in Morocco often use instruments such as the three-stringed sintir.

The region has also produced important writers and artists. For example, Egyptian poetry and other writing date back thousands of years. One of Egypt's most famous writers is Naguib Mahfouz. In 1988 he became the first Arab writer to win the Nobel Prize for Literature.

READING CHECK Analyzing What are some important facts about the people and culture of North Africa?

SUMMARY AND PREVIEW In this section you learned about the history and culture of North Africa. Next, you will learn about the region today.

Section 2 Assessment   hmhsocialstudies.com
ONLINE QUIZ

Reviewing Ideas, Terms, and Places

1. **a. Define** What are hieroglyphics?
   b. Make Inferences What made the city of **Alexandria** important?
   c. Evaluate Why do you think European countries wanted to take over countries in North Africa?
2. **a. Recall** What language do most North Africans speak?
   b. Summarize What is one custom practiced in North Africa?
   c. Elaborate How is Islam a major part of the daily lives of many North Africans?

Critical Thinking

3. **Summarizing** Use your notes to summarize what you learned about the culture of North Africa.

Language	
Religion	
Food	
The Arts	
Literature	

FOCUS ON WRITING

4. **Choosing Details** Which details about North Africa's history and culture will you include in your myth? Write a sentence or two about each detail.

Social Studies Skills

Analyzing a Diagram

Learn

Diagrams are drawings that use lines and labels to explain or illustrate something. Pictorial diagrams show an object in simple form, much like it would look if you were viewing it. Cutaway diagrams, like the one of an Egyptian pyramid below, show the "insides" of an object. These diagrams usually have labels that identify important areas of the diagram.

Practice

Analyze the diagram below, and answer the following questions.

1 What type of diagram is this?

2 What labels in the diagram suggest what this pyramid was used for?

3 Of what materials was the pyramid made?

An Egyptian Pyramid

King's burial chamber

Air shaft

Grand gallery

Tunnel

Apply

Draw a cutaway diagram of your school. Label classrooms, hallways, the cafeteria, and other areas. Use your diagram to answer the following questions.

1. How many stories are in your school?

2. Where is the closest exit located from the classroom you are sitting in now?

3. What are some of the materials your school is made of?

North Africa Today

If YOU lived there...

You live in the colorful city of Marrakesh, Morocco. This is the week of carnival, an exotic celebration where you can stroll among the crowds and see storytellers, musicians, and snake charmers. You may stop at a food stall for a snack and a cup of mint tea. But even in an ordinary week, you can explore the markets and see palaces and gardens with fountains.

Why is Marrakesh an exciting place to live?

BUILDING BACKGROUND Several countries and cultures have influenced modern North Africa. Some countries in North Africa were once colonies of France or Italy. As a result, the region is still linked with events in Europe.

Egypt

With a population of more than 83 million, Egypt is North Africa's most populous country. Egypt's government faces many challenges today. Most Egyptians are poor farmers because Egypt has limited resources and jobs.

Government and Society

Egypt is a republic that has been heavily influenced by Islamic law. In 2011 a popular revolution overthrew the country's president, who had ruled for three decades. Egypt's military led the country until elections could be held.

Many Egyptians debate over the role of Islam in the country. Some Egyptian Muslims believe Egypt's government, laws, and society should be based on Islamic law. However, some Egyptians worry that such a change in government would mean fewer personal freedoms.

Egyptians are divided over their country's role in the world. Some Egyptians want their government to remain a leader among Arab countries. However, others want their government to focus more on improving their daily life.

What You Will Learn...

Main Ideas

1. Many of Egypt's people are farmers and live along the Nile River.
2. People in the other countries of North Africa are mostly pastoral nomads or farmers, and oil is an important resource in the region.

The Big Idea

Many people of North Africa are farmers, and oil is an important resource.

Key Terms and Places

Cairo, *p. 99*
Maghreb, *p. 100*
souks, *p. 101*
free port, *p. 101*
dictator, *p. 101*

hmhsocialstudies.com
TAKING NOTES

Use the graphic organizer online to take notes on the governments, economies, and cities in Egypt and the other countries of North Africa.

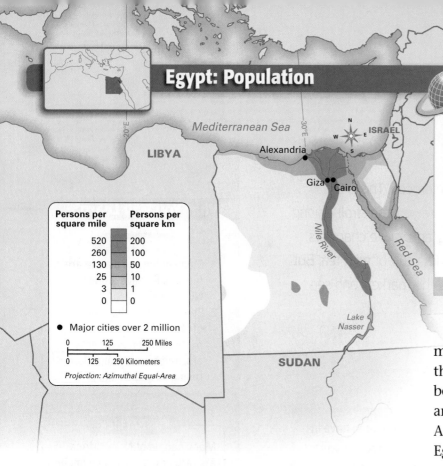

Egypt: Population

Mediterranean Sea

LIBYA

Alexandria

Giza • Cairo

ISRAEL

Nile River

Red Sea

Lake Nasser

SUDAN

Persons per square mile	Persons per square km
520	200
260	100
130	50
25	10
3	1
0	0

● Major cities over 2 million

0   125   250 Miles
0   125   250 Kilometers

Projection: Azimuthal Equal-Area

map zone

Geography Skills

Place Most of Egypt's population lives near the Nile River.

1. **Locate** Which cities have more than 2 million people?
2. **Draw Conclusions** Why do some Egyptians live in rural areas instead of cities?

Some supporters of an Islamic government have turned to violence to advance their cause. Attacks on tourists by members of a radical Islamic group in the 1990s and 2000s were particularly worrisome. A loss of tourism would severely hurt Egypt's economy.

Many Egyptians live in severe poverty. Many do not have clean water for cooking or washing. The spread of disease in crowded cities is also a problem. In addition, about 30 percent of Egyptians cannot read and write. Still, Egypt's government has made progress. Today Egyptians live longer and are much healthier than they were 50 years ago.

Resources and Economy

Egypt is challenged by its limited resources. For example, the country's only farmland is located in the Nile River Valley and Delta. To keep the land productive, farmers must use more and more fertilizer. In addition, salt water drifting up the Nile from the Mediterranean has brought salts to the surface that are harmful to crops. These problems and a rapidly growing population have forced Egypt to import much of its food.

About 32 percent of Egyptians are farmers, but less than 3 percent of the land is used for farming. Most farming is located

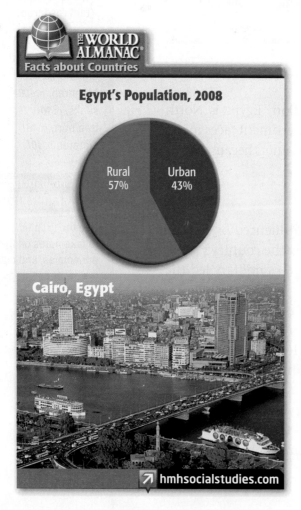

THE WORLD ALMANAC®
Facts about Countries

Egypt's Population, 2008

Rural 57%

Urban 43%

Cairo, Egypt

↗ hmhsocialstudies.com

along the Nile Delta, which is extremely fertile. A warm, sunny climate and water for irrigation make the delta ideal for growing cotton. Farmlands along the Nile River are used for growing vegetables, grain, and fruit.

The Suez Canal is an important part of Egypt's economy. The canal makes about $5 billion a year by requiring tolls from ships that pass through the canal. Thousands of ships use the canal each year to avoid making long trips around Southern Africa. This heavy traffic makes the canal one of the world's busiest waterways.

Egypt's economy depends mostly on agriculture, petroleum exports, and tourism. To provide for its growing population, Egypt is working to expand its industries. Recently, the government has invested in the country's communications and natural gas industries.

Many Egyptians also depend on money sent home by family members working in other countries. Some Egyptians work in other countries because there are not enough jobs in Egypt. Many Egyptians work in Europe or oil-rich countries in Southwest Asia.

Cities and Rural Life

Most North Africans live in cities along the Mediterranean coast or in villages in the foothills of the Atlas Mountains. Although, in Egypt 99 percent of the population lives in the Nile Valley and Delta. Egypt's capital, **Cairo**, is located in the Nile Delta.

With almost 12 million people, Cairo is the largest urban area in North Africa. The city is crowded, poor, and polluted. Cairo continues to grow as people move into the city from Egypt's rural areas in search of work. For centuries, Cairo's location at the southern end of the Nile Delta helped the city grow. The city also lies along old trading routes.

The Nile River

From space, the Nile looks like a river of green. Actually, the areas that appear green in this satellite image are thousands of irrigated fields that line the banks of the river. The river deposits silt along its banks, which makes the land extremely fertile. Farmers also depend on the Nile's waters to irrigate their crops. Without water, they could not farm in the desert.

Notice how the river appears smaller at the bottom of this image. The Aswan High Dam controls the river's flow here, which prevents flooding and provides electricity.

Drawing Conclusions How is the Nile important to Egypt's people?

Today the landscape of Cairo is a mixture of modern buildings, historic mosques, and small, mud-brick houses. However, there is not enough housing in Cairo for its growing population. Many people live in makeshift housing in the slums or boats along the Nile. Communities have even developed in cemeteries, where people convert tombs into bedrooms and kitchens.

HISTORY

VIDEO
Lake Nassar

hmhsocialstudies.com

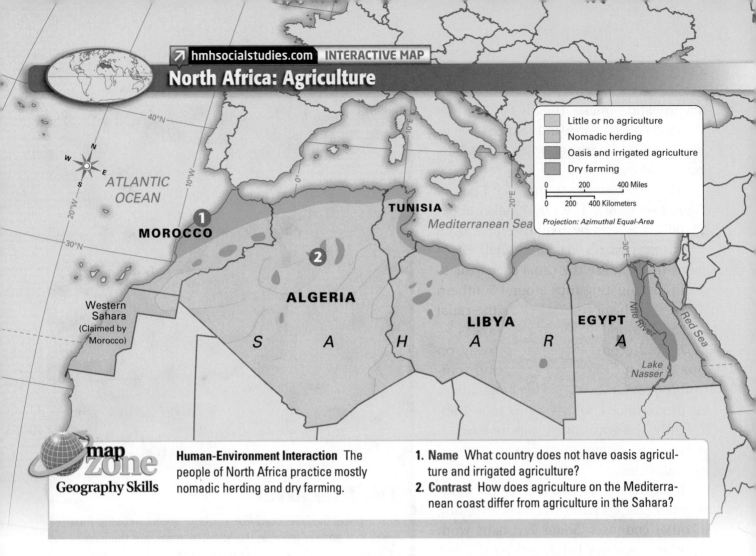

Little or no agriculture
Nomadic herding
Oasis and irrigated agriculture
Dry farming

0   200   400 Miles
0   200   400 Kilometers

Projection: Azimuthal Equal-Area

ATLANTIC OCEAN

MOROCCO

TUNISIA

Mediterranean Sea

Western Sahara (Claimed by Morocco)

ALGERIA

LIBYA

EGYPT

S   A   H   A   R   A

Nile River

Red Sea

Lake Nasser

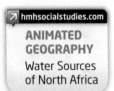

map zone

Geography Skills

Human-Environment Interaction The people of North Africa practice mostly nomadic herding and dry farming.

1. **Name** What country does not have oasis agriculture and irrigated agriculture?
2. **Contrast** How does agriculture on the Mediterranean coast differ from agriculture in the Sahara?

FOCUS ON READING

Think about what details are important in a summary of Egypt's government, economy, and cities.

↗ hmhsocialstudies.com

ANIMATED GEOGRAPHY

Water Sources of North Africa

Alexandria is Egypt's second-largest city. The city was founded by Alexander the Great. Known in ancient times for its spectacular library, it is now the home to a large university and many industries. Its location on the Mediterranean Sea has made it a major seaport. The home of some 4 million people, Alexandria is as poor and crowded as Cairo.

More than half of all Egyptians live in small villages and other rural areas. Most rural Egyptians are farmers called fellahin (fel-uh-HEEN). These farmers own very small plots of land along the Nile River. Some fellahin also work large farms owned by powerful families.

READING CHECK **Finding Main Ideas** What are some of the challenges Cairo faces today?

Other Countries of North Africa

Western Libya, Tunisia, Algeria, and Morocco are often called the **Maghreb** (MUH-gruhb). This Arabic word means "west" or "the direction of the setting sun." Since most of the Maghreb is covered by the Sahara, cities and farmland are located in narrow bands along the coast.

Government and Economy

A major challenge in North Africa is the conflict over the role of Islam in society. For example, in Algeria some groups want a government based on Islamic principles and laws. In 1992 the government canceled elections that many believed would be won by Islamic groups.

1 Dry farming In Morocco, hungry goats climb an argan nut tree. These trees and other hardy crops thrive without much water.

2 Oasis agriculture In Algeria, oases in the desert provide enough water to irrigate crops and date palms.

Oil, mining, and tourism are important industries for the countries of North Africa. Oil is the most important resource, particularly in Libya and Algeria. Money from oil pays for schools, health care, food, social programs, and military equipment. The region's countries also have large deposits of natural gas, iron ore, and lead. The largest trade partners of Algeria, Libya, and Morocco are European Union members.

Agriculture is a major economic activity in North Africa. About one in six workers in Libya, Tunisia, and Algeria is a farmer. In Morocco, farmers make up about 40 percent of the labor force. North Africa's farmers grow and export wheat, olives, fruits, and nuts. Tourism is also an important economic activity in the region, especially in Morocco and Tunisia.

Cities

Many North African cities have large marketplaces, or **souks**. The souks are located in the old district of a city called the Casbah. These souks sell various goods such as spices, carpets, and copper teapots. The Casbah in Algeria's capital, Algiers, is a maze of winding alleys and tall walls.

Libya and Tunisia's cities and most of its population are found in the coastal areas. Libya is the most urbanized country in the region. About 77 percent of Libya's roughly 6 million people live in cities. The largest cities are Benghazi and the capital, Tripoli. Tunisia's capital and largest city, Tunis, lies on the Mediterranean coast.

Morocco's largest city, Casablanca, has about 3.2 million people. Another Moroccan city, Tangier, overlooks the Strait of Gibraltar. This beautiful city was once a Spanish territory. Today tourists can take a quick ferry ride from Spain across the strait to Tangier, a free port. A **free port** is a city in which almost no taxes are placed on goods sold there.

The Countries Today

In addition to sharing similar economies, the countries of North Africa also share similar challenges. Some countries are dealing with violence, while others are strengthening their trading relationships with the United States and Europe.

Libya From 1969 to 2011, Libya was ruled by a dictator, General Mu'ammar al-Gadhafi. A **dictator** is someone who rules a country with complete power. Gadhafi supported acts of violence against Israel and its neighbors. As a result, many countries limited their economic relations with Libya. Relations with the West improved after Libya's government spoke out against terrorism and gave up weapons programs. A popular uprising overthrew Gadhafi in 2011.

Algiers, Algeria

Algeria's capital and major port, Algiers, sits on the Mediterranean Sea.

Algeria Violence between Algeria's government and some Islamic groups claimed thousands of lives in the 1990s. Today, Algeria is trying to recover from the violence and strengthen the country's economy with exports to Europe.

Tunisia Tunisia's government has granted Tunisian women more rights than women in any other North African country. Tunisia has close economic relationships with European countries. Today about two-thirds of Tunisia's imported goods are from European Union countries.

Morocco Morocco is the only North African country with little oil. Today, the country is an important producer and exporter of fertilizer.

READING CHECK **Summarizing** What are some of the challenges these countries face?

SUMMARY AND PREVIEW In this section you learned about North Africa today. In the next chapter you will learn about the region of West Africa.

Section 3 Assessment

hmhsocialstudies.com
ONLINE QUIZ

Reviewing Ideas, Terms, and Places

1. **a. Define** What is a **souk**?
   b. Draw Conclusions Why is housing scarce in **Cairo**?
   c. Predict In what ways do you think Egypt's government can help solve the country's poverty?
2. **a. Recall** What countries in North Africa make up the **Maghreb**?
   b. Compare and Contrast How is Libya similar to and different from Morocco?
   c. Evaluate How do you think the countries of North Africa can improve their economies?

Critical Thinking

3. **Comparing** Use your notes to compare Egypt with the other countries of North Africa.

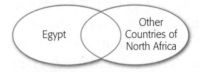

FOCUS ON WRITING

4. **Taking Notes on North Africa** Are there any characteristics of North Africa today that you might feature in your myth? Write down your ideas.

Chapter Review

Geography's Impact
video series
Review the video to answer the closing question:
What are two benefits and two consequences of the Aswan High Dam?

Visual Summary

Use the visual summary below to help you review the main ideas of the chapter.

QUICK FACTS

The Sahara is a major physical feature of North Africa.

One of the world's earliest civilizations thrived on the Nile River in ancient Egypt.

Most major cities in North Africa are located on the Mediterranean Sea.

Reviewing Vocabulary, Terms, and Places

Unscramble each group of letters below to spell a term or place that matches the given definition.

1. **sasoi**—wet, fertile area in a desert where a spring or well provides water

2. **ashraa**—the largest desert in the world that covers most of North Africa

3. **ipmtac**—effect, result

4. **enli virer**—the world's longest river that empties into the Mediterranean Sea in Egypt

5. **oicar**—a city founded more than 1,000 years ago on the Nile and is the capital of Egypt today

6. **uahtroyti**—power; right to rule

7. **tidrotca**—someone who rules a country with complete power

8. **ksuos**—marketplaces

9. **efer tpro**—a city in which almost no taxes are placed on goods sold there

Comprehension and Critical Thinking

SECTION 1 *(Pages 86–89)*

10. **a. Describe** What is the Nile River Valley like? Describe the river and the landscape.

    b. Draw Conclusions How important are oases to people traveling through the Sahara?

    c. Elaborate Why do you think few people live in the Sahara? What role does climate play in where people live? Explain your answer.

SECTION 2 *(Pages 90–95)*

11. **a. Recall** What types of monuments did the ancient Egyptians build?

    b. Make Inferences Why did European countries want to control most of North Africa?

    c. Elaborate Why do you think some groups living in North Africa are nomadic people?

SECTION 3 *(Pages 97–102)*

12. a. Define What is the Maghreb? What physical feature covers this region?

b. Contrast How does Egypt's economy differ from the economies of the other countries of North Africa?

c. Predict In what ways do you think Egypt could improve the lives of its people, who are mostly poor? Explain your answer.

Using the Internet

13. Activity: Exploring the Sahara The Sahara is the largest desert in the world and is covered by great seas of sand dunes. One of the most inhospitable, hostile places on Earth, few people live in the Sahara, and few people even travel through it. Through the online book, take a journey through the Sahara. See pictures of the Sahara and learn more about its history and geography. Imagine what it would be like to cross the desert. Then create a PowerPoint presentation or a visual display that summarizes your adventures across the great Sahara.

Social Studies Skills

Analyzing a Diagram Use the diagram of an Egyptian pyramid on this chapter's Social Studies Skills page to answer the following questions.

14. From looking at the title of the diagram, who built this pyramid?

15. How did the pyramid builders get to the king's burial chamber?

16. In what kind of climate is the pyramid located?

Map Activity

17. North Africa On a separate sheet of paper, match the letters on the map with their correct labels.

Nile River

Atlas Mountains

Cairo

Tripoli

Strait of Gibraltar

FOCUS ON READING AND WRITING

18. Summarizing Re-read the paragraphs under Physical Features in Section 1. Create a short summary of each paragraph, then combine these paragraph summaries into a summary of the whole passage.

19. Writing a Myth Choose one physical feature of North Africa to be the subject of your myth. Then write two to three paragraphs describing the characteristics of the physical feature and how you think ancient peoples would find it mysterious. Use your imagination! For example, your myth might explain why it rarely rains in the Sahara or why the Nile flows north to the Mediterranean Sea.

Standardized Test Prep

DIRECTIONS: Read questions 1 through 7 and write the letter of the best response. Question 8 will require a brief essay.

1 **What physical feature covers most of North Africa?**

A the Nile

B the Sahara

C Sinai Peninsula

D Atlas Mountains

2 **The Nile flows through Egypt and empties into the**

A Red Sea.

B Atlantic Ocean.

C Mediterranean Sea.

D Sahara.

3 **The ancient Egyptians built pyramids to bury their**

A relatives.

B pharaohs.

C pets.

D valuable goods.

4 **What language do the majority of North Africans speak?**

A English

B French

C Italian

D Arabic

5 **Most North Africans are**

A Christians.

B Buddhists.

C Muslims.

D Hindus.

North Africa

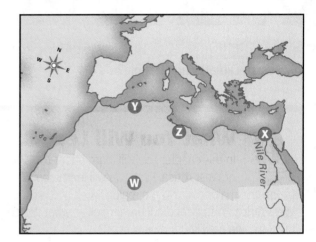

6 **Use the map to answer the following question. Ancient Egyptian civilization thrived in North Africa at the location marked on the map by the letter**

A W.

B Z.

C X.

D Y.

7 **What do ships use to avoid sailing around Southern Africa?**

A the Nile

B the Suez Canal

C the Aswan High Dam

D the Strait of Gibraltar

8 **Extended Response** Look at the physical map in Section 1. Write a short essay describing the physical features of North Africa. Explain why people live only in certain areas of the region.

West Africa

Essential Question How is West Africa shaped by its diverse climates and people?

What You Will Learn...

In this chapter you will learn about the 17 countries of West Africa. First, you will learn about the dry plains and major rivers in the region. Then you will learn about West Africa's history and culture as well as what the countries in the region are like today.

FOCUS ON READING AND SPEAKING

Understanding Comparison-Contrast Comparing and contrasting, or looking for similarities and differences, can help you more fully understand the subject you are studying. As you read, look for ways to compare and contrast the information in your text. **See lesson, Understanding Comparison-Contrast, on page 198.**

Giving an Oral Description Storytelling is an important part of West Africa's history and culture. Storytellers pass along information to the community about events, places, and people. As you read this chapter, imagine that you are a storyteller. You are going to pass on some information about a person who lives, or has lived, in this region.

History People such as the Dogon cliff dwellers have been living in Mali for hundreds of years.

West Africa: Political

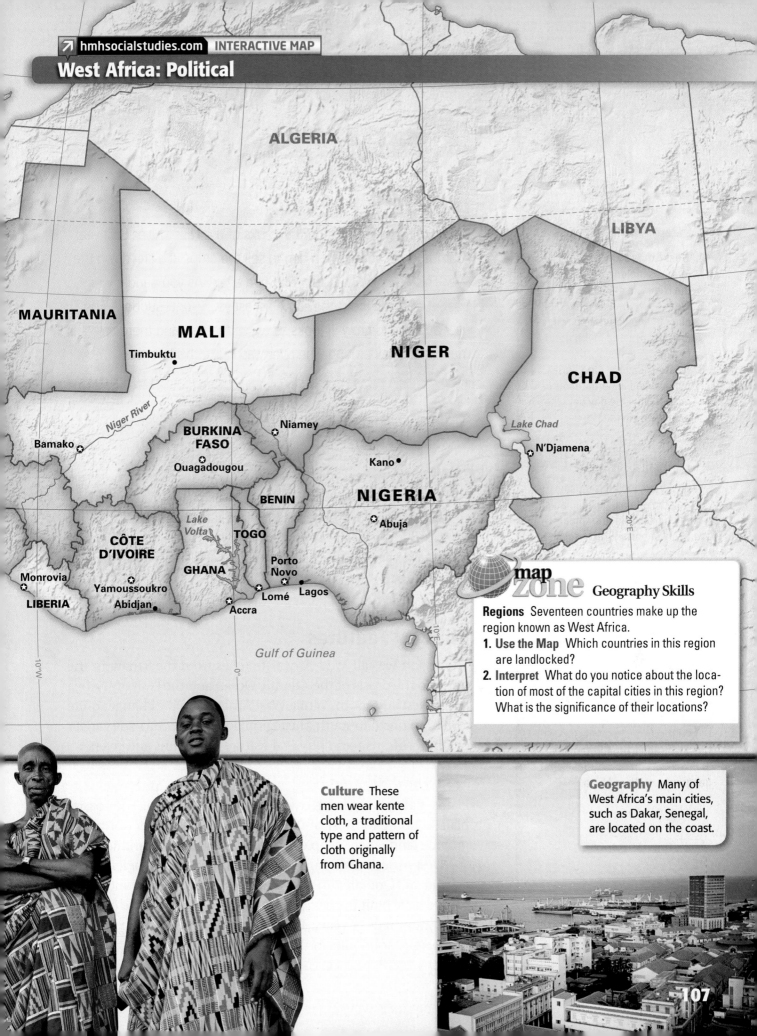

ALGERIA

LIBYA

MAURITANIA

MALI

Timbuktu

NIGER

CHAD

Niger River

BURKINA FASO

Niamey

Lake Chad

Bamako

N'Djamena

Ouagadougou

Kano

BENIN

NIGERIA

Lake Volta

TOGO

Abuja

CÔTE D'IVOIRE

GHANA

Porto Novo

Monrovia

Yamoussoukro

Lomé

Lagos

LIBERIA

Abidjan

Accra

Gulf of Guinea

map zone Geography Skills

Regions Seventeen countries make up the region known as West Africa.

1. **Use the Map** Which countries in this region are landlocked?
2. **Interpret** What do you notice about the location of most of the capital cities in this region? What is the significance of their locations?

Culture These men wear kente cloth, a traditional type and pattern of cloth originally from Ghana.

Geography Many of West Africa's main cities, such as Dakar, Senegal, are located on the coast.

107

Physical Geography

What You Will Learn...

Main Ideas

1. West Africa's key physical features include plains and the Niger River.
2. West Africa has distinct climate and vegetation zones that go from arid in the north to tropical in the south.
3. West Africa has good agricultural and mineral resources that may one day help the economies in the region.

The Big Idea

West Africa, which is mostly a region of plains, has climates ranging from arid to tropical and has important resources.

Key Terms and Places

Niger River, *p. 109*
zonal, *p. 110*
Sahel, *p. 110*
desertification, *p. 110*
savanna, *p. 110*

hmhsocialstudies.com
TAKING NOTES

Use the graphic organizer online to take notes on the physical geography of West Africa.

If YOU lived there...

Your family grows crops on the banks of the Niger River. Last year, your father let you go with him to sell the crops in a city down the river. This year you get to go with him again. As you paddle your boat, everything looks the same as last year—until suddenly the river appears to grow! It looks as big as the sea, and there are many islands all around. The river wasn't like this last year.

What do you think caused the change in the river?

BUILDING BACKGROUND The Niger River is one of West Africa's most important physical features. It brings precious water to the region's dry plains. Much of the interior of West Africa experiences desertlike conditions, but the region's rivers and lakes help to support life there.

Physical Features

The region we call West Africa stretches from the Sahara in the north to the coasts of the Atlantic Ocean and the Gulf of Guinea in the west and south. While West Africa's climate changes quite a bit from north to south, the region does not have a wide variety of landforms. Its main physical features are plains and rivers.

Plains and Highlands

Plains, flat areas of land, cover most of West Africa. The coastal plain is home to most of the region's cities. The interior plains provide land where people can raise a few crops or animals.

West Africa's plains are vast, interrupted only by a few highland areas. One area in the southwest has plateaus and cliffs. People have built houses directly into the sides of these cliffs for many hundreds of years. The region's only high mountains are the Tibesti Mountains in the northeast.

The Niger River

As you can see on the map below, many rivers flow across West Africa's plains. The most important river is the Niger (NY-juhr). The **Niger River** starts in some low mountains not too far from the Atlantic Ocean. From there, it flows 2,600 miles (4,185 km) into the interior of the region before emptying into the Gulf of Guinea.

The Niger brings life-giving water to West Africa. Many people farm along its banks or fish in its waters. It is also an important transportation route, especially during the rainy season. At that time, the river floods and water flows smoothly over its rapids.

Part of the way along its route the river divides into a network of channels, swamps, and lakes. This watery network is called the inland delta. Although it looks much like the delta where a river flows into the sea, this one is actually hundreds of miles from the coast in Mali.

READING CHECK **Summarizing** Why is the Niger River important to West Africa?

FOCUS ON READING
The word *although* signals contrast in this paragraph. What is being contrasted?

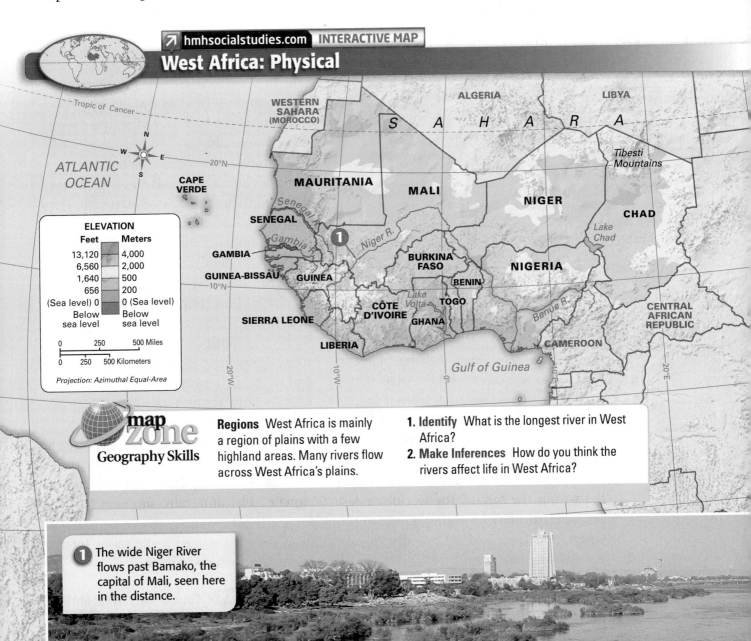

↗ hmhsocialstudies.com **INTERACTIVE MAP**

West Africa: Physical

ELEVATION

Feet	Meters
13,120	4,000
6,560	2,000
1,640	500
656	200
(Sea level) 0	0 (Sea level)
Below sea level	Below sea level

0   250   500 Miles
0   250   500 Kilometers

Projection: Azimuthal Equal-Area

map zone

Geography Skills

Regions West Africa is mainly a region of plains with a few highland areas. Many rivers flow across West Africa's plains.

1. **Identify** What is the longest river in West Africa?
2. **Make Inferences** How do you think the rivers affect life in West Africa?

1 The wide Niger River flows past Bamako, the capital of Mali, seen here in the distance.

West Africa: Climate

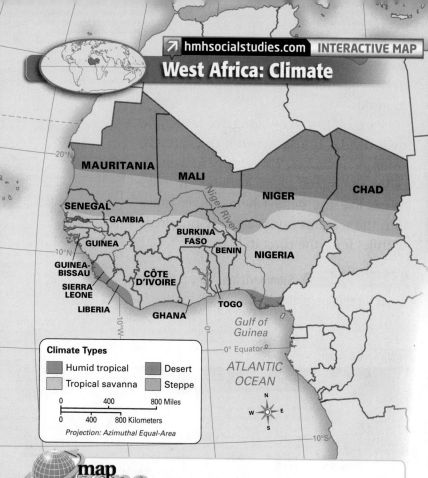

Climate Types

- Humid tropical
- Tropical savanna
- Desert
- Steppe

```
0        400        800 Miles
0     400      800 Kilometers
Projection: Azimuthal Equal-Area
```

map zone Geography Skills

Regions Four climate types stretch across West Africa in horizontal bands.
1. Identify What countries have desert climates?
2. Make Inferences What areas do you think get the most rainfall?

Sahel Vegetation in the semiarid Sahel is limited, but it does support some grazing animals.

Climate and Vegetation

West Africa has four different climate regions. As you can see on the map above, these climate regions stretch from east to west in bands or zones. Because of this, geographers say the region's climates are **zonal**, which means "organized by zone."

The northernmost zone of the region lies within the Sahara, the world's largest desert. Hardly any vegetation grows in the desert, and large areas of this dry climate zone have few or no people.

South of the Sahara is the semiarid **Sahel** (SAH-hel), a strip of land that divides the desert from wetter areas. It has a steppe climate. Rainfall there varies greatly from year to year. In some years it never rains. Although the Sahel is quite dry, it does have enough vegetation to support hardy grazing animals.

However, the Sahel is becoming more like the Sahara. Animals have overgrazed the land in some areas. Also, people have cut down trees for firewood. Without these plants to anchor the soil, wind blows soil away. These conditions, along with drought, are causing desertification in the Sahel. **Desertification** is the spread of desertlike conditions.

To the south of the Sahel is a savanna zone. A **savanna** is an area of tall grasses and scattered trees and shrubs. When rains fall regularly, farmers can do well in this region of West Africa.

The fourth climate zone lies along the coasts of the Atlantic and the Gulf of Guinea. This zone has a humid tropical climate. Plentiful rain supports tropical forests. However, many trees have been cut from these forests to make room for the region's growing populations.

READING CHECK **Categorizing** What are the region's four climate zones?

Savanna Grasses and scattered trees grow on the savanna. This region can be good for farming.

Tropical Forest Thick forests are found along the coasts of West Africa. The tall trees provide homes for many animals.

Resources

West Africa has a variety of resources. These resources include agricultural products, oil, and minerals.

The climate in parts of West Africa is good for agriculture. For example, Ghana is the world's leading producer of cacao, which is used to make chocolate. Coffee, coconuts, and peanuts are also among the region's main exports.

Oil, which is found off the coast of Nigeria, is the region's most valuable resource. Nigeria is a major exporter of oil. West Africa also has mineral riches, such as diamonds, gold, iron ore, and bauxite. Bauxite is the main source of aluminum.

READING CHECK **Summarizing** What are some of the region's resources?

SUMMARY AND PREVIEW West Africa is mostly covered with plains. Across these plains stretch four different climate zones, most of which are dry. In spite of the harsh climate, West Africa has some valuable resources. Next, you will learn about West Africa's history and culture.

hmhsocialstudies.com
ONLINE QUIZ

Section 1 Assessment

Reviewing Ideas, Terms, and Places

1. a. Describe What is the inland delta on the **Niger River** like?
b. Summarize What is the physical geography of West Africa like?
c. Elaborate Why do you think most of West Africa's cities are located on the coastal plain?
2. a. Recall Why do geographers say West Africa's climates are **zonal**?
b. Compare and Contrast What is one similarity and one difference between the **Sahel** and the **savanna**?
c. Evaluate How do you think **desertification** affects people's lives in West Africa?
3. a. Identify What is the most valuable resource in West Africa?
b. Make Inferences Where do you think most of the crops in West Africa are grown?

Critical Thinking

4. Identifying Cause and Effect
Review your notes on climate. Using a graphic organizer like the one here, identify the causes and effects of desertification.

| Causes | → | Desertification | → | Effects |

FOCUS ON SPEAKING

5. Describing the Physical Geography The person you will describe will live or have lived in this region. How might the physical geography have affected his or her life?

History and Culture

What You Will Learn...

Main Ideas

1. In West Africa's history, trade made great kingdoms rich, but this greatness declined as Europeans began to control trade routes.
2. The culture of West Africa includes many different ethnic groups, languages, religions, and housing styles.

The Big Idea

Powerful early kingdoms, European slave trade and colonization, and traditions from a mix of ethnic groups have all influenced West African culture.

Key Terms and Places

Timbuktu, *p. 113*
animism, *p. 114*
extended family, *p. 115*

hmhsocialstudies.com
TAKING NOTES

Use the graphic organizer online to take notes on West Africa's history and culture.

If **YOU** lived there...

When you were a small child, your family moved to Lagos, the largest city in Nigeria. You live in a city apartment now, but you still visit your aunts and uncles and cousins in your home village. There are more types of activities in the city, but you also remember that it was fun to have all your family members around.

Do you want to stay in the city or move back to your village? Why?

BUILDING BACKGROUND West African societies are changing as people like this family move to cities where they meet people whose habits and language are strange to them. West Africa has been home to many different ethnic groups throughout its history.

History

Much of what we know about West Africa's early history is based on archaeology. Archaeology is the study of the past based on what people left behind. Oral history—a spoken record of past events—offers other clues.

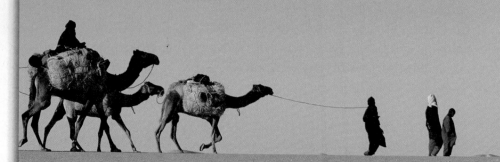

Merchants from North Africa crossed the Sahara to trade for West African gold and salt.

Great Kingdoms

Ancient artifacts suggest that early trading centers developed into great kingdoms in West Africa. One of the earliest kingdoms was Ghana (GAH-nuh). By controlling the Sahara trade in gold and salt, Ghana became rich and powerful by about 800.

According to legend, Ghana fell to a mighty warrior from a neighboring kingdom in about 1300. Under this leader, the empire of Mali (MAH-lee) replaced Ghana. Mali gained control of the Sahara trade routes. Mali's most famous king, Mansa Musa, used wealth from trade to support artists and scholars. However, invasions caused the decline of Mali by the 1500s.

As Mali declined, the kingdom of Songhai (SAWNG-hy) came to power. With a university, mosques, and more than 100 schools, the Songhai city of **Timbuktu** was a cultural center. By about 1600, however, invasions had weakened this kingdom.

The great West African trade cities also faded when the Sahara trade decreased. Trade decreased partly because Europeans began sailing along the west coast of Africa. They could trade for gold on the coast rather than with the North African traders who carried it through the desert.

The Slave Trade

For a while, both Europeans and Africans profited from trade with each other. However, in the 1500s the demand for labor in Europe's American colonies changed this relationship. European traders met the demand for labor by selling enslaved Africans to colonists.

The slave trade was profitable for these traders, but it devastated West Africa. Many families were broken up when members were kidnapped and enslaved. Africans often died on the voyage to the Americas. By the end of the slave trade in the 1800s, millions of Africans had been enslaved.

Primary Source

BOOK
I Speak of Freedom

As European colonizers left West Africa, some people believed that Africa should not be divided into independent countries. Kwame Nkrumah, a future leader of Ghana, explained in 1961 why he thought Africans should unite.

❝It is clear that we must find an African solution to our problems, and that this can only be found in African unity. Divided we are weak; united, Africa could become one of the greatest forces for good in the world.**❞**

—Kwame Nkrumah, from *I Speak of Freedom: A Statement of African Ideology*

ANALYSIS SKILL **ANALYZING PRIMARY SOURCES**

Why did Kwame Nkrumah think Africa would be better off united than divided?

Colonial Era and Independence

Even with the end of the slave trade, Europeans wanted access to West Africa's resources. To ensure that access, France, Britain, Germany, and Portugal all claimed colonies in the region in the 1800s.

Some Europeans moved to West Africa to run the colonies. They built schools, roads, and railroads. However, they also created new and difficult problems for the people of West Africa. For example, many West Africans gave up farming and instead earned only low wages working in the new commercial economy.

After World War II, Africans worked for independence. Most of the colonies became independent during the 1950s and 1960s. All were independent by 1974.

FOCUS ON READING

What words in the discussion of the slave trade signal comparison or contrast?

READING CHECK **Summarizing** What impact did Europeans have on West Africa?

Culture

West African societies are very diverse. Their culture reflects three main influences —traditional African cultures, European culture, and Islam.

People and Languages

West Africa's people belong to hundreds of different ethnic groups. In fact, Nigeria alone is made up of more than 250 ethnic groups. The biggest ethnic groups there are Hausa and Fulani, Yoruba, and Igbo. Members of some ethnic groups in West Africa still live in their traditional villages. Other ethnic groups mix with each other in the region's cities.

Because of the way the European colonizers drew political boundaries, country borders sometimes separated members of the same ethnic group. Other borders grouped together peoples that did not get along. As a result, many West Africans are more loyal to their own ethnic groups than they are to their countries.

Because of the huge number of ethnic groups, hundreds of different languages are spoken in West Africa. In some areas, using the colonial languages of French, English, or Portuguese helps people from different groups communicate with each other. Also, West African languages that many people share, such as Fula and Hausa, help with communication in the region.

Religion

Like peoples and languages, many forms of religion exist in West Africa. Traditional religions of West Africa have often been forms of animism. **Animism** is the belief that bodies of water, animals, trees, and other natural objects have spirits. Animists also honor the memories of ancestors.

The two most common religions came from outside the region. They are Islam and Christianity. North African traders brought Islam to West Africa. Europeans introduced Christianity. Today most West Africans of the Sahel practice Islam. Many towns there have mosques built of mud. Christianity is the most common religion south of the Sahel.

Clothing, Families, and Homes

West Africans wear a mix of traditional and modern clothing styles. Some West Africans, particularly in the cities, wear Western-style clothing. Traditional robes, pants, blouses, and skirts are made from colorful cotton fabrics. Women often wear beautiful wrapped headdresses. Because of the warm climate, most clothing is loose.

CONNECTING TO the Arts

Masks

Masks are one of the best-known West African arts. They are traditionally carved out of wood only by skilled and respected men. The colors and shape of a mask have specific meanings. For example, the color white represents the spirit world.

Masks are used in ceremonies to call spirits or to prepare boys and girls for adulthood. Ceremony participants often wear a mask as part of a costume that completely hides the body. The wearer is believed to become what the mask represents.

Drawing Inferences Why would someone want to wear a mask?

A West African Village

These homes are in Burkina Faso. Trees are scarce in the Sahel and savanna so there is little wood for construction.

Women are responsible for painting and decorating the walls of the homes.

These homes are made of a mixture of mud, water, and cow dung.

Rural homes are small and simple. Many homes in the Sahel and savanna zones are circular. Straw or tin roofs sit atop mud, mud-brick, or straw huts. Large extended families often live close together in the same village. An **extended family** includes the father, mother, children, and close relatives in one household.

In urban areas also, members of an extended family may all live together. However, in West Africa's cities you will find modern buildings. People may live in houses or high-rise apartments.

READING CHECK Generalizing What are some features of West African culture?

SUMMARY AND PREVIEW Great kingdoms and European colonists once ruled West Africa. These historical influences still affect West Africa's diverse cultures. Next, you will learn about the countries of West Africa today.

hmhsocialstudies.com
ONLINE QUIZ

Section 2 Assessment

Reviewing Ideas, Terms, and Places

1. **a. Identify** What was the significance of **Timbuktu**?
   b. Explain How did the slave trade affect West Africa?
   c. Evaluate Do you think West Africans mostly appreciated or disliked the European colonizers? Explain your answer.
2. **a. Recall** What do people who believe in **animism** think about natural objects?
   b. Analyze How did European colonizers affect tension between ethnic groups?

Critical Thinking

3. **Sequencing** Look over your notes on the history of West Africa. Then, using a diagram like the one here, put major events in chronological order.

FOCUS ON SPEAKING

4. **Describing History and Culture** What details about West Africa's history might affect the daily life of someone in the area? Many aspects of culture in the region would affect someone in West Africa. What religion would this person practice? How would he or she dress? List some ideas for your description.

Geography and History

The Atlantic Slave Trade

Between 1500 and 1870, British, French, Dutch, Portuguese, and Spanish traders sent millions of enslaved Africans to colonies in the Americas. The highest number of slaves went to British and French colonies in the West Indies. The climate in the colonies was good for growing crops like cotton, tobacco, and sugarcane. These crops required a great deal of labor to grow and process. The colonists relied on enslaved Africans to meet this demand for labor.

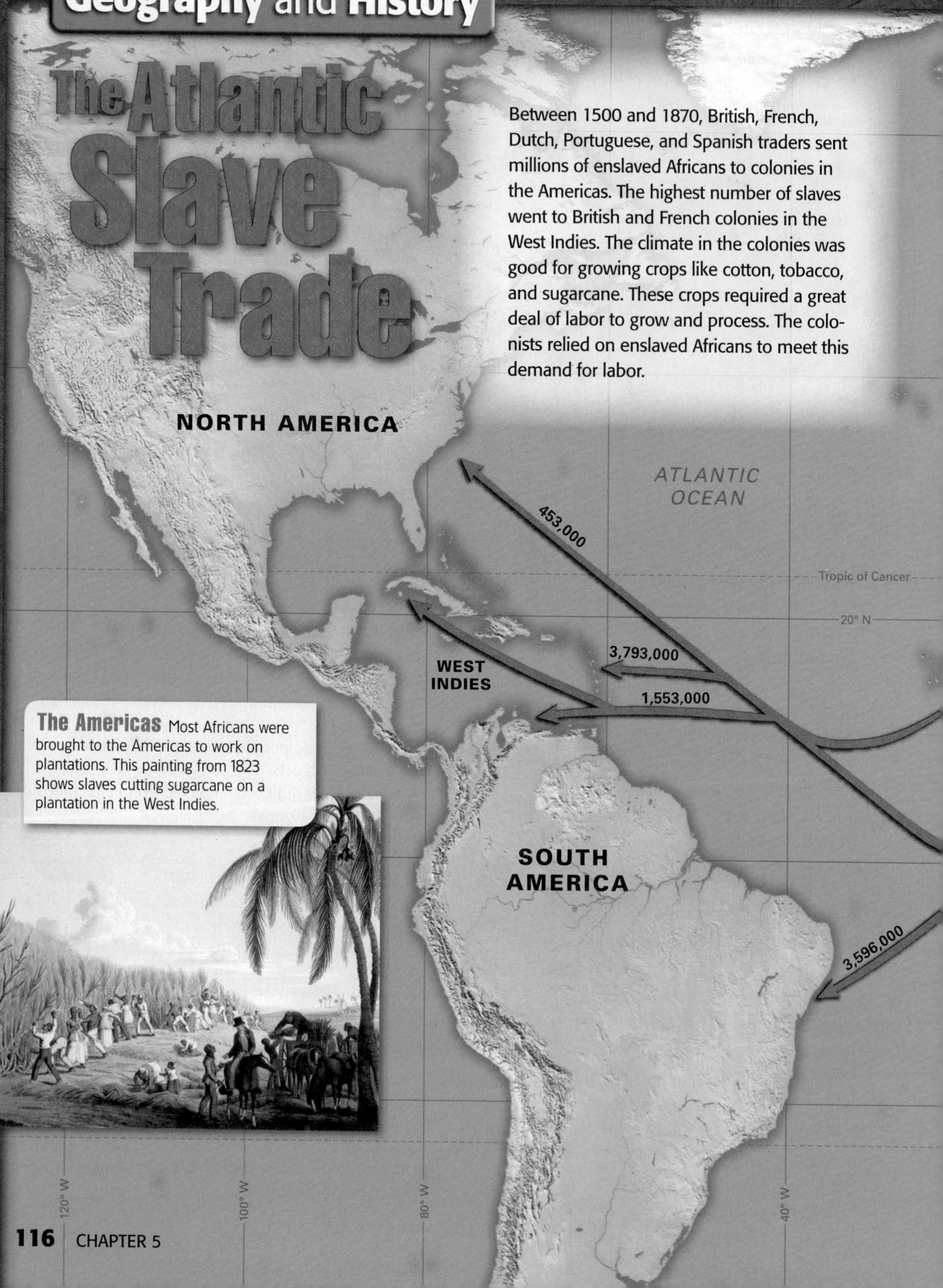

NORTH AMERICA
ATLANTIC OCEAN
453,000
Tropic of Cancer
20° N
3,793,000
WEST INDIES
1,553,000
SOUTH AMERICA
3,596,000
120° W
100° W
80° W
40° W

The Americas Most Africans were brought to the Americas to work on plantations. This painting from 1823 shows slaves cutting sugarcane on a plantation in the West Indies.

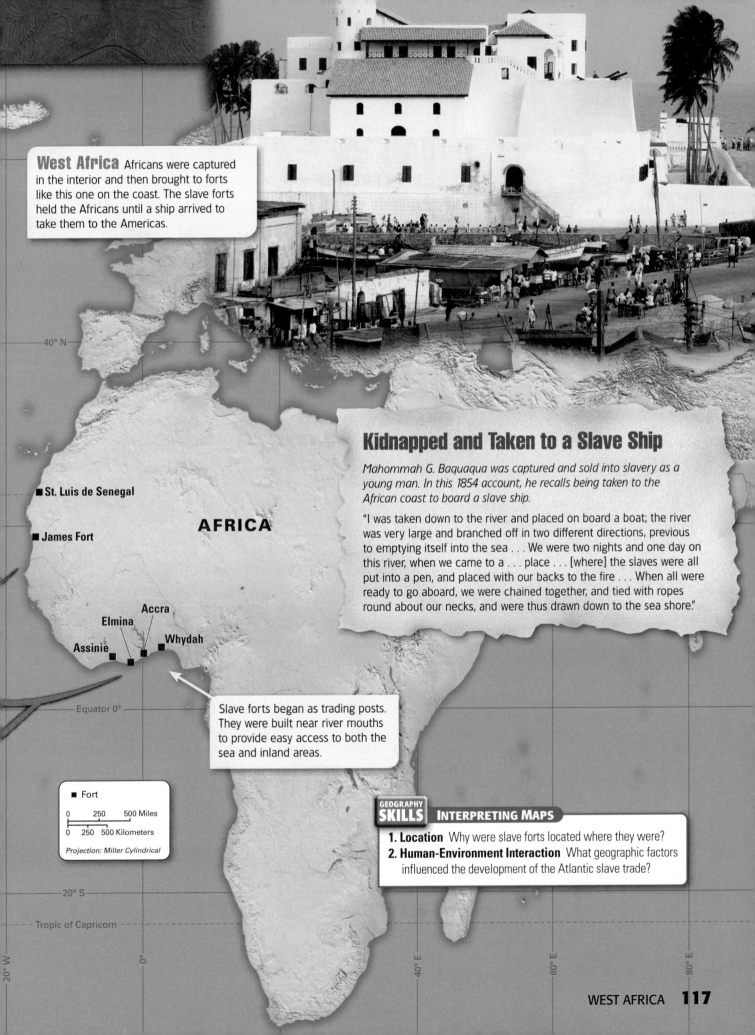

West Africa Africans were captured in the interior and then brought to forts like this one on the coast. The slave forts held the Africans until a ship arrived to take them to the Americas.

AFRICA

■ St. Luis de Senegal

■ James Fort

Accra

Elmina

Assinie

Whydah

Equator 0°

Kidnapped and Taken to a Slave Ship

Mahommah G. Baquaqua was captured and sold into slavery as a young man. In this 1854 account, he recalls being taken to the African coast to board a slave ship.

"I was taken down to the river and placed on board a boat; the river was very large and branched off in two different directions, previous to emptying itself into the sea . . . We were two nights and one day on this river, when we came to a . . . place . . . [where] the slaves were all put into a pen, and placed with our backs to the fire . . . When all were ready to go aboard, we were chained together, and tied with ropes round about our necks, and were thus drawn down to the sea shore."

Slave forts began as trading posts. They were built near river mouths to provide easy access to both the sea and inland areas.

■ Fort

0   250   500 Miles

0   250 500 Kilometers

Projection: Miller Cylindrical

GEOGRAPHY SKILLS **INTERPRETING MAPS**

1. **Location** Why were slave forts located where they were?
2. **Human-Environment Interaction** What geographic factors influenced the development of the Atlantic slave trade?

20° S

Tropic of Capricorn

20° W

0°

40° E

60° E

80° E

West Africa Today

If YOU lived there...

You live in the Sahel country of Niger, where your family herds cattle. You travel with your animals to find good grazing land for them. In the past few years, however, the desert has been expanding. It is getting harder and harder to find good grass and water for your cattle. You worry about the coming years.

How does this environment affect your life and your future?

BUILDING BACKGROUND The countries of West Africa are very different from one another. Some, such as Niger, have poor soils, little rain, and few resources. Others, such as Nigeria, have good natural resources. None of these countries is wealthy, however.

Nigeria

Nigeria is the second largest country in West Africa. With almost 150 million people, it has Africa's largest population, its second largest city, and one of the strongest economies.

People and Government

Like many other former colonies, Nigeria has many different ethnic groups within its borders. Conflicts have often taken place among those ethnic groups. In the 1960s one conflict became so serious that one ethnic group, the Igbo, tried to secede from Nigeria. To **secede** means to break away from the main country. This action led to a bloody civil war, which the Igbo eventually lost.

Ethnic and regional conflicts have continued to be an issue in Nigeria. Avoiding conflict was important in choosing a site for a new capital in the 1990s. Leaders chose Abuja (ah-BOO-jah) because it was centrally located in an area of low population density. A low population density meant that there would be fewer people to cause conflicts. Nigeria's government is now a democracy after years of military rule.

Crowding in Lagos

Lagos is a busy seaport and industrial center. Overcrowding leads to problems common in big cities such as traffic jams and poor housing.

ANALYZING VISUALS What activities are these people participating in?

Economy

Nigeria has some of Africa's richest natural resources. Major oil fields, the country's most important resource, are located in the Niger River delta and just off the coast. Oil accounts for about 95 percent of the country's export earnings. Income from oil exports has allowed Nigeria to build good roads and railroads for transporting oil. The oil industry is centered around **Lagos** (LAY-gahs). Also the former capital, Lagos is the most populous city in West Africa.

Although Nigeria is rich in resources, many Nigerians are poor. One cause of the poverty there is a high birthrate. Nigeria cannot produce enough food for its growing population. Another cause of Nigeria's poverty is a history of bad government. Corrupt government officials have used their positions to enrich themselves.

READING CHECK Drawing Inferences What are some obstacles to progress in Nigeria?

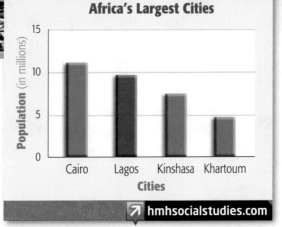

THE WORLD ALMANAC®
Facts about the World

Africa's Largest Cities

Bar chart showing Population (in millions) on the y-axis (0 to 15) and Cities on the x-axis: Cairo (~11), Lagos (~9.5), Kinshasa (~7.5), Khartoum (~4.5)

hmhsocialstudies.com

Other Coastal Countries

Several West African countries lie along the Atlantic Ocean and the Gulf of Guinea. Many of these countries have struggling economies and unstable governments.

Senegal and Gambia

Senegal wraps around Gambia. The odd border was created by French and British diplomats during the colonial era. Senegal is larger and richer than Gambia, but the two countries do have many similarities. For example, peanuts are their major crops. Also, tourism is becoming more important in both countries.

FOCUS ON READING
How are Senegal and Gambia similar?

Many people in Senegal and Gambia speak a language called Wolof (WOH-lawf). Griots (GREE-ohz), or storytellers, are important to the Wolof speakers there and to other West Africans.

Guinea, Guinea-Bissau, and Cape Verde

Guinea and its small neighbor, Guinea-Bissau (GI-nee bi-SOW), are poor countries. Guinea's main natural resource is bauxite, which is used to make aluminum. Guinea-Bissau has undeveloped mineral resources.

Cape Verde (VUHRD) is a group of volcanic islands in the Atlantic. It is West Africa's only island country. Once a Portuguese colony, Cape Verde now has one of the most stable democratic governments in Africa. Services such as tourism form the main part of the country's economy.

Liberia and Sierra Leone

Liberia is Africa's oldest republic. Americans founded it in the 1820s as a home for freed slaves. The freed slaves who settled in Liberia and their descendants lived in towns on the coast. They often clashed with Africans already living there. Those Africans were usually poorer and lived in rural areas. In the 1980s these conflicts led to a civil war, which ended in 2003.

Sierra Leone (lee-OHN) also experienced violent civil war, from 1991 to 2002. The fighting wrecked the country's economy, killed thousands of people, and forced millions from their homes.

Now, both Liberia and Sierra Leone are trying to rebuild. They do have natural resources on which to build stronger economies. Liberia exports rubber and iron ore while Sierra Leone exports diamonds.

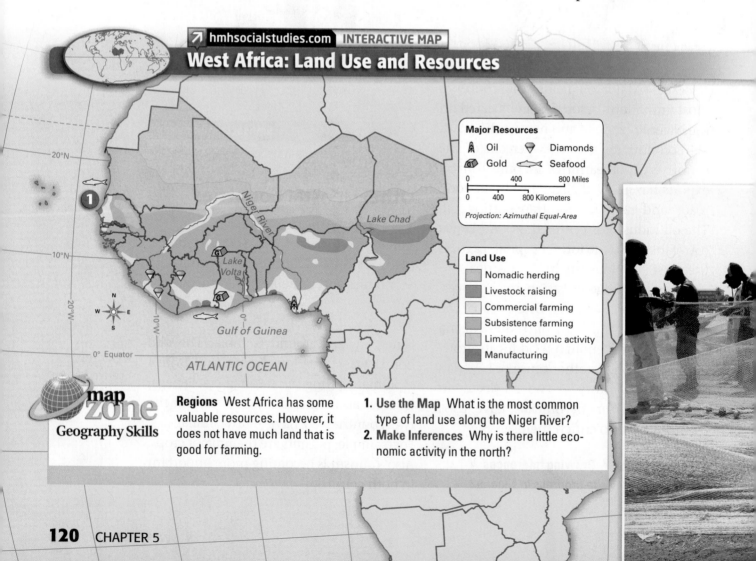

↗ hmhsocialstudies.com INTERACTIVE MAP

West Africa: Land Use and Resources

Major Resources

- Oil
- Diamonds
- Gold
- Seafood

0 — 400 — 800 Miles
0 — 400 — 800 Kilometers

Projection: Azimuthal Equal-Area

Land Use

- Nomadic herding
- Livestock raising
- Commercial farming
- Subsistence farming
- Limited economic activity
- Manufacturing

20°N · 10°N · 20°W · 10°W · 0° Equator

Niger River · Lake Chad · Lake Volta · Gulf of Guinea · ATLANTIC OCEAN

map zone Geography Skills

Regions West Africa has some valuable resources. However, it does not have much land that is good for farming.

1. **Use the Map** What is the most common type of land use along the Niger River?
2. **Make Inferences** Why is there little economic activity in the north?

Ghana and Côte d'Ivoire

Ghana is named for an ancient kingdom. Côte d'Ivoire (koht-dee-VWAHR) is a former French colony whose name means "Ivory Coast" in English. Côte d'Ivoire boasts Africa's largest Christian church building.

These two countries have rich natural resources. Gold, timber, and cacao (kuh-KOW) are major products of Ghana. Côte d'Ivoire is a world leader in export of cacao and coffee. However, civil war there has hurt the economy.

Togo and Benin

Unstable governments have troubled Togo and Benin (buh-NEEN) since independence. These two countries have experienced periods of military rule. Their fragile economies have contributed to their unstable and sometimes violent politics.

Both Togo and Benin are poor. The people depend on farming and herding for income. Palm products, cacao, and coffee are the main crops in both countries.

READING CHECK **Generalizing** What are the economies of the coastal countries like?

1 Fishing is an important industry in the coastal countries of West Africa.

Sahel Countries

The Sahel region of West Africa includes some of the poorest and least developed countries in the world. Drought and the expanding desert make feeding the people in these countries difficult.

Mauritania, Niger, and Chad

Most Mauritanians were once nomadic herders. Today the expanding Sahara has driven more than half of the nomads into cities. People in these cities, as well as the rest of the country, are very poor. Only in the far south, near the Senegal River, can people farm. Near the Atlantic Ocean, people fish for a living. Corrupt governments and ethnic tensions between blacks and Arabs add to Mauritania's troubles.

In Niger, only about 11 percent of the land is good for farming. The country's only farmland lies along the Niger River and near the Nigerian border. Farmers there grow staple, or main, food crops, such as millet and sorghum.

In 2005, locusts and drought destroyed Niger's crops. The loss of crops caused widespread **famine**, or an extreme shortage of food. International groups provided some aid, but it was impossible to **distribute** food to all who needed it. In 2007, fighting broke out between Tuareg rebels and government forces. In 2009, President Mamadou Tandja used his emergency powers to dissolve the government. He then instituted changes that would allow him to serve a third term as president.

Chad has more land for farming than Mauritania or Niger, and conditions there are somewhat better than in the other two countries. In addition to farming, Lake Chad once had a healthy fishing industry and supplied water to several countries. However, drought has evaporated much of the lake's water in the past several years.

ACADEMIC VOCABULARY
distribute to divide among a group of people

Water well

Dry Croplands

This aerial view shows how, with just a little water, people can farm in the dry Sahel.

The future may hold more promise for Chad. A long civil war finally ended in the 1990s. Also, oil was recently discovered there, and Chad began to export this valuable resource in 2004.

Mali and Burkina Faso

The Sahara covers about 40 percent of the land in Mali. The scarce amount of land available for farming makes Mali among the world's poorest countries. The available farmland lies in the southwest, along the Niger River. Most people in Mali fish or farm in this small area along the river. Cotton and gold are Mali's main exports.

Mali's economy does have some bright spots, however. A fairly stable democratic government has begun economic reforms. Also, the ancient cities of Timbuktu and Gao (GOW) continue to attract tourists.

Burkina Faso is also a poor country. It has thin soil and few mineral resources. Few trees remain in or near the capital, Ouagadougou (wah-gah-DOO-goo), because they have been cut for firewood and building material. Jobs in the city are also scarce. To support their families many men try to find work in other countries. Thus, when unrest disrupts work opportunities in other countries, Burkina Faso's economy suffers.

READING CHECK **Summarizing** What are the challenges facing Chad and Burkina Faso?

SUMMARY AND PREVIEW Countries in West Africa struggle with poor economies. In addition, many have faced political instability since independence. In the next chapter, you will learn about how the countries in East Africa face some similar issues.

Section 3 Assessment

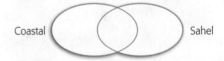

hmhsocialstudies.com
ONLINE QUIZ

Reviewing Ideas, Terms, and Places

1. **a. Recall** Why did the Igbo try to **secede**?
   b. Evaluate What do you think were some benefits and drawbacks to Nigeria's leaders moving the capital from **Lagos** to Abuja?
2. **a. Identify** What is West Africa's only island country?
   b. Compare What are some similarities between Togo and Benin?
   c. Elaborate Why do you think countries with poor economies often have unstable governments?
3. **a. Describe** What caused **famine** in Niger?
   b. Evaluate What do you think is the biggest problem facing the Sahel countries? Explain.

Critical Thinking

4. **Compare and Contrast** Review your notes on the coastal countries and the Sahel countries. Then use a diagram like the one here to compare and contrast the two regions.

Coastal   Sahel

FOCUS ON SPEAKING

5. **Describing Countries of West Africa** Think about the countries of West Africa. Which one might be a good location for the person you are going to describe? Take some notes about that place.

from
AKÉ: The Years of Childhood

by Wole Soyinka

Merchants from North Africa sometimes traded brass objects in West Africa.

About the Reading *In this excerpt from* Aké: The Years of Childhood, *Nigerian-born Wole Soyinka describes some traders who came to his childhood home in Aké. As a young boy, he was fascinated with the appearance of the exotic goods.*

AS YOU READ Notice the variety of goods the traders brought to the author's house.

It was a strange procedure, one which made little sense to me. ❶ They spread their wares in front of the house and I had to be prised off them. There were brass figures, horses, camels, trays, bowls, ornaments. Human figures spun on a podium, balanced by weights at the end of curved light metal rods. We spun them round and round, yet they never fell off their narrow perch. The smell of fresh leather filled the house as pouffs, handbags, slippers and worked scabbards were unpacked. There were bottles encased in leather, with leather stoppers, . . . scrolls, glass beads, bottles of scent with exotic names—I never forgot, from the first moment I read it on the label—Bint el Sudan, with its picture of a turbanned warrior by a kneeling camel. A veiled maiden offered him a bowl of fruits. They looked unlike anything in the orchard and Essay said they were called dates. ❷ I did not believe him; dates were figures which appeared on a calendar on the wall, so I took it as one of his jokes.

GUIDED READING

WORD HELP

wares goods
prised taken by force
pouff fluffy clothing or accessory
scabbard a case to hold a knife
turbanned wearing a turban, or wrapped cloth, on the head

❶ The author is describing a visit by the Hausa traders who came from northwestern Africa.

❷ Essay is the author's father.

Connecting Literature to Geography

1. **Drawing Inferences** The author describes many unusual things. What descriptions or comments lead you to believe that the trader traveled to Aké from far away?

2. **Analyzing** Think about the way the author described the goods. What senses did the author use as a child to discover the goods the traders brought?

Social Studies Skills

Analyzing a Precipitation Map

Learn

A precipitation map shows how much rain or snow typically falls in a certain area over a year. Studying a precipitation map can help you understand a region's climate.

To read a precipitation map, first look at the legend to see what the different colors mean. Compare the legend to the map to see how much precipitation different areas get.

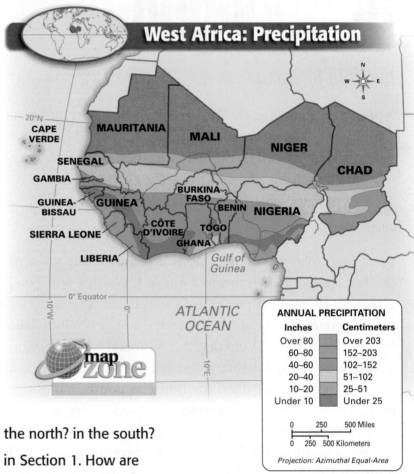

West Africa: Precipitation

ANNUAL PRECIPITATION

Inches		Centimeters
Over 80		Over 203
60–80		152–203
40–60		102–152
20–40		51–102
10–20		25–51
Under 10		Under 25

0   250   500 Miles
0   250 500 Kilometers

Projection: Azimuthal Equal-Area

Practice

Use the map on this page to answer the following questions.

1. What countries have areas that get over 80 inches of rain every year?

2. In what part of the region does the least amount of rain fall?

3. What do you think vegetation is like in the north? in the south?

4. Compare this map to the climate map in Section 1. How are the two maps similar?

Apply

Using an atlas or the Internet, find a precipitation map of the United States. Use that map to answer the following questions.

1. What area of the country gets the most precipitation?

2. What area of the country gets the least precipitation?

3. How much annual precipitation does Hawaii get?

Chapter Review

Geography's Impact
video series
Review the video to answer the closing question:
What are some of the ways desertification can be slowed, stopped, or even reversed?

Visual Summary

Use the visual summary below to help you review the main ideas of the chapter.

QUICK FACTS

West Africa has four distinct climate zones. In the dry Sahel, people try to farm or herd cattle.

Masks are just one example of traditional African culture that can be seen in West Africa today.

Most West African countries are poor. Fishing is important to the economy along rivers and in coastal areas.

Reviewing Vocabulary, Terms, and Places

For each statement below, write T if it is true and F if it is false. If the statement is false, write the correct term that would make the sentence a true statement.

1. West Africa's climate is described as <u>savanna</u> because it is organized by zone.

2. <u>Animism</u>, a belief that natural objects have spirits, is a traditional religion in West Africa.

3. An <u>extended family</u> is one that includes a mother, father, children, and close relatives in one household.

4. International aid agencies have tried to <u>distribute</u> food in Niger.

5. <u>Timbuktu</u> is the largest city in Nigeria.

6. The <u>Niger River</u> flows through many countries in West Africa and empties into the Gulf of Guinea.

7. The spread of desertlike conditions is <u>famine</u>.

8. Some animals can graze in the <u>Sahel</u>.

Comprehension and Critical Thinking

SECTION 1 *(Pages 108–111)*

9. **a. Identify** What are the four climate zones of West Africa?

   b. Make Inferences What are some problems caused by desertification?

   c. Elaborate West Africa has valuable resources such as gold and diamonds. Why do you think these resources have not made West Africa a rich region?

SECTION 2 *(Pages 112–115)*

10. **a. Recall** What religion do most people in the Sahel practice?

   b. Analyze What role did trade play in the early West African kingdoms and later in West Africa's history?

   c. Elaborate What might be some advantages of living with an extended family?

11. a. Identify Which country in West Africa has an economy based nearly entirely on oil?

b. Compare and Contrast What is one similarity and one difference between the cause of civil war in Nigeria and its cause in Liberia?

c. Predict How might the recent discovery of oil in Chad affect that country in the future?

Using the Internet

12. Activity: Creating a Postcard Come and learn about the mighty baobab tree. This unique tree looks as if it has been plucked from the ground and turned upside down. These trees are known not only for their unique look but also for their great size. Some are so big that a chain of 30 people is needed to surround one tree trunk! Through the online book, visit Web sites about baobab trees in West Africa. Then create a postcard about this strange wonder of nature.

↗ **hmhsocialstudies.com**

Map Activity

13. West Africa On a separate sheet of paper, match the letters on the map with their correct labels.

Niger River	Senegal River
Lagos, Nigeria	Mali
Gulf of Guinea	

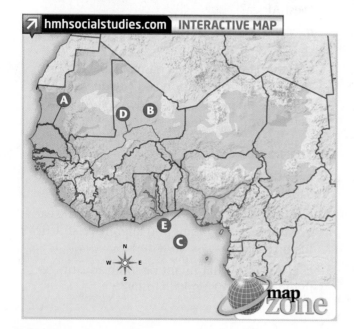

↗ **hmhsocialstudies.com** **INTERACTIVE MAP**

Social Studies Skills

Analyzing a Precipitation Map *Use the precipitation map in the Social Studies Skills lesson to answer the following questions.*

14. What countries have areas that receive under 10 inches of rain every year?

15. Where in West Africa does the most rain typically fall?

16. How would you describe annual precipitation in Chad?

17. How would you describe annual precipitation in Benin?

FOCUS ON READING AND SPEAKING

Understanding Comparison-Contrast *Look over your notes or re-read Section 1. Use the information on climate and vegetation to answer the following questions.*

18. How are the Sahara and the Sahel similar?

19. How are the Sahara and the Sahel different?

20. Compare the Sahel and the savanna zone. How are they similar?

21. Contrast the savanna region and the humid tropical region along the coast. How are these areas different?

22. Giving an Oral Description Read over your notes. Then prepare a brief oral presentation about a day in the life of someone from West Africa. Tell about the land, climate, and vegetation. Describe the culture, including family life. Tell what this person does for a living. Practice your presentation several times before you give it so you can make frequent eye contact with your audience. During your presentation, remember to speak loudly and clearly. Use good descriptive language to interest your audience in your topic.

Standardized Test Prep

DIRECTIONS: Read questions 1 through 6 and write the letter of the best response. Then read question 7 and write your own well-constructed response.

1 The climate zone just south of the Sahara is called the

A desert.

B savanna.

C Sahel.

D tropical forest.

2 Which West African country was named for an ancient kingdom in the region?

A Liberia

B Nigeria

C Chad

D Ghana

3 Which of the following statements about the slave trade is false?

A European slave traders built schools and railroads in West Africa.

B European slave traders profited from it.

C It broke up families in West Africa.

D Enslaved Africans were sent to the Americas to meet the increased demand for labor there.

4 Which country in West Africa has an economy based on oil?

A Niger

B Nigeria

C Mauritania

D Mali

5 Which country has one of the most stable democratic governments in Africa?

A Nigeria

B Liberia

C Cape Verde

D Sierra Leone

West Africa: Population

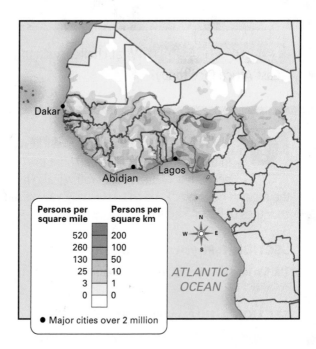

6 Based on the map above, which of the following sentences is true?

A West Africa has only one city with a population over 2 million.

B West Africa's highest population density is in the Sahel countries.

C Most of the region's population is in the south.

D The region around Dakar has a population density of over 520 people per square mile.

7 **Extended Response** Compare the map above to the climate map in Section 1. Then write a brief essay explaining factors that affect human settlement in West Africa. One paragraph should explain how the two maps are related. Another paragraph should describe physical factors that influence settlement.

East Africa

Essential Question What challenges and conflicts does East Africa face today?

- ✪ National capital
- • Other cities

0   150   300 Miles

0   150   300 Kilometers

Projection: Lambert Equal-Area

20°N

0° Equator

10°S

? What You Will Learn...

In this chapter you will learn about the physical geography of East Africa. You will also learn about the region's rich history and culture. Finally, you will study the countries of East Africa today.

Focus on Reading and Writing

Identifying Supporting Details Supporting details are the facts and examples that provide information to support the main ideas of a chapter, section, or paragraph. At the beginning of each section in this book, there is a list of main ideas. As you read this chapter, look for the details that support each section's main ideas. **See the lesson, Identifying Supporting Details, on page 199.**

Writing a Letter Home Imagine that you are spending your summer vacation visiting the countries of East Africa. You want to wite a letter home to a friend in the United States describing the land and its people. As you read this chapter, you will gather information that you can include in your letter.

ATLANTIC OCEAN

History This gold artifact is from the early Nubian civilization of northern Sudan.

East Africa: Political

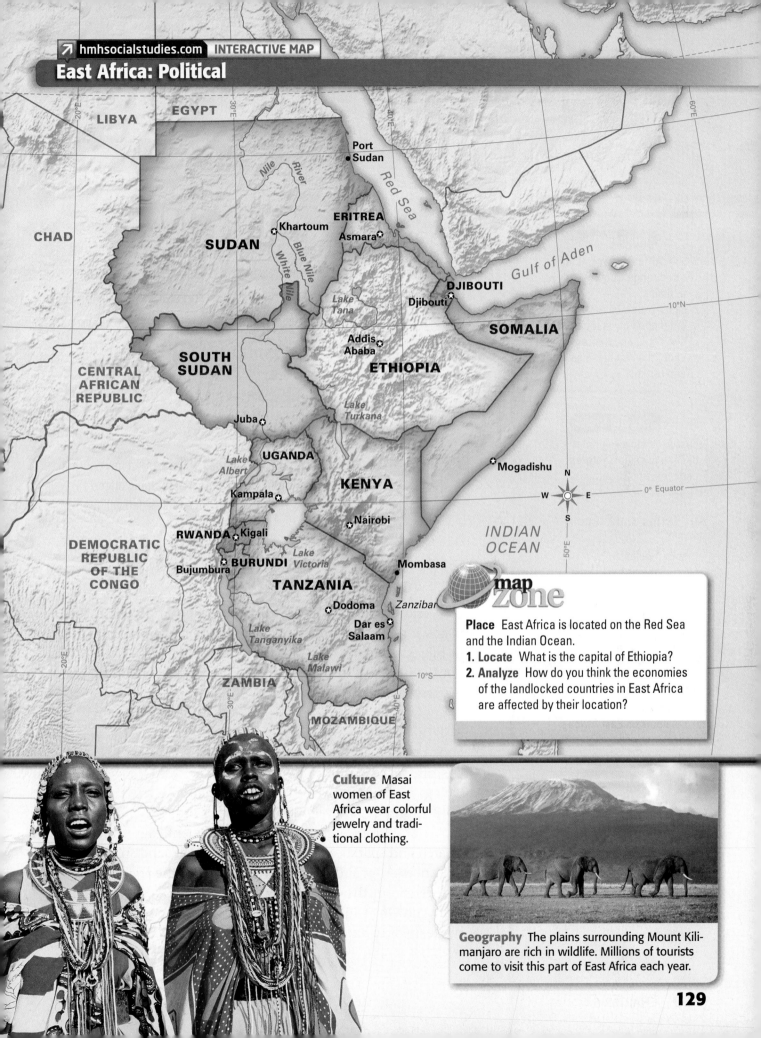

LIBYA

EGYPT

CHAD

30°E

Nile

River

Port
Sudan

Red Sea

SUDAN

Khartoum

Blue Nile

White Nile

ERITREA

Asmara

40°E

60°E

Gulf of Aden

DJIBOUTI

Djibouti

10°N

CENTRAL
AFRICAN
REPUBLIC

SOUTH
SUDAN

Lake
Tana

Addis
Ababa

ETHIOPIA

SOMALIA

Juba

Lake
Turkana

UGANDA

Lake
Albert

KENYA

Kampala

Mogadishu

0° Equator

N

W   E

S

50°E

RWANDA Kigali

Nairobi

INDIAN
OCEAN

DEMOCRATIC
REPUBLIC
OF THE
CONGO

Bujumbura

BURUNDI

Lake
Victoria

Mombasa

20°E

TANZANIA

map
zone

Lake
Tanganyika

Dodoma

Zanzibar

Dar es
Salaam

Lake
Malawi

ZAMBIA

10°S

30°E

40°E

MOZAMBIQUE

Place East Africa is located on the Red Sea
and the Indian Ocean.
1. **Locate** What is the capital of Ethiopia?
2. **Analyze** How do you think the economies
   of the landlocked countries in East Africa
   are affected by their location?

Culture Masai
women of East
Africa wear colorful
jewelry and tradi-
tional clothing.

Geography The plains surrounding Mount Kilimanjaro are rich in wildlife. Millions of tourists
come to visit this part of East Africa each year.

129

Physical Geography

If YOU lived there...

You and your friends are planning to hike up Mount Kilimanjaro, near the equator in Tanzania. It is hot in your camp at the base of the mountain. You're wearing shorts and a T-shirt, but your guide tells you to pack a fleece jacket and jeans. You start your climb, and soon you understand this advice. The air is much colder, and there's snow on the nearby peaks.

Why is it cold at the top of the mountain?

BUILDING BACKGROUND The landscapes of East Africa have been shaped by powerful forces. The movement of tectonic plates has stretched the Earth's surface here, creating steep-sided valleys and huge lakes.

Physical Features

East Africa is a region of spectacular landscapes and wildlife. Vast plains and plateaus stretch throughout the region. In the north lie huge deserts and dry grasslands. In the southwest, large lakes dot the plateaus. In the east, sandy beaches and colorful coral reefs run along the coast.

The Rift Valleys

Look at the map on the next page. As you can see, East Africa's rift valleys cut from north to south across the region. **Rift valleys** are places on Earth's surface where the crust stretches until it breaks. Rift valleys form when Earth's tectonic plates move away from each other. This movement causes the land to arch and split along the rift valleys. As the land splits open, volcanoes erupt and deposit layers of rock in the region.

Seen from the air, the **Great Rift Valley** looks like a giant scar. The Great Rift Valley is the largest rift on Earth and is made up of two rifts—the eastern rift and the western rift.

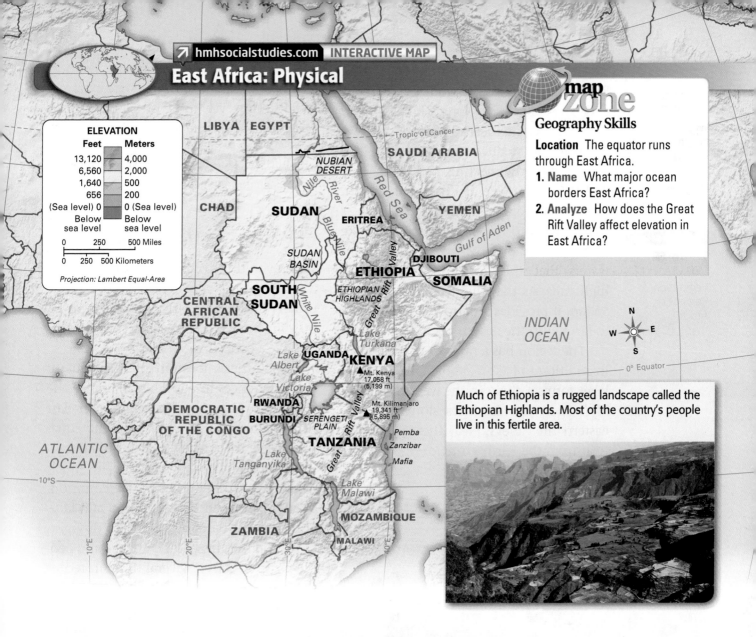

East Africa: Physical

map zone

Geography Skills

Location The equator runs through East Africa.
1. **Name** What major ocean borders East Africa?
2. **Analyze** How does the Great Rift Valley affect elevation in East Africa?

ELEVATION

Feet	Meters
13,120	4,000
6,560	2,000
1,640	500
656	200
(Sea level) 0	0 (Sea level)
Below sea level	Below sea level

0   250   500 Miles

0   250 500 Kilometers

Projection: Lambert Equal-Area

Much of Ethiopia is a rugged landscape called the Ethiopian Highlands. Most of the country's people live in this fertile area.

The rift walls are usually a series of steep cliffs. These cliffs rise as much as 6,000 feet (2,000 m).

Mountains and Highlands

The landscape of East Africa has many high volcanic mountains. The highest mountain in Africa, **Mount Kilimanjaro** (ki-luh-muhn-JAHR-oh), rises to 19,340 feet (5,895 m). Despite Kilimanjaro's location near the equator, the mountain's peak has long been covered in snow. This much colder climate is caused by Kilimanjaro's high elevation.

Other areas of high elevation in East Africa include the Ethiopian Highlands.

These highlands, which lie mostly in Ethiopia, are very rugged. Deep river valleys cut through this landscape.

Plains

Even though much of East Africa lies at high elevations, some areas are flat. For example, plains stretch as far as the eye can see along the eastern rift in Tanzania and Kenya. Tanzania's **Serengeti Plain** is one of the largest plains. It is here that an abundance of wildlife thrives. The plain's grasses, trees, and water provide nutrition for wildlife that includes elephants, giraffes, lions, and zebras. To protect this wildlife, Tanzania established a national park.

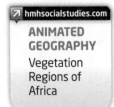

FOCUS ON READING

What details in this paragraph support this section's second main idea?

hmhsocialstudies.com

ANIMATED GEOGRAPHY
Vegetation Regions of Africa

Rivers and Lakes

East Africa also has a number of rivers and large lakes. The world's longest river, the Nile, begins in East Africa and flows north to the Mediterranean Sea. The Nile is formed by the meeting of the Blue Nile and the White Nile at Khartoum, Sudan. The White Nile is formed by the water that flows into Africa's largest lake, **Lake Victoria**. The Blue Nile is formed from waters that run down from Ethiopia's highlands. As the Nile meanders through Sudan, it provides a narrow, fertile lifeline to farmers in the desert.

The region has a number of great lakes in addition to Lake Victoria. One group of lakes forms a chain in the western rift valleys. There are also lakes along the drier eastern rift valleys. Near the eastern rift, heat from the Earth's interior makes some lakes so hot that no human can swim in them. In addition, some lakes are extremely salty. However, some of these rift lakes provide algae for the region's flamingos.

READING CHECK **Evaluating** What river is the most important in this region? Why?

Climate and Vegetation

When you think of Africa, do you think of it as being a hot or cold place? Most people usually think all of Africa is hot. However, they are mistaken. Some areas of East Africa have a cool climate.

East Africa's location on the equator and differences in elevation influence the climates and types of vegetation in East Africa. For example, areas near the equator receive the greatest amount of rainfall. Areas farther from the equator are much drier and seasonal droughts are common. **Droughts** are periods when little rain falls, and crops are damaged. During a drought, crops and the grasses for cattle die and people begin to starve. Several times in recent decades droughts have affected the people of East Africa.

Further south of the equator the climate changes to tropical savanna. Tall grasses and scattered trees make up the savanna landscape. Here the greatest climate changes occur along the sides of the rift valleys. The rift floors are dry with grasslands and thorn shrubs.

North of the equator, areas of plateaus and mountains have a highland climate and dense forests. Temperatures in the highlands are much cooler than temperatures on the savanna. The highlands experience heavy rainfall because of its high elevation, but the valleys are drier. This mild climate makes farming possible. As a result, most of the region's population lives in the highlands.

Satellite View

Great Rift Valley

This satellite image of part of the Great Rift Valley in Ethiopia was created by using both infrared light and true color. The bright blue dots are some of the smaller lakes that were created by the rifts. Once active volcanoes, some of these lakes are very deep. Vegetation appears as areas of green. Bare, rocky land appears pink and gray.

Analyzing How were the lakes in the Great Rift Valley created?

Ancient volcanoes surround Uganda's Lake Mutanda. Here villagers rely on the lake's plentiful supply of fish.

Areas east of the highlands and on the Indian Ocean coast are at a much lower elevation. These areas have desert and steppe climates. Vegetation is limited to shrubs and hardy grasses that are adapted to water shortages.

READING CHECK **Categorizing** What are some of East Africa's climate types?

SUMMARY AND PREVIEW In this section you learned about East Africa's rift valleys, mountains, highlands, plains, rivers, and lakes. You also learned that the region's location and elevation affect its climate and vegetation. In the next section you will learn about East Africa's history and culture.

Section 1 Assessment

Reviewing Ideas, Terms, and Places

1. **a. Define** What are **rift valleys**?
   b. Explain Why is there snow on **Mount Kilimanjaro**?
   c. Elaborate What are some unusual characteristics of the lakes in the **Great Rift Valley**?
2. **a. Recall** What is the climate of the highlands in East Africa like?
   b. Draw Conclusions What are some effects of **drought** in the region?
   c. Develop How are the climates of some areas of East Africa affected by elevation?

Critical Thinking

3. **Categorizing** Using your notes and this chart, place details about East Africa's physical features into different categories.

Physical Features			
Rift Valleys	Mountains and Highlands	Plains	Rivers and Lakes

FOCUS ON WRITING

4. **Describing the Physical Geography** Note the physical features of East Africa that you can describe in your letter. How do these features compare to the features where you live?

History and Culture

What You Will Learn...

Main Ideas

1. The history of East Africa is one of religion, trade, and European influence.
2. East Africans speak many different languages and practice several different religions.

The Big Idea

East Africa is a region with a rich history and diverse cultures.

Key Terms and Places

Nubia, *p. 134*
Zanzibar, *p. 135*
imperialism, *p. 135*

hmhsocialstudies.com
TAKING NOTES

Use the graphic organizer online to take notes on East Africa's history and culture.

If YOU lived there...

You live on the island of Zanzibar, part of the country of Tanzania. Your hometown has beautiful beaches, historic palaces, and sites associated with the East African slave trade. Although you and your friends learn English in school, you speak the African language of Swahili to each other.

How has your country's history affected your life today?

BUILDING BACKGROUND For almost a century, nearly all the countries of East Africa were controlled by European countries. Before that, however, the region's people had close trade ties with Arabs from Southwest Asia. This Arab influence blended with native African cultures to form a new culture and language.

History

Early civilizations in East Africa were highly developed. Later, Christianity and Islam influenced the lives of many East Africans. Other influences included trade, the arrival of Europeans, ethnic conflict, and independence.

Christianity and Islam

Christian missionaries from Egypt first introduced Christianity to Ethiopia as early as the AD 300s. About 200 years later Christianity spread into **Nubia**, an area of Egypt and Sudan today.

In the early 1200s, a powerful Christian emperor named Lalibela ruled Ethiopia. Lalibela is best known for the 11 rock churches he built during his reign. He claimed that God told him to carve the churches out of the rocky ground. Today, the town where the churches are located is called Lalibela.

By about AD 700, Islam was a major religion in Egypt and other parts of North Africa. Gradually, Muslim Arabs from Egypt

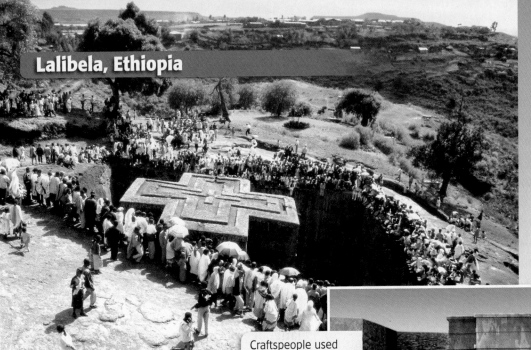

Lalibela, Ethiopia

In the 1200s, highly skilled Ethiopian architects and craftspeople built this Christian church at Lalibela.

ANALYZING VISUALS What Christian symbol does the church resemble?

Workers dug deep trenches to carve out the church.

Craftspeople used special tools to carve windows and doors out of solid rock.

spread into northern Sudan and brought their Islamic faith with them. At the same time, Islam spread to the Indian Ocean coast of what is now Somalia. City-states such as Mogadishu and Mombasa became major Islamic centers and controlled trade on the coast.

The Slave Trade

The slave trade along the Indian Ocean coast dates back more than 1,000 years. East Africans, Arabs, and Europeans all participated in the slave trade in East Africa. They kidnapped Africans, enslaved them, and shipped them to ports throughout Africa and Southwest Asia. Most of these slaves went to Islamic countries. By the early 1500s the Portuguese had begun setting up forts and settlements on the East African coast to support the slave trade.

In the late 1700s the East African island of **Zanzibar** became an international slave-trading center. Later, large plantations with slave labor were set up by Europeans in the interior. They grew crops of cloves and sugarcane.

European Influence and Conflict

Most European nations ended slavery in the early 1800s. They focused instead on trading products such as gold, ivory, and rubber. To get these goods, Europeans believed they needed to dominate regions of Africa rich in these natural resources. Europeans also wanted to expand their empires by establishing more colonies. The British were the most aggressive, and they gained control over much of East Africa.

In the 1880s Britain and other European powers divided up most of Africa. They drew boundaries that separated some ethnic groups. To maintain power over their colonies, Europeans used **imperialism**, a practice that tries to dominate other countries' government, trade, and culture.

hmhsocialstudies.com

ANIMATED GEOGRAPHY
Colonies in Africa 1913

FOCUS ON READING

In the second paragraph under Languages, find at least two details to support the main idea in the first sentence.

Within East Africa, just Kenya was settled by large numbers of Europeans. Under imperialism, colonial rulers usually controlled their countries through African deputies. Many of the deputies were traditional chiefs. These chiefs were loyal to their own peoples, which tended to strengthen ethnic rivalries. Today governments are trying to influence feelings of national identity, but ethnic conflict is still strong in many countries.

In the early 1960s, most East African countries gained independence from European colonizers. Ethiopia was never colonized. Its mountains provided natural protection, and its peoples resisted European colonization.

Independence, however, did not solve all of the problems of the former colonies. In addition, new challenges faced the newly independent countries. For example, some countries experienced ethnic conflicts.

READING CHECK **Evaluating** Why was Ethiopia never a European colony?

Culture

Over thousands of years of human settlement, East Africa developed a great diversity of people and ways of life. As a result, East Africans speak many different languages and practice several religions.

Language

East Africa's history of European imperialism influenced language in many countries in the region. For example, French is an official language in Rwanda, Burundi, and Djibouti today. English is the primary language of millions of people in Uganda, Kenya, and Tanzania.

In addition to European languages, many East Africans also speak African languages. Swahili is the most widely spoken African language in the region. As East Africans traded with Arabic speakers from Southwest Asia, Swahili developed. In fact, Swahili comes from the Arabic word meaning "on the coast." Today about 80 million people speak Swahili. Ethiopians speak Amharic, and Somalians speak Somali.

FOCUS ON CULTURE

The Swahili

For more than 1,000 years, a culture unlike any other has thrived along the coast of modern-day Kenya and Tanzania. In the AD 700s, trade contacts between East Africans and Arab traders began. Over time these interactions led to the creation of a unique language and culture known as Swahili.

The Swahili adopted some cultural traits from Arab traders. For example, many East Africans converted to the religion of the Arab traders—Islam. African languages blended with Arabic to form the Swahili language.

Generalizing What effects did Arab traders have on Swahili culture?

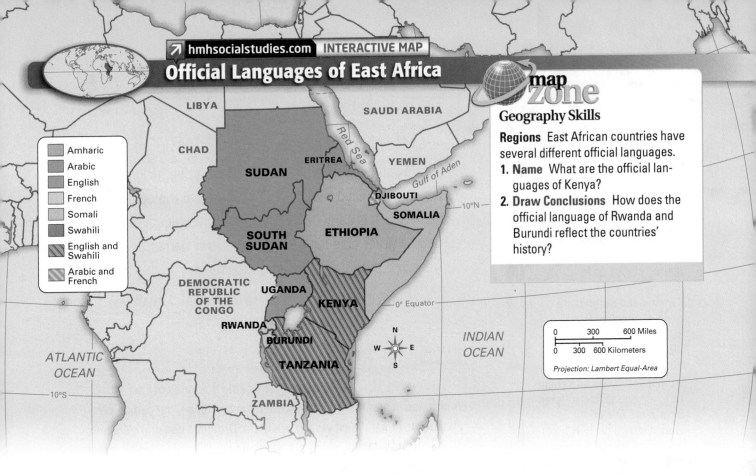

Official Languages of East Africa

map zone

▢	Amharic
▢	Arabic
▢	English
▢	French
▢	Somali
▢	Swahili
▨	English and Swahili
▨	Arabic and French

Geography Skills

Regions East African countries have several different official languages.

1. **Name** What are the official languages of Kenya?
2. **Draw Conclusions** How does the official language of Rwanda and Burundi reflect the countries' history?

0   300   600 Miles
0   300   600 Kilometers
Projection: Lambert Equal-Area

Religion

Religion is an important aspect of culture for many East Africans. While the religions in East Africa vary greatly, most of them place emphasis on honoring ancestors.

Many East Africans are followers of animist religions. Animists believe the natural world contains spirits. Some people also combine animist worship with religions such as Christianity. Most Christians in East Africa live in Ethiopia. Islam is also practiced in the region. Sudan and Somalia are predominantly Muslim.

READING CHECK **Analyzing** Why might people in East Africa speak a European language?

SUMMARY AND PREVIEW In this section you learned about the history and culture of East Africa. Next, you will learn about the countries of East Africa today.

Section 2 Assessment

↗ hmhsocialstudies.com
ONLINE QUIZ

Reviewing Ideas, Terms, and Places

1. a. **Define** What is **imperialism**?
   b. **Explain** What did the emperor Lalibela have architects build in Ethiopia?
   c. **Evaluate** Why do you think Europeans wanted colonies in East Africa?
2. a. **Identify** What language do most people in Uganda speak?
   b. **Explain** What do animists believe?
   c. **Elaborate** How have languages and religion influenced culture in East Africa?

Critical Thinking

3. **Summarizing** Using your notes and this chart, write two sentences that summarize what you learned about the region's languages and religions.

Language	
Religion	

FOCUS ON WRITING

4. **Writing about History and Culture** What aspects of the history and culture of East Africa might interest your friend? Note ideas for your letter.

East Africa Today

If **YOU** lived there...

You are a safari guide in one of Kenya's amazing national parks. Your safari van, filled with tourists, is parked at the edge of the vast savanna. It is early evening, and you are waiting for animals to come to a water hole for a drink. As it grows darker, a huge lion appears and then stalks away on huge paws.

What benefits do tourists bring to your country?

What You Will Learn...

Main Ideas

1. National parks are a major source of income for Tanzania and Kenya.
2. Rwanda and Burundi are densely populated rural countries with a history of ethnic conflict.
3. Both Sudan and Uganda have economies based on agriculture, but Sudan has suffered from years of war.
4. The countries of the Horn of Africa are among the poorest in the world.

The Big Idea

East Africa has abundant national parks, but most of the region's countries are poor and recovering from conflicts.

Key Terms and Places

safari, *p. 139*
geothermal energy, *p. 139*
genocide, *p. 141*
Darfur, *p. 141*
Mogadishu, *p. 143*

hmhsocialstudies.com
TAKING NOTES

Use the graphic organizer online to take notes on East Africa's people and economies.

BUILDING BACKGROUND Many of the countries of East Africa are rich in natural resources—including wildlife—but people disagree about the best way to use them. Droughts can make life here difficult. In addition, political and ethnic conflicts have led to unrest and violence in some areas of the region.

Close-up

Serengeti National Park

The Serengeti Plain is home to one of the world's greatest concentrations of wildlife. In Tanzania, part of the plain is a national park. About 100,000 tourists visit the Serengeti each year to view its diverse wildlife.

Each year huge herds of wildebeest migrate across the Serengeti.

ANALYSIS SKILL **ANALYZING VISUALS**

How would you describe the Serengeti landscape?

Tanzania and Kenya Today

The economies of both Tanzania and Kenya rely heavily on tourism and agriculture. However, both countries are among the poorest in the world.

Economy and Resources

Tanzania and Kenya are popular tourist destinations. With about 2 million tourists visiting each year, tourism is a major source of income for both countries. Today many tourists visit Tanzania and Kenya to go on a safari in the countries' numerous national parks. A **safari** is an overland journey to view African wildlife.

In addition to tourism, Tanzania is particularly rich in gold and diamonds. However, it is still a poor country of mainly subsistence farmers. Poor soils and limited technology have restricted productivity.

In Kenya, much of the land has been set aside as national parkland. Many people would like to farm these lands, but farming would endanger African wildlife. Kenya's economy and tourism industry would likely be **affected** as well.

Kenya's economy relies mostly on agriculture. Mount Kilimanjaro's southern slopes are a rich agricultural region. The rich soils here provide crops of coffee and tea for exports.

Kenya's economy also benefits from another natural resource—geothermal energy. **Geothermal energy** is energy produced from the heat of Earth's interior. This heat—in the form of extremely hot steam—comes up to the surface through cracks in the rift valleys.

ACADEMIC VOCABULARY

affect to change or influence

READING CHECK Finding Main Ideas What activity supports the economies of both Tanzania and Kenya?

Tanzanian guides take visitors on a safari to view Serengeti's wildlife.

Watering holes attract wildlife, which includes flamingos, hippos, and giraffes.

East Africa: Population

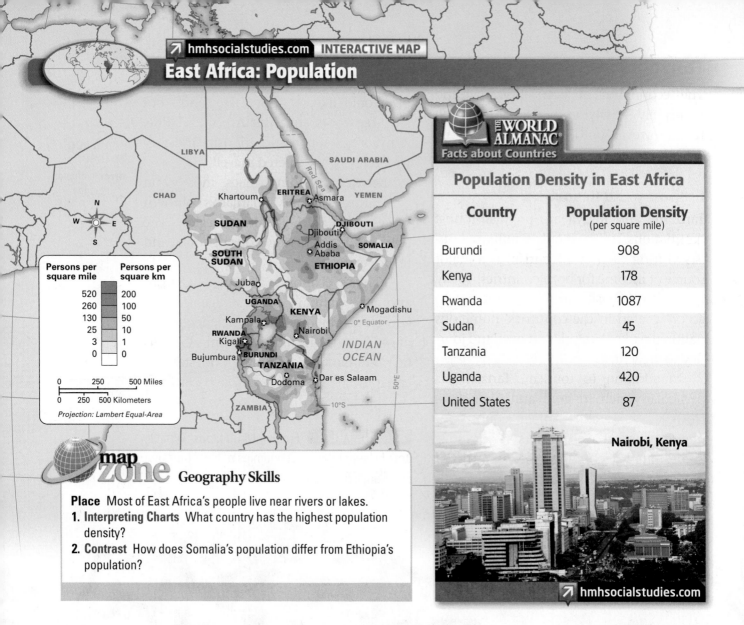

Persons per square mile	Persons per square km
520	200
260	100
130	50
25	10
3	1
0	0

0   250   500 Miles
0   250   500 Kilometers
Projection: Lambert Equal-Area

THE WORLD ALMANAC® Facts about Countries

Population Density in East Africa

Country	Population Density (per square mile)
Burundi	908
Kenya	178
Rwanda	1087
Sudan	45
Tanzania	120
Uganda	420
United States	87

Nairobi, Kenya

↗ hmhsocialstudies.com

map zone Geography Skills

Place Most of East Africa's people live near rivers or lakes.
1. **Interpreting Charts** What country has the highest population density?
2. **Contrast** How does Somalia's population differ from Ethiopia's population?

Cities

Imagine a large city with businesspeople hurrying to work, colorful outdoor markets, soaring skyscrapers, and beautiful parks. The capitals of Tanzania and Kenya both fit this description of a vibrant, modern African city.

Tanzania's official capital is Dodoma. The Tanzanian government began moving its capital from Dar es Salaam to Dodoma in the mid-1970s. Dar es Salaam, a port city with about 3 million people, is located on the Indian Ocean and is Tanzania's business center.

Kenya's capital, Nairobi, also serves as the country's industrial center. In addition,

Nairobi is well connected with the rest of East Africa by a network of railways. By rail, Kenya transports tea and other major crops to the major port of Mombasa.

Even though Kenya and Tanzania are peaceful countries, Dar es Salaam and Nairobi have both endured terrorist attacks. In 1998 members of the al Qaeda terrorist group bombed the U.S. embassies in Dar es Salaam and Nairobi. Most of the more than 250 people killed and the thousands injured were Africans.

READING CHECK **Draw Conclusions** Why do you think it would be important for the railroad to link Kenya's cities?

Rwanda and Burundi Today

Rwanda and Burundi are mostly populated by two ethnic groups—the Tutsi and the Hutu. Since gaining their independence from Belgium, Rwanda and Burundi have experienced conflict between the Tutsi and Hutu ethnic groups. These conflicts have roots in the region's history. The colonial borders of Rwanda and Burundi drawn by Europeans often lumped different ethnic groups into one country.

In Rwanda in the 1990s, hatred between the Hutu and the Tutsi led to genocide. A **genocide** is the intentional destruction of a people. The Hutu tried to completely wipe out the Tutsi. Armed bands of Hutu killed hundreds of thousands of Tutsi.

Rwanda and Burundi are two of the most densely populated countries in all of Africa. These two countries are located in fertile highlands and share a history as German and, later, Belgian colonies. Both countries lack resources and rely on coffee and tea exports for economic earnings.

READING CHECK **Analyzing** What contributed to the region's ethnic conflict?

Sudan and Uganda Today

Sudan is a mainly agricultural country with few mineral resources. Arab Muslims make up the majority of Sudan's population and control political power from the capital, Khartoum.

Sudan suffered from decades of religious and ethnic conflict between Muslims in the North and Christians in the South. More recently, a genocide occurred in a region of Sudan called **Darfur**. Ethnic conflict there resulted in tens of thousands of black Sudanese being killed by an Arab militia group. Millions more fled Darfur and are scattered throughout the region as refugees. In 2011, South Sudan gained independence, becoming Africa's newest country.

Today Uganda is still recovering from several decades of a military dictatorship. Since 1986 Uganda has become more democratic, but economic progress has been slow. About 80 percent of Uganda's workforce is employed in agriculture, with coffee as the country's major export.

READING CHECK **Summarizing** What ethnic group dominates northern Sudan?

FOCUS ON READING

In the paragraphs under Rwanda and Burundi, what details support the main idea that these countries have a history of ethnic conflict?

Refugees in Sudan

People from Sudan who fled the country's Darfur region receive food and aid at a refugee camp.

People of the Horn of Africa

More than half of Eritrea's population are Christian and belong to the Ethiopian Orthodox Church.

In Ethiopia, boys help their families herd sheep.

A teacher in Somalia shows a student how to use the school's new computer.

The Horn of Africa

Four East African countries located on the Red Sea and the Indian Ocean are called the Horn of Africa. This area is called the Horn because it resembles the horn of a rhinoceros. The Horn's people, economies, and resources vary by country.

Ethiopia

Unlike the other countries of the Horn of Africa, Ethiopia has never been under foreign rule. The country's mountains have protected the country from invasion.

In addition to providing a natural defense barrier, Ethiopia's rugged mountain slopes and highlands have rich volcanic soil. As a result, agriculture is Ethiopia's chief economic activity. Ethiopia's economy benefits from exports of coffee, livestock, and oilseeds. Many people also herd sheep and cattle.

During the last 30 years Ethiopia has experienced serious droughts. In the 1980s, drought caused the loss of crops and the starvation of several million people. In contrast, Ethiopia has experienced plenty of rainfall in recent years. Farmers are now able to grow their crops.

Most Ethiopians living in the highlands are Christian, while most of the lowland people are Muslim. Many Ethiopians speak Amharic, the country's official language.

Eritrea

In the late 1800s the Italians made present-day Eritrea a colony. In the 1960s it became an Ethiopian province.

After years of war with Ethiopia, Eritrea broke away from Ethiopia in 1993. Since then the economy has slowly improved. The country's Red Sea coastline is lined with spectacular coral reefs, which attract tourists to the country. Most Eritreans are farmers or herders. The country's economy relies largely on cotton exports.

Somalia

Somalia is a country of deserts and dry savannas. Much of the land is not suitable for farming. As a result, Somalis are nomadic herders.

Somalia is less diverse than most other African countries. Most people in the country are members of a single ethnic group, the Somali. In addition, most Somalis are Muslims and speak the same African language, also called Somali.

Somalia has been troubled by violence in the past. In addition, the country has often had no central government of any kind. Different clans have fought over grazing rights and control of port cities such as **Mogadishu**.

In the 1990s Somalis experienced widespread starvation caused by a civil war and a severe drought. The United Nations sent aid and troops to the country. U.S. troops also assisted with this operation. In recent years, Somali pirates have captured several cargo ships off the coast of Somalia. The pirates have demanded and received millions of dollars in ransom money.

Djibouti

Djibouti (ji-BOO-tee) is a small, desert country. It lies on the Bab al-Mandab, which is the narrow strait that connects the Red Sea and the Indian Ocean. The strait lies along a major shipping route.

In the 1860s the French took control of Djibouti. It did not gain independence from France until 1977. The French government still contributes economic and military support to the country. As a result, French is one of Djibouti's two official languages. The other is Arabic.

The country's capital and major port is also called Djibouti. The capital serves as a port for landlocked Ethiopia. Since Djibouti has very few resources, the port is a major source of the country's income.

The people of Djibouti include two major ethnic groups—the Issa and the Afar. The Issa are closely related to the people of Somalia. The Afar are related to the people of Ethiopia. Members of both groups are Muslim. In the early 1990s, a civil war between the Afar and Issa broke out. In 2001 the two groups signed a peace treaty, which ended the fighting.

READING CHECK **Generalizing** What do the people of Djibouti have in common with people from other countries in East Africa?

SUMMARY AND PREVIEW The countries of East Africa are poor, but rich in wildlife and resources. Next, you will learn about the region of Central Africa.

Section 3 Assessment
hmhsocialstudies.com
ONLINE QUIZ

Reviewing Ideas, Terms, and Places

1. **a. Define** What is **geothermal energy**?
   b. Make Generalizations Why are Kenyans not allowed to farm in national parks?
2. **a. Define** What is **genocide**?
   b. Explain What are the two ethnic groups that make up the population of Rwanda and Burundi?
3. **a. Identify** What is the newest country in Africa?
   b. Analyze Why are millions of Sudanese refugees?
4. **a. Recall** What two major world religions are practiced in Ethiopia?
   b. Analyze How do you think Djibouti's location has helped its economy?

Critical Thinking

5. **Summarize** Draw a chart like this one. Using your notes, summarize in at least two sentences what you learned about each country.

Ethiopia	→	
Eritrea	→	
Somalia	→	
Djibouti	→	

FOCUS ON WRITING

6. **Writing About East Africa Today** Think about what it would be like to travel through the East African countries. What would you want to tell your friend about their people, their governments, and their economies? Make a list of details you would share.

Doing Fieldwork and Using Questionnaires

Learn

To a geographer, fieldwork means visiting a place to learn more about it. While there, the geographer might visit major sites or talk to people to learn about their lives. He or she might also distribute a questionnaire.

A questionnaire is a document that asks people to provide information. Geographers use them to find out specific details about the people in an area, such as what languages they speak. Governments and other groups also use questionnaires to learn more about the people they serve.

Practice

The questionnaire to the right is one that might have been created by the government of Kenya. Study it to answer the questions below.

❶ What details does the questionnaire ask about people living in the household?

❷ How are the questions organized? Why do you think that is?

❸ Why would asking for the person's age be an important question?

Republic of Kenya Population and Housing Census Form A: Information Regarding All Persons

Name
What are the names of all persons who live in this household?

_____

Relationship
What is your relationship to the head of the household? (circle one)

1 Head
2 Spouse
3 Son
4 Daughter
5 Brother/Sister
6 Father/Mother
7 Other relative
8 Non-relative

Age
How old are you?

Tribe Nationality
What is your tribe or nationality?

Religion
What is your religion? (circle one)

1 Catholic
2 Protestant
3 Other Christian
4 Muslim
5 Traditionalist
6 Other Religion
7 No Religion

Birthplace
Where were you born?

_____

Apply

Work with a group of classmates to create a questionnaire about popular music. Think of five questions about popular music that you could ask your fellow students. Try to ask only multiple-choice and yes-or-no questions. These types of questions are easier to study than other questions are. Once you have completed your questionnaire, write a short explanation of what you hope to learn from each question.

Geographers doing fieldwork travel to distant places to learn more about them.

Geography's Impact
video series
Review the video to answer the closing question:
How might the loss of Mount Kilimanjaro's glaciers affect people living in the area?

Visual Summary

Use the visual summary below to help you review the main ideas of the chapter.

QUICK FACTS

East Africa is a land of spectacular mountains, highlands, and lakes.

East Africa's history includes European imperialism and independence.

Even though many countries in East Africa are very poor, they are trying to improve educational opportunities.

Reviewing Vocabulary, Terms, and Places

Choose one word from each word pair to correctly complete each sentence below.

1. A_____(rift valley/plain) is a place on Earth's surface where the crust stretches until it breaks.

2. The tallest mountain in Africa is_____. (Mount Kilimanjaro/Mount Kenya)

3. _____means to change or influence. (geothermal energy/affect)

4. A_____is an overland journey that is taken to view African wildlife. (drought/safari)

5. _____has experienced serious droughts over the past 30 years. (Ethiopia/Kenya)

6. _____are periods when little rain falls and crops are damaged. (flood/drought)

7. The intentional destruction of a people is called_____. (murder/genocide)

8. _____is a practice which tries to dominate other countries' government, trade, and culture. (imperialism/influence)

9. A genocide committed by an Arab militia occured in the region of Sudan known as _____. (Darfur/Khartoum)

10. _____is an East African island that was an international slave-trading center in the late 1700s. (Madagascar/Zanzibar)

Comprehension and Critical Thinking

SECTION 1 *(Pages 130–133)*

11. a. **Identify** What is the Great Rift Valley? What is it made of?

   b. **Draw Conclusions** How is the Nile necessary for farming in the desert?

   c. **Predict** How do you think the effects of drought can be avoided in the future?

SECTION 2 (Pages 134–137)

12. a. Recall In which East African country did an emperor build 11 rock churches?

b. Contrast How does the major religion practiced in Ethiopia differ from other religions practiced in East Africa?

c. Elaborate How did the African language of Swahili develop?

SECTION 3 (Pages 138–143)

13. a. Define What is a safari?

b. Draw Conclusions What economic activity do both Kenya and Tanzania rely on?

c. Evaluate Why do you think the al Qaeda terrorist group bombed U.S. embassies in Dar es Salaam and Nairobi?

Using the Internet

14. Activity: Understanding Cultures In the East African countries you read about in this chapter, there are hundreds of different ethnic groups. Through the online book, discover some ethnic groups of East Africa as you visit Web sites about their culture. Then create a graphic organizer or chart that compares East African ethnic groups. It might include comparisons of language, beliefs, traditions, foods, and more.

↗ **hmhsocialstudies.com**

Social Studies Skills

15. Doing Fieldwork and Using Questionnaires As in Kenya, the United States conducts a census of its population. Research what kinds of questions the U.S. Census asks Americans every 10 years. Go to the official U.S. Census Bureau's Web site at www.census.gov. There you will find examples of the questionnaires used in the 2000 Census. How do you think the questionnaires on the next U.S. Census in 2010 will be the same or different than the questions that were asked on the 2000 Census?

Map Activity

16. East Africa On a separate sheet of paper, match the letters on the map with their correct labels.

Great Rift Valley   Mount Kilimanjaro

Lake Victoria   Nile River

Indian Ocean

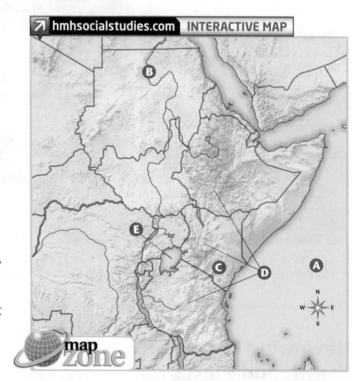

↗ hmhsocialstudies.com   INTERACTIVE MAP

FOCUS ON READING AND WRITING

17. Identifying Supporting Details Look back over the paragraphs under the Culture heading in Section 2. Then make a list of details you find to support the section's main ideas. Make sure you include details about the different languages spoken in East Africa today.

18. Writing a Letter Now that you have information about East Africa, you need to organize it. Think about your audience, a friend at home, and what would feel natural if you had been traveling. Would you organize by topics like physical geography and culture? Or would you organize by country? After you organize your information, write a one-page letter.

Standardized Test Prep

DIRECTIONS: *Read questions 1 through 7 and write the letter of the best response. Then read question 8 and write your own well-constructed response.*

1 **What physical feature of East Africa is usually covered with snow and ice?**

  A Serengeti Plain

  B Mount Kilimanjaro

  C Great Rift Valley

  D Mount Kenya

2 **What is one cause of the cool climate in some areas of East Africa?**

  A elevation

  B drought

  C Indian Ocean

  D Great Rift Valley

3 **The Swahili language developed through trade contacts between East Africans and**

  A the Chinese.

  B Europeans.

  C Arabs.

  D West Africans.

4 **Tourism is a large part of the economy in**

  A Tanzania and Kenya.

  B Sudan and Uganda.

  C Ethiopia and Eritrea.

  D Rwanda and Burundi.

5 **Which East African country used to be a province of Ethiopia?**

  A Djibouti

  B Somalia

  C Eritrea

  D Kenya

> "Then they were over the first hills and the wildebeeste were trailing up them, and then they were over the mountains with sudden depths of green-rising forest and solid bamboo slopes, and then the heavy forest again, sculptured into peaks and hollows until they crossed, and hills sloped down and then another plain, hot now, and purple brown, bumpy with heat..."
>
> —Ernest Hemingway, "The Snows of Kilimanjaro"

6 **In the passage above, Hemingway describes the view of the Mount Kilimanjaro landscape from a plane. The landscape he describes is filled with**

  A rivers.

  B lakes.

  C deserts.

  D forests.

7 **In the passage above, the climate of the plain is described as**

  A hot.

  B dry.

  C wet.

  D cold.

8 **Extended Response** Look at the table and map of East Africa's population density in Section 3. Write a paragraph explaining why you think some areas of East Africa are more populated than other areas. Identify at least two reasons.

CHAPTER 7

Central Africa

Essential Question How is poverty impacting the nations of Central Africa?

What You Will Learn...

In this chapter you will learn about the rivers, forests, and resources of Central Africa. This region has been influenced by native traditions and Europeans, and you will read about how these influences have affected Central Africa's culture. Finally, you will learn about the different countries in Central Africa and some of the challenges these countries face.

FOCUS ON READING AND WRITING

Using Word Parts Many English words have little word parts at the beginning (prefixes) or the end (suffixes) of the word. When you come to an unfamiliar word in your reading, see if you can recognize a prefix or suffix to help you figure out the meaning of the word. **See the lesson, Using Word Parts, on page 200.**

Writing an Acrostic An acrostic is a type of poem in which the first letters of each line spell a word. The lines of the poem describe that word. As you read the chapter, think of a word—maybe a country name or a physical feature—that you would like to describe in your acrostic.

ATLANTIC OCEAN

0° Equator

⊗ National capital
● Other cities

0   200   400 Miles
0   200   400 Kilometers

Projection: Lambert Azimuthal Equal-Area

map zone Geography Skills

Regions The region we call Central Africa consists of 10 countries.
1. **Identify** Which country includes land on the mainland and on islands?
2. **Make Inferences** Why do you think a small part of Angola is separated from the main part of the country?

Culture Drums and horns are used in traditional music from Central Africa. These musicians are from Cameroon.

Central Africa: Political

CHAD

SUDAN

NIGERIA

10°N

SOUTH
SUDAN

CENTRAL
AFRICAN REPUBLIC

CAMEROON

Bangui ✪

Douala
Malabo ✪   ✪ Yaoundé

EQUATORIAL
GUINEA

Congo River

Kisangani ●   UGANDA

São Tomé ✪   ✪ Libreville

Kasindi ●

SÃO TOMÉ
AND PRÍNCIPE   GABON

REPUBLIC
OF THE
CONGO

DEMOCRATIC
REPUBLIC OF
THE CONGO

RWANDA

BURUNDI

Brazzaville ✪

Pointe Noire ●   ✪ Kinshasa

Cabinda
(ANGOLA)

N
W ✦ E
S

Luanda ✪

TANZANIA
10°S

Lubumbashi ●

ANGOLA

Lilongwe ✪

ZAMBIA   MALAWI

Lusaka ✪

Zambezi River

MOZAMBIQUE

NAMIBIA   ZIMBABWE

10°E   20°E   30°E

Geography Many towns in Central Africa rely on the Congo River for trade and transportation.

History People in Central Africa have been making copper statues for hundreds of years. This one is meant to represent an ancestor.

Physical Geography

Main Ideas

1. Central Africa's major physical features include the Congo Basin and plateaus surrounding the basin.
2. Central Africa has a humid tropical climate and dense forest vegetation.
3. Central Africa's resources include forest products and valuable minerals such as diamonds and copper.

The Big Idea

The Congo River, tropical forests, and mineral resources are important features of Central Africa's physical geography.

Key Terms and Places

Congo Basin, *p. 150*
basin, *p. 150*
Congo River, *p. 151*
Zambezi River, *p. 151*
periodic market, *p. 153*
copper belt, *p. 153*

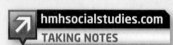

hmhsocialstudies.com
TAKING NOTES

Use the graphic organizer online to note characteristics of Central Africa's physical geography.

If **YOU** lived there...

You are on a nature hike with a guide through the forests of the Congo Basin. It has been several hours since you have seen any other people. Sometimes your guide has to cut a path through the thick vegetation, but mostly you try not to disturb any plants or animals. Suddenly, you reach a clearing and see a group of men working hard to load huge tree trunks onto big trucks.

How do you feel about what you see?

BUILDING BACKGROUND Much of Central Africa, particularly in the Congo Basin, is covered with thick, tropical forests. The forests provide valuable resources, but people have different ideas about how the forests should be used. Forests are just one of the many types of landscapes in Central Africa.

Physical Features

Central Africa is bordered by the Atlantic Ocean in the west. In the east, it is bordered by a huge valley called the Western Rift Valley. The land in between has some of the highest mountains and biggest rivers in Africa.

Landforms

You can think of the region as a big soup bowl with a wide rim. Near the middle of the bowl is the **Congo Basin**. In geography, a **basin** is a generally flat region surrounded by higher land such as mountains and plateaus.

Plateaus and low hills surround the Congo Basin. The highest mountains in Central Africa lie farther away from the basin, along the Western Rift Valley. Some of these snowcapped mountains rise to more than 16,700 feet (5,090 m). Two lakes also lie along the rift—Lake Nyasa and Lake Tanganyika (tan-guhn-YEE-kuh). Lake Nyasa is also called Lake Malawi.

Rivers

The huge **Congo River** is fed by hundreds of smaller rivers. They drain the swampy Congo Basin and flow into the river as it runs toward the Atlantic. Many rapids and waterfalls lie along its route, especially near its mouth. These obstacles make it impossible for ships to travel from the interior of Central Africa all the way to the Atlantic. The Congo provides an important transportation route in the interior, however.

In the southern part of the region, the **Zambezi** (zam-BEE-zee) **River** flows eastward toward the Indian Ocean. Many rivers in Angola and Zambia, as well as water from Lake Nyasa, flow into the Zambezi. The Zambezi also has many waterfalls along its route, the most famous of which are the spectacular Victoria Falls.

READING CHECK **Finding Main Ideas** Where is the highest land in Central Africa?

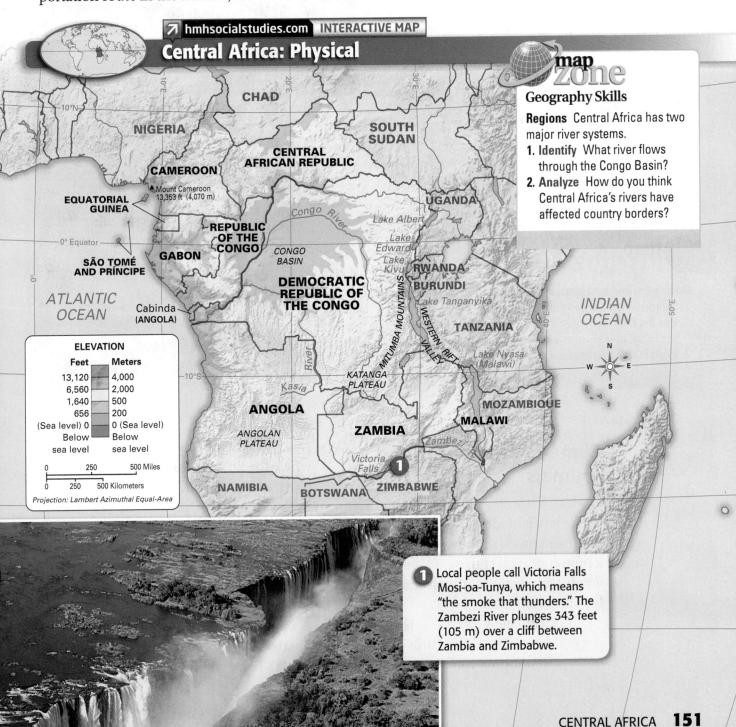

↗ hmhsocialstudies.com **INTERACTIVE MAP**

Central Africa: Physical

map zone

Geography Skills

Regions Central Africa has two major river systems.
1. **Identify** What river flows through the Congo Basin?
2. **Analyze** How do you think Central Africa's rivers have affected country borders?

ELEVATION

Feet	Meters
13,120	4,000
6,560	2,000
1,640	500
656	200
(Sea level) 0	0 (Sea level)
Below sea level	Below sea level

0   250   500 Miles
0   250   500 Kilometers
Projection: Lambert Azimuthal Equal-Area

Mount Cameroon 13,353 ft (4,070 m)

1 Local people call Victoria Falls Mosi-oa-Tunya, which means "the smoke that thunders." The Zambezi River plunges 343 feet (105 m) over a cliff between Zambia and Zimbabwe.

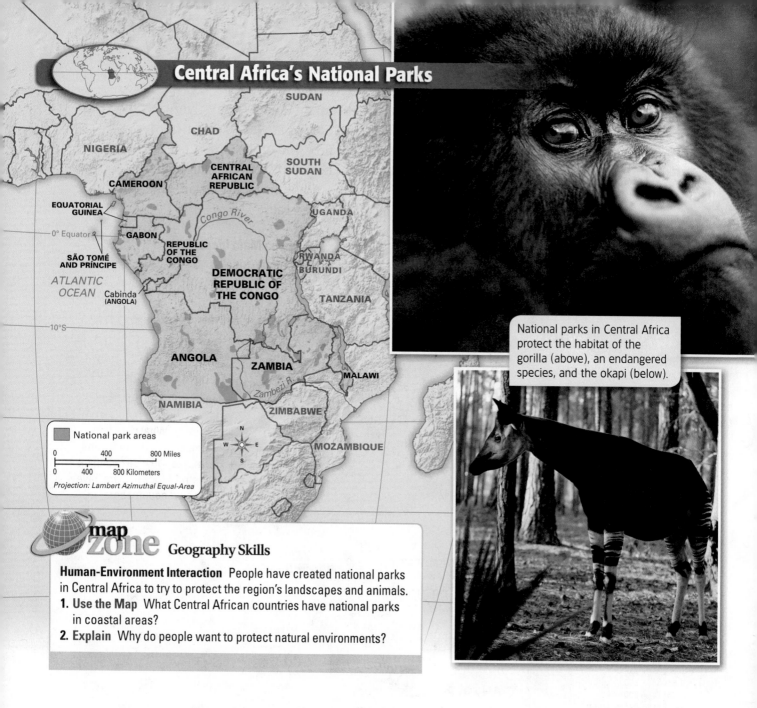

Central Africa's National Parks

SUDAN

CHAD

NIGERIA

CENTRAL AFRICAN REPUBLIC

SOUTH SUDAN

CAMEROON

EQUATORIAL GUINEA

Congo River

UGANDA

0° Equator

GABON

REPUBLIC OF THE CONGO

SÃO TOMÉ AND PRÍNCIPE

RWANDA

BURUNDI

ATLANTIC OCEAN

Cabinda (ANGOLA)

DEMOCRATIC REPUBLIC OF THE CONGO

TANZANIA

10°S

ANGOLA

ZAMBIA

MALAWI

Zambezi R.

NAMIBIA

ZIMBABWE

MOZAMBIQUE

National park areas

0   400   800 Miles
0   400   800 Kilometers
Projection: Lambert Azimuthal Equal-Area

National parks in Central Africa protect the habitat of the gorilla (above), an endangered species, and the okapi (below).

map zone Geography Skills

Human-Environment Interaction People have created national parks in Central Africa to try to protect the region's landscapes and animals.

1. **Use the Map** What Central African countries have national parks in coastal areas?
2. **Explain** Why do people want to protect natural environments?

Climate, Vegetation, and Animals

Central Africa lies along the equator and in the low latitudes. Therefore, the Congo Basin and much of the Atlantic coast have a humid tropical climate. These areas have warm temperatures all year and receive a lot of rainfall.

This climate supports a large, dense tropical forest. The many kinds of tall trees in the forest form a complete canopy. The canopy is the uppermost layer of the trees where the limbs spread out. Canopy leaves block sunlight to the ground below.

Such animals as gorillas, elephants, wild boars, and okapis live in the forest. The okapi is a short-necked relative of the giraffe. However, since little sunlight shines through the canopy, only a few animals live on the forest floor. Some animals, such as birds, monkeys, bats, and snakes, live in the trees. Many insects also live in Central Africa's forest.

The animals in Central Africa's tropical forests, as well as the forests themselves, are in danger. Large areas of forest are being cleared rapidly for farming and logging. Also, people hunt the large animals in the forests to get food. To promote protection of forests and other natural environments, governments have set up national park areas in their countries.

North and south of the Congo Basin are large areas with a tropical savanna climate. Those areas are warm all year, but they have distinct dry and wet seasons. There are grasslands, scattered trees, and shrubs. The high mountains in the east have a highland climate. Dry steppe and even desert climates are found in the far southern part of the region.

READING CHECK **Summarizing** What are the climate and vegetation like in the Congo Basin?

Resources

The tropical environment of Central Africa is good for growing crops. Most people in the region are subsistence farmers. However, many farmers are now beginning to grow crops for sale. Common crops are coffee, bananas, and corn. In rural areas, people trade agricultural and other products in periodic markets. A **periodic market** is an open-air trading market that is set up once or twice a week.

Central Africa is rich in other natural resources as well. The large tropical forest provides timber, while the rivers provide a way to travel and to trade. Dams on the rivers produce hydroelectricity, an important energy resource. Other energy resources in the region include oil, natural gas, and coal.

Central Africa also has many valuable minerals, including copper, uranium, tin, zinc, diamonds, gold, and cobalt. Of these, copper is the most important. Most of

Africa's copper is found in an area called the **copper belt**. The copper belt stretches through northern Zambia and southern Democratic Republic of the Congo. However, poor transportation systems and political problems have kept the region's resources from being fully developed.

READING CHECK **Analyzing** Why are Central Africa's rivers an important natural resource?

FOCUS ON READING
What prefix do you recognize in *promote*?

SUMMARY AND PREVIEW Mighty rivers, the tropical forest of the Congo Basin, and mineral resources characterize the physical geography of Central Africa. These landscapes have influenced the region's history. Next, you will read about Central Africa's history and culture.

Section 1 Assessment

hmhsocialstudies.com
ONLINE QUIZ

Reviewing Ideas, Terms, and Places

1. **a. Describe** What is the **Congo Basin**?
   b. Elaborate How do you think the **Congo River**'s rapids and waterfalls affect the economy of the region?
2. **a. Recall** What part of Central Africa has a highland climate?
   b. Explain Why have governments in the region set up national parks?
   c. Evaluate Is it more important to use the forest's resources or to protect the natural environment? Why?
3. **a. Define** What is a **periodic market**?
   b. Elaborate What kinds of political problems might keep mineral resources from being fully developed?

Critical Thinking

4. **Contrasting** Use your notes and a graphic organizer like this one to list differences between the Congo Basin and the areas surrounding it in Central Africa.

Congo Basin   Surrounding Areas

FOCUS ON WRITING

5. **Describing Physical Geography** What topics in this section might work well in your acrostic? Jot down notes on one or two topics you could feature in your poem.

Mapping Central Africa's Forests

Essential Elements

The World in Spatial Terms
Places and Regions
Physical Systems
Human Systems
Environment and Society
The Uses of Geography

Background Imagine taking a walk along a street in your neighborhood. Your purpose is to see the street in spatial terms and gather information to help you make a map. While you walk, you ask the kinds of questions geographers ask. How many houses, apartment buildings, or businesses are on the street? What kinds of animals or trees do you see? Your walk ends, and you organize your data. Now imagine that you are going to gather data on another walk. This walk will be 2,000 miles long.

A 2,000-Mile Walk In September 1999, an American scientist named Michael Fay began a 465-day, 2,000-mile walk through Central Africa's forests. He and his team followed elephant trails through thick vegetation. They waded through creeks and mucky swamps.

On the walk, Fay gathered data on the number and kinds of animals he saw. He counted elephant dung, chimpanzee nests, leopard tracks, and gorillas. He counted the types of trees and other plants along his

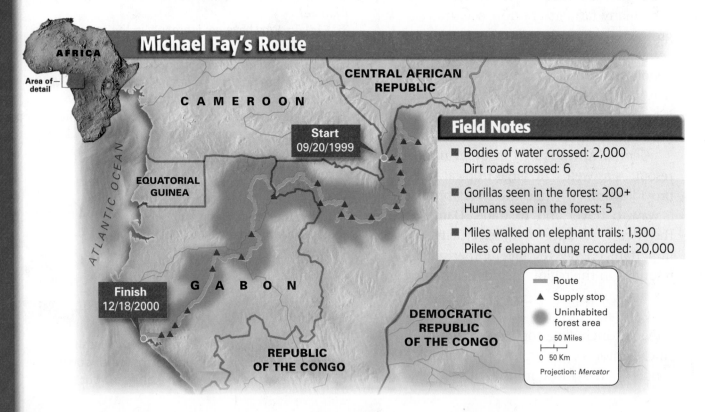

Michael Fay's Route

AFRICA

Area of detail

CENTRAL AFRICAN REPUBLIC

CAMEROON

ATLANTIC OCEAN

EQUATORIAL GUINEA

Start
09/20/1999

Finish
12/18/2000

GABON

REPUBLIC OF THE CONGO

DEMOCRATIC REPUBLIC OF THE CONGO

Field Notes

- Bodies of water crossed: 2,000
  Dirt roads crossed: 6

- Gorillas seen in the forest: 200+
  Humans seen in the forest: 5

- Miles walked on elephant trails: 1,300
  Piles of elephant dung recorded: 20,000

— Route
▲ Supply stop
● Uninhabited forest area

0   50 Miles
0   50 Km

Projection: *Mercator*

Michael Fay (above) and his team had to chop their way through thick forest vegetation. In a clearing, they spotted this group of elephants.

route. He also counted human settlements and determined the effect of human activities on the environment.

Fay used a variety of tools to record the data he gathered on his walk. He wrote down what he observed in waterproof notebooks. He shot events and scenes with video and still cameras. To measure the distance he and his team walked each day, he used a tool called a Fieldranger. He also kept track of his exact position in the forest by using a GPS, or global positioning system.

What It Means Michael Fay explained the purpose of his long walk. "The whole idea behind this is to be able to use the data we've collected as a tool." Other geographers can compare Fay's data with their own. Their comparison may help them create more accurate maps. These maps will show where plants, animals, and humans are located in Central Africa's forests.

Fay's data can also help scientists plan the future use of land or resources in a region. For example, Fay has used his data to convince government officials in Gabon to set aside 10 percent of its land to create 13 national parks. The parks will be protected from future logging and farming. They also will preserve many of the plants and animals that Fay and his team observed on their long walk.

Geography for Life Activity

1. Why did Michael Fay walk 2,000 miles?

2. In what practical way has Michael Fay used his data?

3. **Read More about Fay's Walk** Read the three-part article on Michael Fay's walk in *National Geographic* October 2000, March 2001, and August 2001. After you read the article, explain why Fay called his walk a "megatransect."

History and Culture

What You Will Learn...

Main Ideas

1. Great African kingdoms and European colonizers have influenced the history of Central Africa.
2. The culture of Central Africa includes many ethnic groups and languages, but it has also been influenced by European colonization.

The Big Idea

Central Africa's history and culture have been influenced by native traditions and European colonizers.

Key Terms and Places

Kongo Kingdom, *p. 156*
dialects, *p. 158*

hmhsocialstudies.com
TAKING NOTES

Use the graphic organizer online to take notes on Central Africa's history and culture.

If **YOU** lived there...

You live in Central Africa in the 1300s. Over the past year, many new people have moved to your village. They speak a different language—one that you don't understand. They also have some customs that seem strange to you. But they have begun bringing fancy items such as animal skins and shells to your village. Now your village seems very rich.

How do you feel about these new people?

BUILDING BACKGROUND Different groups of people have influenced Central Africa throughout its history. Whether they came from near or far, and whether they stayed in Central Africa for only a few decades or for more than a hundred years, these groups brought their own cultures and customs to the region.

History

Early humans lived in Central Africa many thousands of years ago. However, the descendants of these people have had less impact on the region's history than people from the outside. Tribes from West Africa, and later European colonists, brought their customs to the region and changed the way people lived.

Early History

About 2,000 years ago new peoples began to migrate to Central Africa from West Africa. They eventually formed several kingdoms in Central Africa. Among the most important was the **Kongo Kingdom**. Founded in the 1300s, it was located near the mouth of the Congo River.

The Kongo people established trade routes to western and eastern Africa. Their kingdom grew rich from the trade of animal skins, shells, slaves, and ivory. Ivory is a cream-colored material that comes from elephant tusks.

Ivory Trade

Ivory traders collected elephant tusks for export to Europe.

ANALYZING VISUALS Who was involved in the ivory trade?

In the late 1400s, Europeans came to the region. They wanted the region's forest products and other resources such as ivory. They used ivory for fine furniture, jewelry, statues, and piano keys. Europeans also began to trade with some Central African kingdoms for slaves. Over a span of about 300 years, the Europeans took millions of enslaved Africans to their colonies in the Americas.

Some African kingdoms became richer by trading with Europeans. However, all were gradually changed and weakened by European influence. In the late 1800s, European countries divided all of Central Africa into colonies. The colonial powers were France, Belgium, Germany, Spain, the United Kingdom, and Portugal.

These European powers drew colonial borders that ignored the homelands of different ethnic groups. Many different ethnic groups were lumped together in colonies where they had to interact. These groups spoke different languages and had different customs. Their differences caused conflicts, especially after the colonies won independence.

Modern Central Africa

Central African colonies gained their independence from European powers after World War II. Some of the colonies fought bloody wars to win their independence. The last country to become independent was Angola. It won freedom from Portugal in 1975.

Independence did not bring peace to Central Africa, however. Ethnic groups continued to fight one another within the borders of the new countries. Also, the United States and the Soviet Union used Central Africa as a battleground in the Cold War. They supported different allies in small wars throughout Africa. The wars in the region killed many people and caused great damage.

FOCUS ON READING

What prefix do you recognize in *interact*?

READING CHECK **Summarizing** What role did Europeans play in Central Africa's history?

Culture

Today about 137 million people live in Central Africa. These people belong to many different ethnic groups and have different customs.

People and Language

The people of Central Africa speak hundreds of different languages. They also speak different **dialects**, regional varieties of a language. For example, although many Central Africans speak Bantu languages, those languages can be quite different from one another.

The main reason for this variety is the number of ethnic groups. Most ethnic groups have their own language or dialect. Most people in the region speak traditional African languages in their daily lives. However, the official languages of the region are European because of the influence of the colonial powers. For example, French is the official language of the Democratic Republic of the Congo. Portuguese is the language of Angola. English is an official language in Zambia and Malawi.

Religion

Central Africa's colonial history has also influenced religion. Europeans introduced Christianity to the region. Now many people in the former French, Spanish, and Portuguese colonies are Roman Catholic. Protestant Christianity is most common in former British colonies.

Two other religions came to parts of Central Africa from other regions. Influenced by the Muslim countries of the Sahel, the northern part of Central Africa has many Muslims. Zambia is the home of Muslims as well as Hindus.

The Arts

Central Africa's traditional cultures influence the arts of the region. The region is famous for sculpture, carved wooden masks, and beautiful cotton gowns dyed in bright colors.

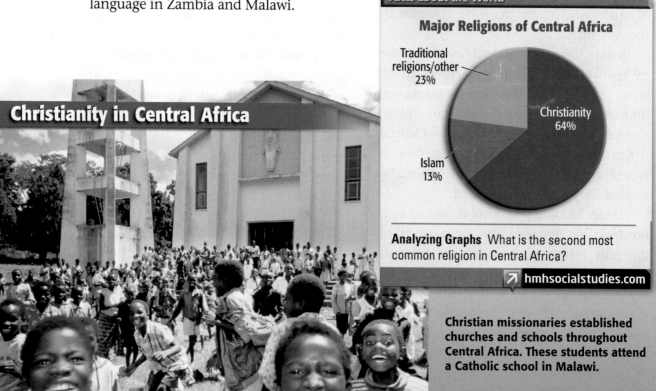

Christianity in Central Africa

THE WORLD ALMANAC
Facts about the World

Major Religions of Central Africa

- Traditional religions/other 23%
- Christianity 64%
- Islam 13%

Analyzing Graphs What is the second most common religion in Central Africa?

hmhsocialstudies.com

Christian missionaries established churches and schools throughout Central Africa. These students attend a Catholic school in Malawi.

Bantu Languages

About 2,000 years ago people who spoke Bantu languages migrated out of West Africa. They moved to Central Africa as well as eastern and southern Africa. The Bantu speakers mixed with peoples who already lived in these lands.

The migration of Bantu speakers had important effects on African life. They brought new ways for growing food. They used tools made of iron, which others also began to use. The Bantu speakers also brought their languages. Today many Central Africans speak one or more of the some 500 Bantu languages such as Rundi, Bemba, or Luba.

Drawing Inferences How do you think the number of languages affects communication in the region?

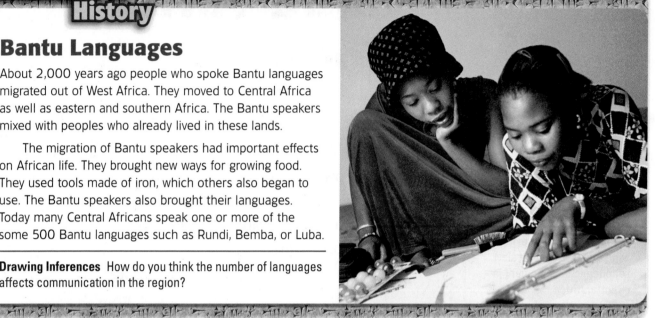

Central Africa also has popular styles of music. The *likembe*, or thumb piano, was invented in the Congo region. Also, a type of dance music called *makossa* originated in Cameroon and has become popular throughout Africa. It can be played with guitars and electric keyboards.

READING CHECK **Generalizing** What are characteristics of culture in Central Africa?

SUMMARY AND PREVIEW Central Africa's history was influenced by great kingdoms that controlled trade and by Europeans, who originally came to the region looking for trade goods. European and traditional African influences have shaped the region's culture. Next, you will learn about the countries of Central Africa and what life is like there today.

hmhsocialstudies.com
ANIMATED GEOGRAPHY
Bantu Migrations

Section 2 Assessment

hmhsocialstudies.com
ONLINE QUIZ

Reviewing Ideas, Terms, and Places

1. **a. Recall** What Central African resource did Europeans value for making jewelry and crafts?
   b. Explain How did the **Kongo Kingdom** become important?
   c. Elaborate How do you think the colonial borders affected Central African countries' fights for independence?
2. **a. Define** What is a **dialect**?
   b. Summarize How did the colonial era affect Central Africa's culture?
   c. Elaborate How might Central Africa's culture be different today if the region had not been colonized by Europeans?

Critical Thinking

3. **Sequencing** Review your notes on Central Africa's history. Using a graphic organizer like this one, put major events in chronological order.

FOCUS ON WRITING

4. **Taking Notes on History and Culture** Your acrostic could describe the region's history and culture as well as physical geography. Take notes on interesting information you might include in your poem.

Central Africa Today

What You Will Learn...

Main Ideas
1. The countries of Central Africa are mostly poor, and many are trying to recover from years of civil war.
2. Challenges to peace, health, and the environment slow economic development in Central Africa.

The Big Idea
War, disease, and environmental problems have made it difficult for the countries of Central Africa to develop stable governments and economies.

Key Terms and Places
Kinshasa, *p. 161*
inflation, *p. 163*
malaria, *p. 164*
malnutrition, *p. 165*

hmhsocialstudies.com
TAKING NOTES

Use the graphic organizer online to take notes on the countries of Central Africa and the challenges facing those countries.

If YOU lived there...

You are an economic adviser in Zambia. Your country is poor, and most people are farmers. But scientists say Zambia has a lot of copper under ground. With a new copper mine, you could sell valuable copper to other countries. However, the mine would destroy a lot of farmland.

Do you support building the mine? Why or why not?

BUILDING BACKGROUND You have already read about Central Africa's great resources. Many countries in the region have the potential for great wealth. However, several factors throughout history have made it difficult for Central African countries to develop their resources.

Countries of Central Africa

Most of the countries in Central Africa are very poor. After years of colonial rule and then civil war, they are struggling to build stable governments and strong economies.

Democratic Republic of the Congo

The Democratic Republic of the Congo was a Belgian colony until 1960. When the country gained independence, many Belgians left. Few teachers, doctors, and other professionals remained in the former colony. In addition, various ethnic groups fought each other for power. These problems were partly to blame for keeping the new country poor.

A military leader named Joseph Mobutu came to power in 1965. He ruled as a dictator. One way Mobutu used his power was to change the name of the country to Zaire—a name that was traditionally African rather than European. He also changed his own name to Mobutu Sese Seko.

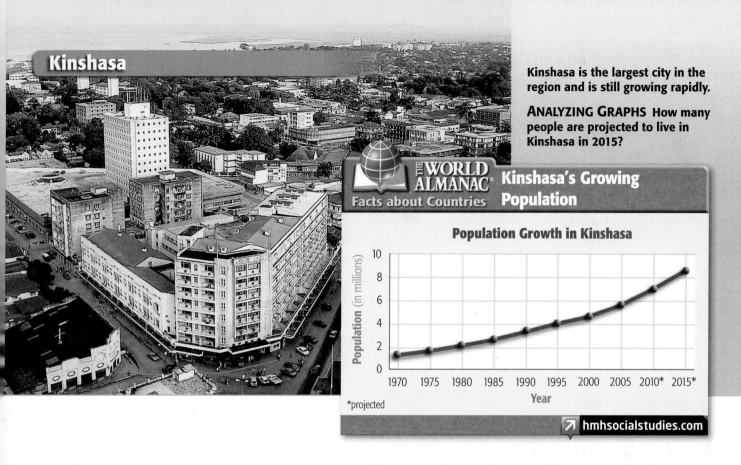

Kinshasa

Kinshasa is the largest city in the region and is still growing rapidly.

ANALYZING GRAPHS How many people are projected to live in Kinshasa in 2015?

THE WORLD ALMANAC® Facts about Countries

Kinshasa's Growing Population

Population Growth in Kinshasa

*projected

hmhsocialstudies.com

During his rule, the government took over foreign-owned industries. It borrowed money from foreign countries to try to expand industry. However, most farmers suffered, and government and business leaders were corrupt. While the economy collapsed, Mobutu became one of the richest people in the world and used violence against people who challenged him.

In 1997, after a civil war, a new government took over. The new government renamed the country the Democratic Republic of the Congo.

The Democratic Republic of the Congo is a treasure chest of minerals that could bring wealth to the country. The south is part of Central Africa's rich copper belt. The country also has gold, diamonds, and cobalt. In addition, the tropical forest provides wood, food, and rubber. However, civil war, bad government, and crime have scared many foreign businesses away. As a result, the country's resources have helped few of its people.

Most people in the Democratic Republic of the Congo are poor. They usually live in rural areas where they must farm and trade for food. Many people are moving to the capital, **Kinshasa**. This crowded city has some modern buildings, but most of the city consists of poor slums.

Central African Republic and Cameroon

North of the Democratic Republic of the Congo is the landlocked country of Central African Republic. Since independence, this country has struggled with military coups, corrupt leaders, and improper elections.

In addition to political instability, the country suffers from a weak economy. Most people there are farmers. Although the country has diamonds and gold, it does not have railroads or ports needed to transport the resources for export. Central African Republic receives some aid from foreign countries, but this is not enough to meet the needs of its people.

FOCUS ON READING

If *–al* means "relating to," what does *political* mean?

Between Central African Republic and the Atlantic Ocean is Cameroon. Unlike most countries in Central Africa, Cameroon is fairly stable. It is a republic. The president is elected and holds most of the power.

Political stability has made economic growth possible. The country has oil reserves and good conditions for farming. Cacao, cotton, and coffee are valuable export crops. A good system of roads and railways helps people transport these goods for export to other countries.

Because of the steady economy, the people of Cameroon have a high standard of living for the region. For example, more people in Cameroon are enrolled in school than in most places in Africa.

Equatorial Guinea and São Tomé and Príncipe

Tiny Equatorial Guinea is divided between the mainland and five islands. The country is a republic. It has held elections, but many have seen the elections as being flawed. These elections have kept the same president ruling the country for more than 25 years. Although the recent discovery of oil has produced economic growth, living conditions for most people are still poor.

The island country of São Tomé and Príncipe has struggled with political instability. In addition, it is a poor country with few resources. It produces much cacao but has to import food. The recent discovery of oil in its waters may help the economy.

Village Architecture

Although Central Africa has several big cities, many people still live in rural villages. Different groups of people have different styles of architecture for their villages. Building materials vary depending on the resources available in the geographic setting.

An extended family lives together in these adobe homes in the mountains of Cameroon.

The strong tropical sun provides power for this hut in Angola.

Gabon and Republic of the Congo

Gabon has had only one president since 1967. For many years, Gabon held no multi-party elections. Gabon's economy provides the highest standard of living in the region. More than half the country's income comes from oil.

Like Gabon, the Republic of the Congo receives much of its income from oil. It also receives income from forest products. Despite these resources, a civil war in the late 1990s hurt the economy.

The Republic of the Congo is mostly urban and growing more so. Many people are moving from villages to cities. The biggest city is the capital, Brazzaville.

Angola

Angola won independence from Portugal in 1975. The country then plunged into a long civil war. Fighting finally ended in 2002, and the country has been more stable since then. Angola is now a republic with an elected president.

Even with peace, Angola's economy is struggling. For about 85 percent of the population, subsistence farming is the only source of income. Even worse, land mines left over from the civil war endanger the farmers. A high rate of **inflation**, the rise in prices that occurs when currency loses its buying power, has also weakened the economy. Finally, corrupt officials have taken large amounts of money meant for public projects.

Angola does have potential, however. The country has diamonds and oil. The oil is found offshore and in Cabinda. Cabinda is a part of Angola that is separated from the rest of the country by the Democratic Republic of the Congo.

Zambia and Malawi

The southernmost countries in Central Africa are Zambia and Malawi. About 85 percent of Zambia's workers are farmers. Though rich with copper mines, Zambia's economy is growing very slowly. It is hurt by high levels of debt and inflation.

Nearly all of Malawi's people farm for a living. About 83 percent of the people live in villages in rural areas. Aid from foreign countries and religious groups has been important to the economy. However, the country has been slow to build factories and industries. In the future, Malawi will probably have to develop its own industries rather than rely on aid from foreign countries.

READING CHECK **Generalizing** What are the economies like in Central African countries?

A family sits outside their home in Zambia.

ANALYSIS SKILL **ANALYZING VISUALS**

How does the construction of the huts help you recognize different climates in Central Africa?

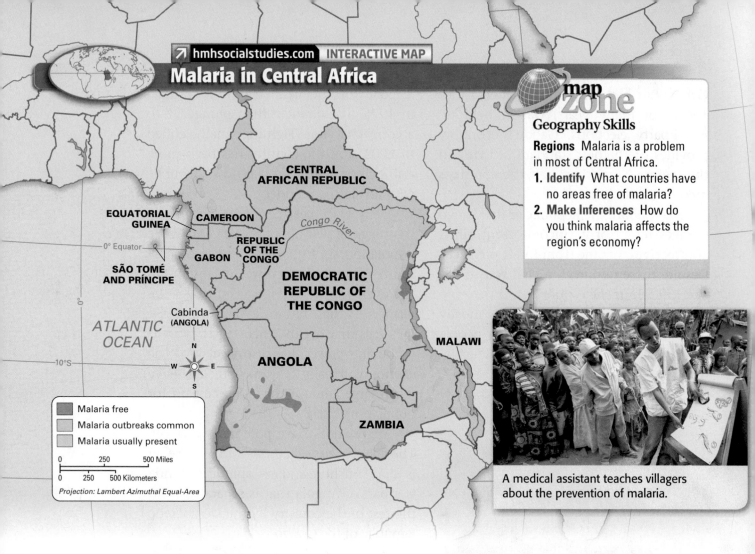

map zone

Geography Skills

Regions Malaria is a problem in most of Central Africa.
1. **Identify** What countries have no areas free of malaria?
2. **Make Inferences** How do you think malaria affects the region's economy?

CENTRAL AFRICAN REPUBLIC

EQUATORIAL GUINEA

CAMEROON

Congo River

0° Equator

REPUBLIC OF THE CONGO

GABON

SÃO TOMÉ AND PRÍNCIPE

DEMOCRATIC REPUBLIC OF THE CONGO

Cabinda (ANGOLA)

ATLANTIC OCEAN

MALAWI

10°S

ANGOLA

N W E S

ZAMBIA

Malaria free
Malaria outbreaks common
Malaria usually present

0   250   500 Miles
0   250   500 Kilometers
Projection: Lambert Azimuthal Equal-Area

A medical assistant teaches villagers about the prevention of malaria.

Issues and Challenges

As you have read, many of the countries in Central Africa have unstable governments and poor economies. These circumstances have been either the cause or effect of other issues and challenges in the region today.

Ethnic and Regional Conflict

A mix of ethnic groups and competing desires for power has led to civil war in many of the region's countries. Thousands of people have been killed in these wars over the past several years.

Wars have also contributed to poor economies in the region. The people killed or injured in the fighting can no longer work. In addition, the fighting destroys land and other resources that could be used in more productive ways.

ACADEMIC VOCABULARY
implement to put in place

Health

Like war, disease kills many people in the region. **Malaria** is a disease spread by mosquitoes that causes fever and pain. Without treatment it can lead to death. In fact, malaria is by far the most common cause of death in Central Africa. A child there dies from malaria every 45 seconds. On the map above, you can see that this disease is a problem almost everywhere.

International health organizations and some national governments have begun to **implement** strategies to control malaria. These strategies include educating people about the disease and passing out nets treated with insecticide. The nets and medicine are expensive, and not everyone can afford them. However, people who sleep under these nets will be protected from mosquitoes and malaria.

While some countries are beginning to control malaria, another disease is spreading rapidly. HIV, the virus that causes AIDS, is very common in Central Africa. Hundreds of thousands of people die of AIDS each year in Central Africa. There is no cure for HIV infection, and medicines to control it are very expensive. International groups are working hard to find a cure for HIV and to slow the spread of the disease.

Partly because so many people die of disease, Central Africa has a very young population. Almost 45 percent of people living in Central Africa are under age 15. For comparison, only about 20 percent of the people in the United States are under age 15. Although many young people in Central Africa work, they do not contribute to the economy as much as older, more experienced workers do.

Resources and Environment

To help their economies and their people, the countries of Central Africa must begin to develop their natural resources more effectively. Agricultural land is one resource that must be managed more effectively. In some places, partly because of war, food production has actually declined. Also, food production cannot keep up with the demands of the growing population. The results are food shortages and malnutrition. **Malnutrition** is the condition of not getting enough nutrients from food.

The environment is another important resource that must be managed. Some of Central Africa's most important industries are destroying the environment. Lumber companies cut down trees in the tropical forest, threatening the wildlife that lives there. Mining is also harming the environment. Diamonds and copper are mined in huge open pits. This mining process removes large areas of land and destroys the landscape.

Many people in Central Africa and around the world are working hard and spending billions of dollars to improve conditions in the region. National parks have been set up to protect the environment. Projects to provide irrigation and prevent erosion are helping people plant more crops. Central Africa's land and people hold great potential for the future.

READING CHECK **Summarizing** What are some threats to Central Africa's environment?

SUMMARY AND PREVIEW Countries in Central Africa are trying to build stable governments and strong economies after years of civil war, but challenges slow economic development. Next, you will learn about the places and people of Southern Africa.

Section 3 Assessment

ONLINE QUIZ

Reviewing Ideas, Terms, and Places

1. a. **Define** What is **inflation**?
   b. **Summarize** What effect did Mobutu Sese Seko's rule have on the Democratic Republic of the Congo?
   c. **Evaluate** Do you think Central African countries would benefit more from a stable government or from a strong economy? Explain your answer.
2. a. **Identify** What causes **malaria**?
   b. **Explain** How are some countries coping with environmental challenges?

Critical Thinking

3. **Evaluating** Look over your notes on Central Africa. Using a graphic organizer like the one here, rank the challenges facing Central Africa. Put the one you see as the biggest challenge first.

Challenges
1.
2.

FOCUS ON WRITING

4. **Describing Countries** You can focus on one country or on the whole region in your acrostic. Review your notes and jot down some ideas for the focus of your acrostic.

Social Studies Skills

Interpreting a Population Pyramid

Learn

A population pyramid shows the percentages of males and females by age group in a country's population. The pyramids are split into two sides. Each bar on the left shows the percentage of a country's population that is male and of a certain age. The bars on the right show the same information for females.

Population pyramids help us understand population trends in countries. Countries that have large percentages of young people have populations that are growing rapidly. Countries with more older people are growing slowly or not at all.

Practice

Use the population pyramid of Angola to answer the following questions.

❶ What age group is the largest?

❷ What percent of Angola's population is made up of 15- to 19-year-old males?

❸ What does this population pyramid tell you about the population trend in Angola?

Ages are listed down the middle of the diagram.

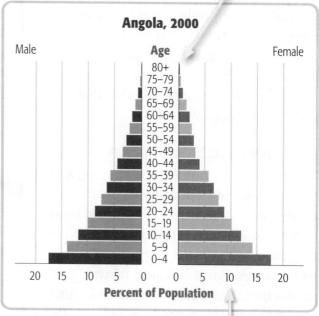

Source: U.S. Census Bureau, International Data Base

Percentages are labeled across the bottom of the diagram.

Apply

Do research at the library or on the Internet to find age and population data for the United States. Use that information to answer the following questions.

1. What age group is the largest?

2. Are there more males or females over age 80?

3. How would you describe the shape of the population pyramid?

Chapter Review

Geography's Impact
video series
Review the video to answer the closing question:
Why do you think the president of Gabon passed a law establishing new national parks?

Visual Summary

Use the visual summary below to help you review the main ideas of the chapter.

QUICK FACTS

The forests of Central Africa's Congo Basin are home to gorillas and many other kinds of animals.

Ivory attracted Europeans to Central Africa. They left their influence on the region's history and culture.

Countries of Central Africa are looking for ways to solve many of their challenges, such as preventing disease.

Reviewing Vocabulary, Terms, and Places

Using your own paper, complete the sentences below by providing the correct term for each blank.

1. The _____ is a low area near the middle of Central Africa.

2. _____ is a disease spread by mosquitoes that causes fever and aching.

3. People who do not get enough nutrients from their food suffer from _____.

4. To _____ a system is to put it in place.

5. _____ is the rise in prices that occurs when currency loses its buying power.

6. A _____ is a regional variety of a language.

7. The river that flows through Central Africa and into the Atlantic Ocean is the _____.

8. A _____ is an open-air market set up once or twice a week.

9. Much of the copper in Central Africa comes from a region known as the _____.

Comprehension and Critical Thinking

SECTION 1 *(Pages 150–153)*

10. **a. Describe** What are the main landforms in Central Africa?

   b. Make Inferences Why would people in rural areas be more likely to shop at periodic markets than at grocery stores?

   c. Elaborate How does the development of national parks affect people in the region? How does it affect people around the world?

SECTION 2 *(Pages 156–159)*

11. **a. Recall** When did European countries divide Central Africa into colonies?

   b. Analyze What factors besides European colonization influenced where different religions are most common in Central Africa today?

   c. Evaluate What do you think was the most significant influence or effect the Europeans had on Central Africa? Explain your answer.

SECTION 3 *(Pages 160–165)*

12. a. Identify What are the diseases that affect many people in Central Africa?

b. Analyze What factors have allowed certain countries like Cameroon and Gabon to have stronger economies than other countries in the region?

c. Evaluate What are the benefits of foreign aid to Central Africa? What might be some possible drawbacks?

Social Studies Skills

Interpreting a Population Pyramid *Use the population pyramid in the Social Studies Skills lesson to answer the following questions.*

13. What age group is the smallest?

14. How would you describe the current population in Angola?

Map Activity

15. Central Africa On a separate sheet of paper, match the letters on the map with their correct labels.

Congo River   Congo Basin

Zambezi River   Lake Nyasa

Angola

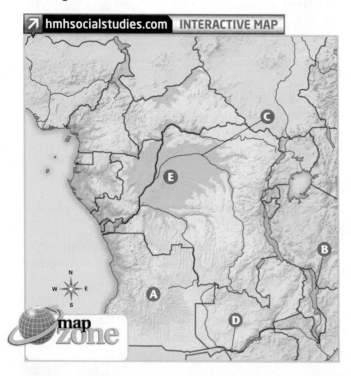

hmhsocialstudies.com **INTERACTIVE MAP**

map zone

Using the Internet

16. Activity: Making a Scrapbook Central Africa is home to many different ethnic groups. Although there are similarities among them, they each have unique characteristics as well. Through the online book, take a journey to Central Africa. Research some of the many groups that live there. Then create an illustrated scrapbook that documents some of the groups that you have met in your travels. Include information on their towns, ways of life, and environments. You may also want to include maps, souvenirs, and pictures from your journey.

hmhsocialstudies.com

FOCUS ON READING AND WRITING

Using Word Parts *Look at the list of prefixes and suffixes and their meanings below. Then answer the questions that follow.*

mal- (bad)	-ous (characterized by)
in- (not)	-ment (result, action)
re- (again)	-ion (action, condition)

17. Which of the following words means "getting only poor nutrients"?

a. nutriment   **c.** renutrition

b. malnutrition   **d.** nutrious

18. Which of the following words means "the condition of being protected"?

a. reprotect   **c.** protection

b. protectment   **d.** protectous

19. Writing Your Acrostic Your poem will describe Central Africa or a part of it. Choose the place you want to describe and write the letters of that word vertically, with one letter on each line of your paper. For each letter, use your notes to write a descriptive word or phrase that tells about your subject. Make a final copy of your acrostic to share with classmates.

Standardized Test Prep

DIRECTIONS: Read questions 1 through 6 and write the letter of the best response. Then read question 7 and write your own well-constructed response.

1 What major river flows through Central Africa and into the Atlantic Ocean?

A Zambezi River

B Congo Basin

C Niger River

D Congo River

2 In rural areas, people are most likely to trade goods at a

A copper belt.

B periodic market.

C supermarket.

D dialect.

3 Why did Europeans become interested in Central Africa?

A They wanted resources and trade goods.

B They wanted to teach people European languages.

C They wanted to divide up ethnic groups.

D They wanted to destroy African kingdoms.

4 What disease is spread by mosquitoes and is very common in Central Africa?

A malnutrition

B HIV

C malaria

D inflation

5 Most people in Zambia and Malawi work in

A copper mines.

B the oil industry.

C cities.

D farming.

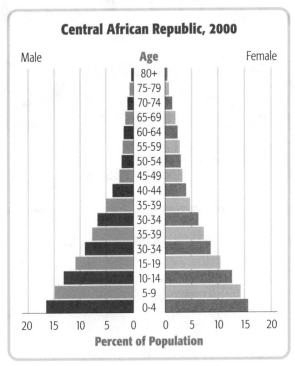

Central African Republic, 2000

Source: U.S. Census Bureau, International Data Base

6 Based on the graph above, which of the following statements is false?

A Females ages 15–19 make up about 10 percent of the population.

B Males and females ages 0–4 each make up over 15 percent of the population.

C The population of Central African Republic is growing at a very slow rate.

D There are more males ages 5–9 than there are females.

7 **Extended Response** Using the graph above and the graph of Population Growth in Kinshasa in Section 3, write a paragraph explaining how Central Africa's population and people's lives in the region are changing.

CHAPTER 8

Southern Africa

Essential Question What role did European imperialism play in the development of Southern Africa?

? What You Will Learn...

In this chapter you will learn about nine countries that are located in the region of Southern Africa—South Africa, Lesotho, Swaziland, Namibia, Botswana, Zimbabwe, Mozambique, Madagascar, and Comoros. You will learn about the region's history, cultures, and economies.

FOCUS ON READING AND VIEWING

Making Generalizations A generalization is a broad, general conclusion drawn from examples, facts, or other information. As you read this chapter, try to make generalizations about the facts and information in the text. Making generalizations will help you understand the meaning of what you are reading. **See the lesson, Making Generalizations, on page 201.**

Viewing a TV News Report You are a journalist covering world news. Your assignment is to create a brief TV news report on something about Southern Africa. As you read this chapter, you will collect information about the region and plan your report. Later you and your classmates will give your TV news reports and evaluate one another's reports.

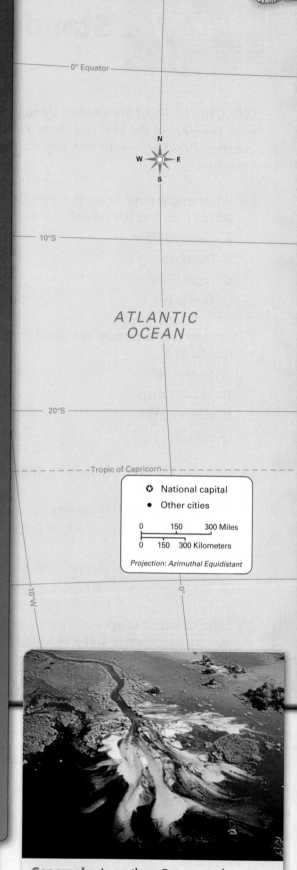

Geography In northern Botswana, the Okavango River forms an enormous inland delta.

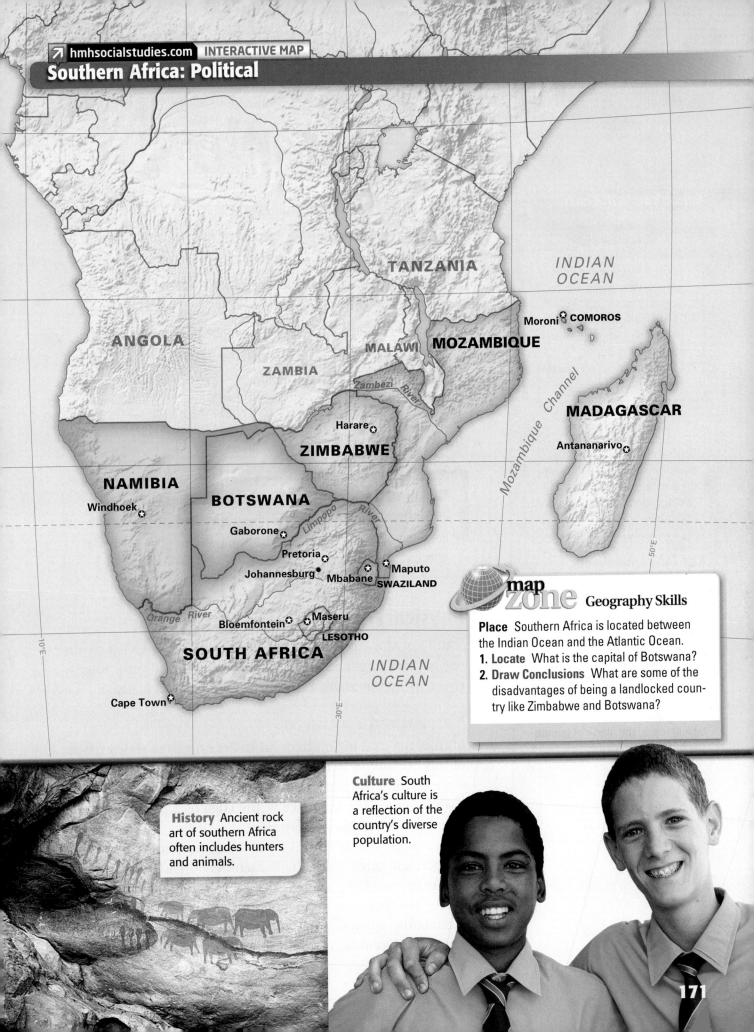

Southern Africa: Political

INDIAN OCEAN

TANZANIA

ANGOLA

ZAMBIA

MALAWI

MOZAMBIQUE

Moroni ⚓ COMOROS

Zambezi River

MADAGASCAR

Antananarivo

Mozambique Channel

Harare

ZIMBABWE

NAMIBIA

BOTSWANA

Windhoek

Limpopo River

Gaborone

Pretoria

Johannesburg

Mbabane

Maputo

SWAZILAND

Orange River

Bloemfontein

Maseru

LESOTHO

SOUTH AFRICA

INDIAN OCEAN

Cape Town

50°E

10°E

30°E

map zone Geography Skills

Place Southern Africa is located between the Indian Ocean and the Atlantic Ocean.
1. **Locate** What is the capital of Botswana?
2. **Draw Conclusions** What are some of the disadvantages of being a landlocked country like Zimbabwe and Botswana?

History Ancient rock art of southern Africa often includes hunters and animals.

Culture South Africa's culture is a reflection of the country's diverse population.

171

Physical Geography

What You Will Learn...

Main Ideas

1. Southern Africa's main physical feature is a large plateau with plains, rivers, and mountains.
2. The climate and vegetation of Southern Africa is mostly savanna and desert.
3. Southern Africa has valuable mineral resources.

The Big Idea

Southern Africa's physical geography includes a high, mostly dry plateau, grassy plains and rivers, and valuable mineral resources.

Key Terms and Places

escarpment, *p. 172*
veld, *p. 174*
Namib Desert, *p. 174*
pans, *p. 174*

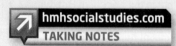
hmhsocialstudies.com
TAKING NOTES

Use the graphic organizer online to take notes on the physical geography of Southern Africa.

If YOU lived there...

You are a member of the San, a people who live in the Kalahari Desert. Your family lives with several others in a group of circular grass huts. You are friends with the other children. Sometimes you help your mom look for eggs or plants to use for carrying water. Your water containers, clothes, carrying bags, and weapons all come from the resources you find in the desert. Next year you will move away to attend school in a town.

How will your life change next year?

BUILDING BACKGROUND Parts of Southern Africa have a desert climate. Little vegetation grows in these areas, but some people do live there. Most of Southern Africa's people live in cooler and wetter areas, such as on the high, grassy plains in the south and east.

Physical Features

Southern Africa has some amazing scenery. On a visit to the region, you might see grassy plains, steamy swamps, mighty rivers, rocky waterfalls, and steep mountains and plateaus.

Plateaus and Mountains

Most of the land in Southern Africa lies on a large plateau. Parts of this plateau reach more than 4,000 feet (1,220 m) above sea level. To form the plateau, the land rises sharply from a narrow coastal plain. The steep face at the edge of a plateau or other raised area is called an **escarpment**.

In eastern South Africa, part of the escarpment is made up of a mountain range called the Drakensberg (DRAH-kuhnz-buhrk). The steep peaks rise as high as 11,425 feet (3,482 m). Farther north, another mountain range, the Inyanga (in-YANG-guh) Mountains, separates Zimbabwe and Mozambique. Southern Africa also has mountains along its western coast.

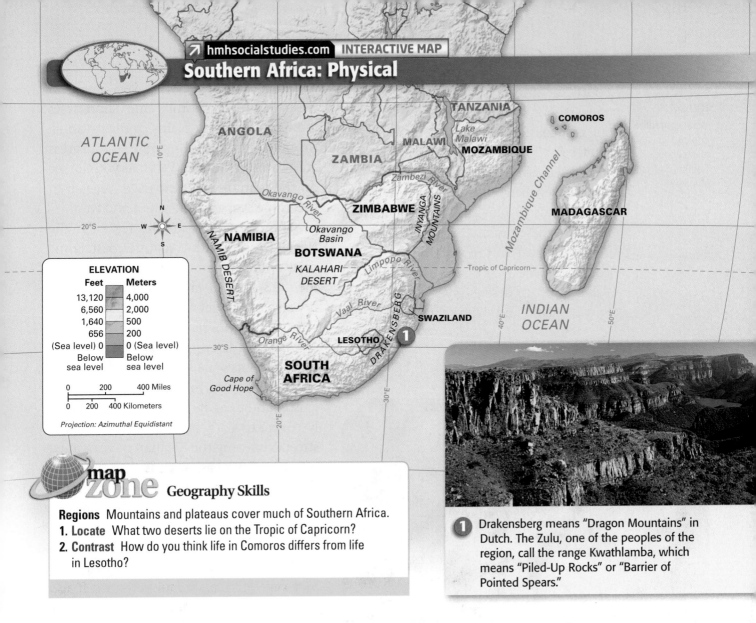

ELEVATION

Feet	Meters
13,120	4,000
6,560	2,000
1,640	500
656	200
(Sea level) 0	0 (Sea level)
Below sea level	Below sea level

0   200   400 Miles
0   200   400 Kilometers

Projection: Azimuthal Equidistant

map zone Geography Skills

Regions Mountains and plateaus cover much of Southern Africa.
1. **Locate** What two deserts lie on the Tropic of Capricorn?
2. **Contrast** How do you think life in Comoros differs from life in Lesotho?

1 Drakensberg means "Dragon Mountains" in Dutch. The Zulu, one of the peoples of the region, call the range Kwathlamba, which means "Piled-Up Rocks" or "Barrier of Pointed Spears."

Plains and Rivers

Southern Africa's narrow coastal plain and the wide plateau are covered with grassy plains. These flat plains are home to animals such as lions, leopards, elephants, baboons, and antelope.

Several large rivers cross Southern Africa's plains. The Okavango River flows from Angola into a huge basin in Botswana. This river's water never reaches the ocean. Instead it forms a swampy inland delta that is home to crocodiles, zebras, hippos, and other animals. Many tourists travel to Botswana to see these wild animals in their natural habitat.

The Orange River passes through the rocky Augrabies (oh-KRAH-bees) Falls as it flows to the Atlantic Ocean. When the water in the river is at its highest, the falls are several miles wide. The water tumbles down 19 separate waterfalls. The Limpopo River is another of the region's major rivers. It flows into the Indian Ocean. **Features** such as waterfalls and other obstacles block ships from sailing up these rivers. However, the rivers do allow irrigation for farmland in an otherwise dry area.

ACADEMIC VOCABULARY

features characteristics

READING CHECK **Generalizing** What are Southern Africa's main physical features?

Climate and Vegetation

FOCUS ON READING

What generalization can you make about Southern Africa's climate?

Southern Africa's climates vary from east to west. The wettest place in the region is the east coast of the island of Madagascar. On the mainland, winds carrying moisture blow in from the Indian Ocean. Because the Drakensberg's high elevation causes these winds to blow upward, the eastern slopes of these mountains are rainy.

In contrast to the eastern part of the continent, the west is very dry. From the Atlantic coast, deserts give way to plains with semiarid and steppe climates.

Satellite View

Namib Desert

One of the world's most unusual deserts, the Namib lies on the Atlantic coast in Namibia. As this satellite image shows, the land there is extremely dry. Some of the world's highest sand dunes stretch for miles along the coast.

In spite of its harsh conditions, some insects have adapted to life in the desert. They can survive there because at night a fog rolls in from the ocean. The insects use the fog as a source of water.

Drawing Conclusions How have some insects adapted to living in the Namib Desert?

Savanna and Deserts

A large savanna region covers much of Southern Africa. Shrubs and short trees grow on the grassy plains of the savanna. In South Africa, these open grassland areas are known as the **veld** (VELT). As you can see on the map on the next page, vegetation gets more sparse in the south and west.

The driest place in the region is the **Namib Desert** on the Atlantic coast. Some parts of the Namib get as little as a half an inch (13 mm) of rainfall per year. In this dry area, plants get water from dew and fog rather than from rain.

Another desert, the Kalahari, occupies most of Botswana. Although this desert gets enough rain in the north to support grasses and trees, its sandy plains are mostly covered with scattered shrubs. Ancient streams crossing the Kalahari have drained into low, flat areas, or **pans**. On these flat areas, minerals left behind when the water evaporated form a glittering white layer.

Tropical Forests

Unlike the mainland, Madagascar has lush vegetation and tropical forests. It also has many animals found nowhere else. For example, some 50 species of lemurs, relatives of apes, live only on this island. However, the destruction of Madagascar's forests has endangered many of the island's animals.

READING CHECK **Summarizing** What is the climate and vegetation like in Southern Africa?

Resources

Southern Africa is rich in natural resources. Madagascar's forests provide timber. The region's rivers supply hydroelectricity and water for irrigation. Where rain is plentiful or irrigation is possible, farmers can grow a wide range of crops.

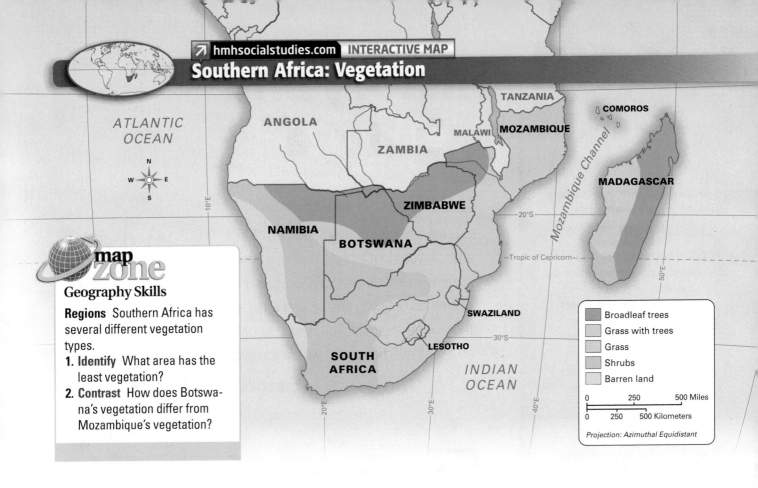

Southern Africa: Vegetation

hmhsocialstudies.com **INTERACTIVE MAP**

ATLANTIC OCEAN

ANGOLA

ZAMBIA

TANZANIA

MALAWI

MOZAMBIQUE

COMOROS

Mozambique Channel

MADAGASCAR

ZIMBABWE

20°S

NAMIBIA

BOTSWANA

Tropic of Capricorn

SWAZILAND

30°S

LESOTHO

SOUTH AFRICA

INDIAN OCEAN

Broadleaf trees
Grass with trees
Grass
Shrubs
Barren land

0   250   500 Miles

0   250   500 Kilometers

Projection: Azimuthal Equidistant

map zone

Geography Skills

Regions Southern Africa has several different vegetation types.

1. **Identify** What area has the least vegetation?
2. **Contrast** How does Botswana's vegetation differ from Mozambique's vegetation?

The region's most valuable resources, however, are minerals. Mines in South Africa produce most of the world's gold. In addition, South Africa, Botswana, and Namibia have productive diamond mines. Other mineral resources in Southern Africa include coal, platinum, copper, uranium, and iron ore. Although mining is very important to the economy of the region, the mines can have damaging effects on the surrounding natural environments.

READING CHECK **Finding Main Ideas** What are the main resources of Southern Africa?

SUMMARY AND PREVIEW Southern Africa is mainly covered with grassy plains and deserts atop a large plateau. Minerals are among the region's main resources. In the next section, you will learn about Southern Africa's history and culture.

Section 1 Assessment

hmhsocialstudies.com
ONLINE QUIZ

Reviewing Ideas, Terms, and Places

1. **a. Define** What is an **escarpment**?
   b. Elaborate How is the Okavango River different from most other rivers you have studied?
2. **a. Recall** Where in Southern Africa is the driest climate?
   b. Explain What caused minerals to collect in **pans** in the Kalahari Desert?
3. **a. Identify** What are Southern Africa's most valuable resources?
   b. Elaborate How do you think the gold and diamond mines have affected South Africa's economy?

Critical Thinking

4. **Categorizing** Review your notes and use a graphic organizer like this one to sort characteristics by location.

	East	West
Physical Features		
Climate and Vegetation		

FOCUS ON VIEWING

5. **Telling about the Physical Geography** Your TV news report might focus on some part of the geography of Southern Africa. Could you focus on the destruction of the rain forest or life in the desert?

History and Culture

What You Will Learn...

Main Ideas

1. Southern Africa's history began with hunter-gatherers, followed by great empires and European settlements.
2. The cultures of Southern Africa are rich in different languages, religions, customs, and art.

The Big Idea

Native African ethnic groups and European settlements influenced the history and culture of Southern Africa.

Key Terms and Places

Great Zimbabwe, *p. 177*
Cape of Good Hope, *p. 177*
Afrikaners, *p. 178*
Boers, *p. 178*
apartheid, *p. 178*
township, *p. 179*

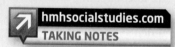
hmhsocialstudies.com
TAKING NOTES

Use the graphic organizer online to take notes on the history and culture of Southern Africa.

If YOU lived there...

You are a hunter living in Southern Africa 10,000 years ago. The animals you hunt include antelope, rhinoceros, and ostrich. A spear is your only weapon. You spend several days following herds of animals until you and several other people are able to surround them. After the hunt, you decide to paint your hunting experience on a rock overhang near where you live.

Why do you paint these images of animals?

BUILDING BACKGROUND Southern Africa's fertile land and its abundance of wildlife have supported different peoples for tens of thousands of years. Hunter-gatherers were the first peoples to thrive in the region. Much later, peoples from West Africa migrated to the region, and then eventually Europeans.

History

As you learned in the previous chapter, Bantu farmers migrated from West Africa to Central Africa as early as 2,000 years ago. These peoples also migrated to Southern Africa at about the same time. Much later, Europeans arrived on the coast of Southern Africa and forever changed the landscape and ways of life of the people in the region.

Early History

For many centuries the Khoisan peoples lived in Southern Africa. Divided into several ethnic groups, the Khoisan were hunter-gatherers and herders. When the early Bantu peoples migrated from West and Central Africa, they brought new languages and iron tools.

One Bantu group, the Shona, built an empire that reached its height in the 1400s. The Shona Empire included much of what is now the countries of Zimbabwe and Mozambique.

The Shona farmed, raised cattle, and traded gold with other groups on the coast.

The Shona are best known for **Great Zimbabwe**, their stone-walled capital. In fact, the name Zimbabwe is the Shona word for stone-walled towns. The builders of Great Zimbabwe used huge granite boulders and rectangular blocks of stone to build the capital's walls.

Founded in the late 1000s, Great Zimbabwe was a small trading and herding center. In the 1100s, the population grew, and both gold mining and farming grew in importance. Great Zimbabwe may have had 10,000 to 20,000 residents. With these resources, the city eventually became the center of a large trading network.

Trade made Great Zimbabwe's rulers wealthy and powerful. However, in the 1400s the gold trade declined. Deprived of its main source of wealth, Great Zimbabwe weakened. By 1500 it was no longer a capital and trading center.

Archaeologists have found Chinese porcelain and other artifacts from Asia at Great Zimbabwe. These artifacts suggest that the Shona traded widely. In addition to trading with peoples of Asia, the Shona apparently traded with the Swahili. The Swahili were Muslim Africans living along the East Africa coast. In effect, all of these peoples were once connected by an Indian Ocean trade network.

Europeans in Southern Africa

In the late 1400s traders from Portugal explored the Southern African coast on their way to Asia to trade for spices. To get to Asia from Portugal, they had to sail around the southern tip of Africa and then cross the Indian Ocean. The trip was long and difficult, so they set up bases on the Southern African coast. These bases provided the ships with supplies.

The Dutch Other Europeans arrived in Southern Africa after the Portuguese. People from the Netherlands, or the Dutch, were the first Europeans to settle in the region. In 1652 the Dutch set up a trade station at a natural harbor near the **Cape of Good Hope**.

Highly skilled craftspeople built several stone walls that surrounded the Shona capital of Great Zimbabwe. Today the ruins are a World Heritage Site.

ANALYZING VISUALS Why do you think Great Zimbabwe was made of stone?

Great Zimbabwe

The Cape sits at the tip of Africa. The land around the Cape lacked the gold and copper of the interior. However, it had a mild climate, similar to the climate the Dutch were used to back home.

This small colony on the Cape provided supplies to Dutch ships sailing between Dutch colonies in the East Indies and the Netherlands. The Dutch eventually brought in slaves from the region and Southeast Asia to work in the colony.

The Afrikaners and the Boers The people of the colony were very diverse. In addition to the Dutch, other Europeans also settled on the Cape. Dutch, French, and German settlers and their descendants in South Africa were called **Afrikaners**. Over time, a new language called Afrikaans emerged in the Cape colony. This language combined Dutch with Khoisan and Bantu words. German, French, and English also influenced the language's development.

Dutch Settlers

This painting shows Dutch settlers arriving at the Cape of Good Hope in Southern Africa.

In the early 1800s, Great Britain took over the area of the Cape. The **Boers**, Afrikaner frontier farmers who had spread out from the original Cape colony, resisted the British. Many Boers packed all their belongings into wagons and soon moved farther east and north.

The Zulu and the British At about the same time, a Bantu-speaking group, the Zulu, became a powerful fighting force in the region. They conquered the surrounding African peoples, creating their own empire. When the Boers moved north of the Cape, they entered Zulu territory. The two sides clashed over control of the land. Eventually the British also wanted Zulu land. After a series of battles, the British defeated the Zulu.

The ending of slavery in the British Empire in the 1830s brought changes to the economy of colonial settlements in the region. Instead of slaves, people traded ivory—the tusks of elephants. Over time, however, hunters wiped out the entire elephant population in some parts of Southern Africa. With ivory in short supply, trade shifted to diamonds and gold, which were discovered in South Africa in the 1860s.

Apartheid

In the early 1900s South Africa's government, which was dominated by white Afrikaners, became increasingly racist. As a result, black South Africans opposed the government. To defend their rights, they formed the African National Congress (ANC) in 1912.

However, the trend toward racial division and inequality continued. South Africa's government set up a policy of separation of races, or **apartheid**, which means "apartness." This policy divided people into four groups: whites, blacks, Coloureds, and Asians.

Music of South Africa

Stomping. Spinning. Swaying. This is the kind of dancing you might see at a performance of South African music. In addition, musicians playing drums, guitars, and traditional flutes provide a rhythmic beat that makes it impossible to stand still.

One of the groups that does it the best are the Mahotella Queens. They are grandmothers who have been singing together for over 40 years. Their songs mix gospel with traditional African music. Performing all over the world, the Queens give unforgettable performances of nonstop singing and dancing.

Drawing Conclusions Why do you think South African music is popular around the world?

Coloureds and Asians were only allowed to live in certain areas. Each African tribe or group was given its own rural "homeland." These homelands generally did not include good farmland, mines, and other natural resources. Those resources were owned by the whites, and blacks had no rights in white areas.

Housing, health care, and schools for blacks were poor compared to those for whites. Schools for Coloureds were poor, but slightly better than the black schools.

During apartheid, many blacks found work in white-owned industries, mines, shops, and farms. Blacks had to live in separate areas called **townships**, which were often crowded clusters of tiny homes. The townships were far from the jobs in the cities and mines.

Independence

Beginning in the 1960s, many colonies gained independence from the European countries that had once colonized them.

Some gained independence rather peacefully, but others struggled. For example, the British colonists in Rhodesia fought native Africans for years. Fighting broke out after the colonists declared their own white-dominated republic in 1970. Finally, in 1980, the Africans won independence and renamed their country Zimbabwe.

Independence also did not come easy for other countries. Despite violent resistance, Namibia continued to be ruled by South Africa until 1990. Mozambique was granted independence in 1975 after 10 years of war against Portuguese rule.

READING CHECK **Generalizing** Why did Europeans settle Southern Africa?

Culture

Over time, many groups of people created a diverse culture in Southern Africa. As a result, the region's culture reflects both European and African influence.

Ndebele Village

The Ndebele are one of many ethnic groups in South Africa who have kept their traditional culture alive. Many live in villages of brightly painted houses.

ANALYSIS **SKILL** ANALYZING VISUALS

What aspect of Ndebele culture do you see in these two photographs?

People

The people of Southern Africa belong to hundreds of different ethnic groups. Some groups are very large. For example, about 9 million people in South Africa are Zulu. Nearly 1.6 million of Botswana's 2 million people belong to a single ethnic group, the Tswana.

Other ethnic groups are small and usually not native to Africa. For example, about 6 percent of Namibia's population is of German descent. In Madagascar people are a mix of 18 small ethnic groups. These Malagasy groups descended from people who migrated across the Indian Ocean from Indonesia.

Languages

FOCUS ON READING

What generalization can you make about the languages spoken in Southern Africa?

Because people in Southern Africa belong to hundreds of different ethnic groups, they speak many languages. Most of the African languages spoken in Southern Africa are related to one of two language families—Khoisan or Bantu.

The early peoples of Southern Africa spoke different Khoisan languages. Khoisan speakers are known for the "click" sounds they make when they speak. Today, the majority of Khoisan speakers belong to the San ethnic group and live in remote areas of Botswana and Namibia.

Most people in Southern Africa speak one of the more than 200 Bantu languages. For example, most of South Africa's 11 official languages are Bantu.

In countries with European influence, European languages are also spoken. For example, English is the official language of Namibia and Zimbabwe. The official language of Mozambique is Portuguese.

Religion

In addition to language, Europeans brought the religion of Christianity to Southern Africa. As a result, millions of people in Southern Africa are Christians. In Namibia and South Africa the majority of the population is Christian.

Painting houses is traditionally the role of Ndebele women. They use colorful geometric patterns.

Artists in Zimbabwe are known for their beautiful stone sculptures of birds and other animals. Traditional crafts of Botswana include ostrich-eggshell beadwork and woven baskets with complex designs. People there also produce colorful wool rugs.

READING CHECK **Analyzing** Why do you think the people of Southern Africa speak several different languages?

SUMMARY AND PREVIEW Southern Africa's ancient history and later European settlement greatly influenced the region's culture. Next, you will learn about the governments and economies of the region's countries today.

Many people in Southern Africa who are not Christian practice traditional African religions. Some of these people believe that ancestors and the spirits of the dead have divine powers. In Zimbabwe, traditional beliefs and Christianity have been mixed together. About half of the people in Zimbabwe practice a combination of traditional beliefs and Christianity.

Celebrations and Art

Southern Africans celebrate many holidays. On Heritage Day, South Africans celebrate their country's diverse population. Most countries in Southern Africa celebrate their countries' independence day. Many Christian holidays such as Christmas Day are also celebrated throughout the region.

Southern Africa's art reflects its many cultures. For example, South African artists make traditional ethnic designs for items such as clothing, lamps, linens, and other products. Artists in Lesotho are famous for their woven tapestries of daily life.

Section 2 Assessment

hmhsocialstudies.com
ONLINE QUIZ

Reviewing Ideas, Terms, and Places

1. **a. Define** What was **apartheid**?
   b. Draw Conclusions Why did the Shona capital of **Great Zimbabwe** decline as a trading center?
   c. Elaborate Why do you think the language of Afrikaans developed among the European colonists?
2. **a. Recall** What ethnic group in Southern Africa speaks languages that use click sounds?
   b. Draw Conclusions How do the religions practiced in Southern Africa reflect the region's history?
   c. Evaluate Why do you think Heritage Day is a national holiday in South Africa?

Critical Thinking

3. **Sequencing** Review your notes on the history of Southern Africa. Then organize your information using a time line like the one below. You may add more dates if you need to.

   AD 1000   1990

FOCUS ON VIEWING

4. **Discussing History and Culture** Which information about the history and culture of Southern Africa might make a good TV news report? What visuals would be interesting?

Southern Africa Today

SECTION 3

What You Will Learn...

Main Ideas

1. South Africa ended apartheid and now has a stable government and strong economy.
2. Some countries of Southern Africa have good resources and economies, but several are still struggling.
3. Southern African governments are responding to issues and challenges such as drought, disease, and environmental destruction.

The Big Idea

Countries of Southern Africa today are trying to use their governments and resources to improve their economies and deal with challenges.

Key Terms and Places

sanctions, *p. 182*
Cape Town, *p. 184*
enclave, *p. 184*

hmhsocialstudies.com
TAKING NOTES

Use the graphic organizer online to take notes on the countries of Southern Africa today and the challenges they face.

If YOU lived there...

You are an economic adviser in Botswana. In recent years your country has made progress toward improving people's lives, but you think there is room for improvement. One way you plan to help the economy is by promoting tourism. Botswana already has amazing natural landscapes and fascinating animals.

What could your country do to attract more tourists?

BUILDING BACKGROUND Some of the countries in Southern Africa are relatively well off, with plentiful resources and good jobs and transportation systems. Others lack these positive conditions. One of the most successful countries in the region is South Africa.

South Africa

Today South Africa has a stable government and the strongest economy in the region. In addition, many South Africans are enjoying new rights and freedoms. The country has made great progress in resolving the problems of its past, but it still faces many challenges.

End of Apartheid

Ending apartheid, the separation of races, has probably been South Africa's biggest challenge in recent years. Many people around the world objected to the country's apartheid laws. For that reason, they put **sanctions**—economic or political penalties imposed by one country on another to force a change in policy—on South Africa. Some countries banned trade with South Africa. Several companies in the United States and Europe refused to invest their money in South Africa. In addition, many international scientific and sports organizations refused to include South Africans in meetings or competitions.

Celebrating Mandela's Freedom

South Africans in Soweto warmly welcomed Nelson Mandela after he was released from prison in 1990.

The sanctions isolated South Africa. As other countries in Southern Africa gained independence, South Africa became even more isolated. Protest within the country increased. In response, the government outlawed the African National Congress (ANC). This group had been formed to protect the rights of black South Africans. Many ANC members were jailed or forced to leave the country.

The antiapartheid protests continued, however. Finally, in the late 1980s South Africa began to move away from the apartheid system. In 1990 the government released its political prisoners, including Nelson Mandela. Mandela was elected president in 1994 after South Africans of all races were given the right to vote.

Today all races have equal rights in South Africa. The country's public schools and universities are open to all people, as are hospitals and transportation. However, economic equality has come more slowly. White South Africans are still wealthier than the vast majority of black South Africans. Still, South Africans now have opportunities for a better future.

BIOGRAPHY

Nelson Mandela
(1918–   )

Because he protested against apartheid, Nelson Mandela was imprisoned for 26 years. In 1990, however, South Africa's President de Klerk released Mandela from prison. Mandela and de Klerk shared the Nobel Peace Prize in 1993. One year later, Mandela became South Africa's first black president. He wrote a new constitution and worked to improve the living conditions of black South Africans.

Summarizing What did Nelson Mandela accomplish when he was South Africa's president?

Government and Economy

South Africa's government and economy are well positioned to create a better future for the country. South Africa's new government is a republic with an elected president. The country's constitution emphasizes equality and human rights.

In working toward equality, the government is trying to create jobs and better conditions for black workers and farmers. Currently, most of South Africa's wealth and industries are still controlled by whites. However, even some officials who favor reform are afraid to **execute** new policies. They fear that rapid change will weaken the economy. They are also concerned that it might cause educated and wealthy whites to leave the country.

ACADEMIC VOCABULARY
execute to perform, to carry out

South Africa's strong economy may help bring economic opportunities to the entire population. The country has more resources and industry than most African countries. For example, South Africa is the world's largest producer of several valuable minerals—gold, platinum, and chromium. The country is also a major exporter of gold and diamonds.

Large cities in South Africa also contribute to the country's economy. Africa's largest industrial area is located in Johannesburg. In addition, beautiful cities such as **Cape Town** attract many tourists.

READING CHECK **Analyzing** Why and how did South Africa do away with apartheid?

Other Countries of Southern Africa

The eight other countries in the region share some characteristics with South Africa. Some, but not all, have strong economies and stable governments.

Lesotho and Swaziland

These two countries are particularly influenced by South Africa. Lesotho and Swaziland are both enclaves. An **enclave** is a small territory surrounded by foreign territory. Lesotho and Swaziland are both located completely, or almost completely, within South Africa. Swaziland shares part of its border with Mozambique.

Close-up

Cape Town

Founded by the Dutch in 1652, Cape Town is a bustling international port city today. It lies on the South Atlantic Ocean and is home to about 3 million people.

Hiking trails lead to the top of Lion's Head for an amazing view of the city.

ANALYSIS SKILL **ANALYZING VISUALS**

What can you see in this photograph that might reveal why Cape Town is popular with tourists?

Because it is so small, Lesotho has few resources or agricultural land. As a result, it is a poor country. Many of its people work in nearby South Africa. In spite of its poverty, Lesotho has the highest female literacy rate in Africa. Most children, including females, get at least a primary education in free schools run by Christian churches.

Swaziland has some important mineral deposits and industry. Cattle raising and farming are also common there. A good transportation system helps Swaziland to participate in foreign trade.

Lesotho and Swaziland are both kingdoms. Although each country has a king as head of state, each is governed by an elected prime minister and a parliament.

The city's buildings are a mix of modern and Dutch colonial architecture.

People jog, bike, and rollerblade on this trail along the ocean.

Namibia

Namibia gained its independence from South Africa as recently as 1990. Now it is a republic with an elected president and legislature. Its capital, Windhoek, is located in the central highlands.

Very few people live in Namibia's deserts in the east and the west, but these areas are the sites of some of the richest mineral deposits in Africa. Most of the country's income comes from the mining of diamonds, copper, uranium, lead, and zinc. Fishing in the Atlantic Ocean and sheep ranching are also important sources of income. In spite of this strong economy, however, most people are still poor.

Botswana

Botswana is one of Africa's success stories, thanks to mineral resources and a stable democratic government. The main economic activities in Botswana are cattle ranching and diamond mining. Recently, international companies have built factories there, and tourism is increasing. Although unemployment is high, the country has had one of the world's highest rates of economic growth since the 1960s.

FOCUS ON READING
In general, what is Botswana's economy like?

Zimbabwe

Zimbabwe has suffered from a poor economy and political instability. Zimbabwe does not lack resources. It has gold and copper mines as well as productive agriculture and manufacturing. However, high inflation, debts, and war have hurt the economy.

In addition, there is much inequality. Although white residents made up less than 1 percent of the population, they owned most of the large farms and ranches. In 2000 the president began a program to take farmland from white farmers and give the land to black residents. This action led many white farmers to leave the country and caused food shortages.

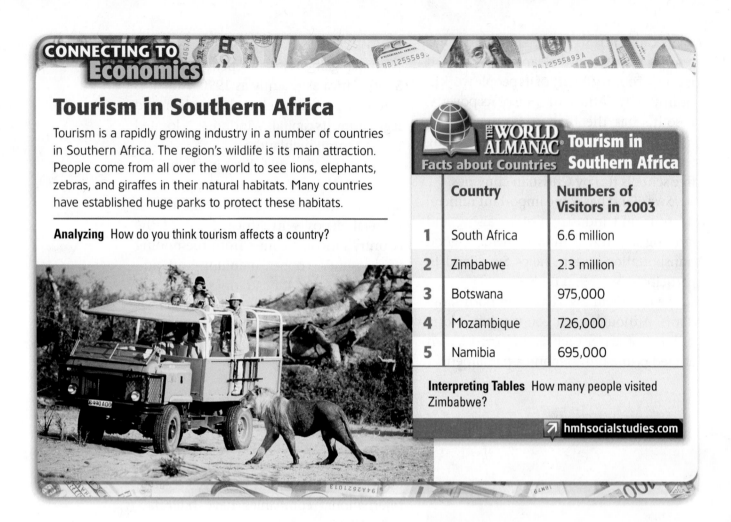

CONNECTING TO Economics

Tourism in Southern Africa

Tourism is a rapidly growing industry in a number of countries in Southern Africa. The region's wildlife is its main attraction. People come from all over the world to see lions, elephants, zebras, and giraffes in their natural habitats. Many countries have established huge parks to protect these habitats.

Analyzing How do you think tourism affects a country?

THE WORLD ALMANAC Facts about Countries — Tourism in Southern Africa

	Country	Numbers of Visitors in 2003
1	South Africa	6.6 million
2	Zimbabwe	2.3 million
3	Botswana	975,000
4	Mozambique	726,000
5	Namibia	695,000

Interpreting Tables How many people visited Zimbabwe?

hmhsocialstudies.com

The attempt at land reform, the poor economy, and violent acts against political opponents have made people in Zimbabwe unhappy with the president. Although he was re-elected in 2002 and 2008, most people think the elections were flawed.

Mozambique

Mozambique is one of the world's poorest countries. The economy has been badly damaged by civil war, but it is improving. Mozambique's ports ship many products from the interior of Africa. Taxes collected on these shipments are an important source of income. Also, plantations grow cashews, cotton, and sugar for export. The country must import more than it exports, however, and it relies on foreign aid.

Madagascar and Comoros

Madagascar was ruled for more than 20 years by a socialist dictator. Today the elected president is working to improve the struggling economy. Most of the country's income comes from exports of coffee, vanilla, sugar, and cloves. Madagascar also has some manufacturing, and the country is popular with tourists who come to see the unique plants and animals.

Comoros is a country made up of four tiny islands. It suffers from a lack of resources and political instability. The government of Comoros is struggling to improve education and promote tourism.

READING CHECK **Contrasting** In what ways are Botswana and Zimbabwe different?

Issues and Challenges

Although conditions in many countries of Southern Africa are better than they are on much of the continent, the region has its own challenges. One of the most serious problems facing Southern Africa is poverty. Terrible droughts often destroy food crops. In addition, many of Southern Africa's people are unemployed.

Disease is another problem. Southern Africa has high numbers of people infected with HIV. The region's governments are trying to educate people to slow the spread of disease.

Another challenge is environmental destruction. For example, in Madagascar, deforestation leads to erosion. There is hope for the future, though. Namibia was the first country in the world to put environmental protection in its constitution. Also, the African Union (AU) works to promote cooperation among African countries. The AU tries to solve problems across the continent.

READING CHECK **Generalizing** What main challenges does Southern Africa face?

Baobab trees line a street in Madagascar.

SUMMARY Southern Africa has valuable mineral resources and landscapes popular with tourists. Some countries have more stable governments and economies than much of Africa. However, the region still faces many challenges.

Section 3 Assessment

hmhsocialstudies.com
ONLINE QUIZ

Reviewing Ideas, Terms, and Places

1. **a. Describe** What effect did **sanctions** have on South Africa?
   b. Interpret What have been two effects of the end of apartheid?
2. **a. Recall** Which country's president began a program to take farmland from white farmers?
   b. Make Inferences Why might being an **enclave** affect a country's economy?
   c. Rank Besides South Africa, which two countries in the region seem to have the best economies?
3. **a. Describe** How does terrible drought lead to poverty?
   b. Explain How are people in Southern Africa addressing the challenges in the region?

Critical Thinking

4. **Summarizing** Review your notes on South Africa. Then using a graphic organizer like this one, describe what the country has been like at each different period.

Before the 1990s	The 1990s	Today

Focus on Viewing

5. **Telling about Southern Africa Today** Would you try to include information about all of Southern Africa in your report? Or would you just focus on one country? Take notes on your ideas.

Social Studies Skills

Evaluating a Web Site

Learn

The Internet is one of the most valuable tools available for research today. However, not everything that you find on the Internet is useful or accurate. You have to be careful and analyze the sites you use.

A good Web site should be accurate and up-to-date. Before you use a site for research, find out who produced it. The author should be qualified and unbiased. Also, check to see when the site was last updated. If it has not been updated recently, the information it contains may no longer be accurate.

Practice

Study this page taken from a Web site and then answer these questions.

1. Who do you think produced this Web site? How can you tell?

2. What kinds of information can you find on this site?

3. Do you think this would be a good site for research? Why or why not?

A country's official Web site is usually a good source for information.

Check to see how current the articles on the Web site are. Have they been updated regularly?

Notice what type of information is present on the Web site. Is the site biased or unbalanced?

Apply

Search the Internet to find a Web page about one of the countries of Southern Africa. Analyze the site and determine whether you think it would be a good site for research. Write a paragraph to explain your decision. Make sure to include the site's URL and the date on which you visited it in your report.

Geography's Impact
video series
Review the video to answer the closing question:
What are some ways South Africans could continue working together?

Visual Summary

Use the visual summary below to help you review the main ideas of the chapter.

QUICK FACTS

The Drakensberg rises to meet a high plateau that dominates the physical geography of Southern Africa.

Traditional African and European cultures mix in Southern Africa. Music and dance are very important.

Countries such as South Africa have strong economies and modern cities. Other countries struggle with poverty.

Reviewing Vocabulary, Terms, and Places

Match the words with their definitions.

1. Great Zimbabwe
2. features
3. Boers
4. apartheid
5. sanctions
6. townships
7. escarpment
8. enclave

a. the steep face at the edge of a plateau or other raised area

b. economic or political penalties imposed by one country on another to force a change in policy

c. a large, stone-walled town built by the Shona

d. Afrikaner frontier farmers in South Africa

e. a small territory surrounded by foreign territory

f. characteristics

g. South Africa's policy of separation of races

h. separate areas with clusters of tiny homes for black South Africans

Comprehension and Critical Thinking

SECTION 1 *(Pages 172–175)*

9. a. **Identify** What are the two main deserts in Southern Africa?

b. **Contrast** How is the eastern part of Southern Africa different from the western part?

c. **Elaborate** How do you think the geography of Southern Africa has affected settlement patterns in the region?

SECTION 2 *(Pages 176–181)*

10. a. **Define** Who are the Afrikaners? What country do they live in?

b. **Contrast** How does the origin of Khoisan languages differ from Bantu languages? What is unusual about Khoisan languages?

c. **Elaborate** What was life like for non-whites under the policy of apartheid? What rights were blacks, Coloureds, and Asians denied?

SECTION 3 *(Pages 182–187)*

11. **a. Identify** Which countries are enclaves?

b. Analyze In what ways has South Africa changed with the end of apartheid? In what ways has it stayed the same?

c. Evaluate Poverty is the most serious challenge facing Southern Africa. Do you agree or disagree with this statement? Explain your answer.

Social Studies Skills

12. **Analyzing a Web Site** Search the Internet to find two Web sites about topics in Southern Africa. One Web site should be one you would consider good to use for research. The other site should be one you do not consider to be a good source of information for research. Write a paragraph comparing and contrasting the two sites. Be sure to explain why one site seems more useful and accurate than the other.

Map Activity

13. **Southern Africa** On a separate sheet of paper, match the letters on the map with their correct labels.

Cape of Good Hope	Namib Desert
Okavango Basin	Drakensberg
Orange River	

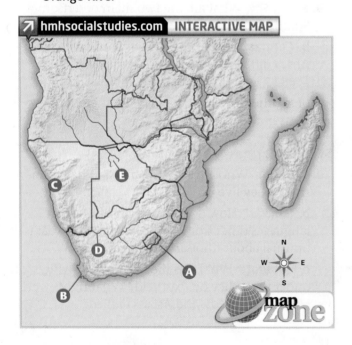

↗ **hmhsocialstudies.com** INTERACTIVE MAP

Using the Internet

14. **Activity: Researching Apartheid** From 1948 until 1994, many people in South Africa were legally discriminated against under the policy known as apartheid. Imagine that you are a reporter writing an article on the history of apartheid. Through the online book, use both primary and secondary sources to research who started apartheid, how people struggled against it, and when it finally came to an end. Using that information, create an outline for your article. Be sure to include details from your research that support the main ideas.

↗ **hmhsocialstudies.com**

FOCUS ON READING AND VIEWING

15. **Making Generalizations** Re-read the information about South Africa today in Section 3. Based on the specific information you read, make one generalization about the country's economy and one about its resources.

16. **Presenting a TV News Report** Review your notes and decide on a topic for your report. Next, identify the point you want to make about your topic—your purpose. Your purpose may be to share interesting information—a recently celebrated holiday, for example. Or your purpose may be more serious—perhaps the need to reduce poverty. Decide what images you will show and what you will say to make your point.

Write a script and in it, identify which visuals go with what content. Present your report to the class using visuals, just as though you were on the TV news. Listen and watch your classmates' reports. Evaluate their reports based on accuracy of the content and visual interest.

Standardized Test Prep

DIRECTIONS: Read questions 1 through 7 and write the letter of the best response. Then read question 8 and write your own well-constructed response.

1 **Most of the land in Southern Africa lies on a**

A mountain range.

B coastal plain.

C plateau.

D delta.

2 **The Dutch first settled in Southern Africa in 1652 near the**

A Inyanga Mountains.

B Cape of Good Hope.

C Okavango Basin.

D Namib Desert.

3 **Who were the first Europeans to explore the southern coast of Africa?**

A Portuguese

B Dutch

C French

D German

4 **Which country had a policy called apartheid to separate different races?**

A Zimbabwe

B Madagascar

C Namibia

D South Africa

5 **Which of the following statements about the end of apartheid is false?**

A Sanctions helped bring the end of apartheid.

B Black people and white people now have economic equality.

C Both black people and white people can vote.

D Public schools and universities are open to all people.

Madagascar: Climate

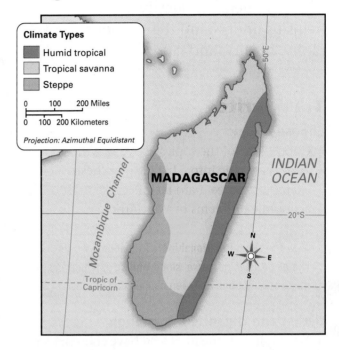

6 **Based on the map above, where would Madagascar's tropical forests likely be located?**

A in the east

B in the west

C on the savanna

D in the north

7 **Which two countries are enclaves?**

A South Africa and Lesotho

B Madagascar and Comoros

C Lesotho and Swaziland

D Zimbabwe and Mozambique

8 **Extended Response** Choose two countries from the table in Section 3 on Tourism in Southern Africa. Think about the information in this chart and what you know about the resources in these two countries. Write a paragraph explaining reasons for the differences and similarities in the number of tourists who visit each country.

Explaining Cause or Effect

"Why did it happen?" "What were the results?" Questions like these help us identify causes and effects. This, in turn, helps us understand the relationships among physical geography, history, and culture.

Assignment

Write a paper about one of these topics:

- causes of economic problems in West Africa
- effects of European colonization in Southern Africa

1. Prewrite

Choose a Topic

- Choose one of the topics above to write about.
- Turn that topic into a big idea, or thesis. For example, "Three main factors cause most of the economic problems in West Africa."

> **TIP** **What Relationships?** Transitional words like *as a result, because, since,* and *so* can help make connections between causes and effects.

Gather and Organize Information

- Depending on the topic you have chosen, identify at least three causes or three effects. Use your textbook, the library, or the Internet.
- Organize causes or effects in their order of importance. To have the most impact on your readers, put the most important cause or effect last.

2. Write

Use a Writer's Framework

A Writer's Framework

Introduction
- Start with an interesting fact or question related to your big idea, or thesis.
- State your big idea and provide background information.

Body
- Write at least one paragraph, including supporting facts and examples, for each cause or effect.
- Organize your causes or effects by order of importance.

Conclusion
- Summarize the causes or effects.
- Restate your big idea.

3. Evaluate and Revise

Review and Improve Your Paper

- Re-read your paper and use the questions below to determine how to make your paper better.
- Make changes to improve your paper.

Evaluation Questions for a Cause and Effect Explanation

1. Do you begin with a fact or question related to your big idea, or thesis?
2. Does your introduction identify your big idea and provide any needed background?
3. Do you have at least one paragraph for each cause or effect?
4. Do you include facts and details to support the connections between causes and effects?
5. Do you explain the causes or effects in order of importance?
6. Do you summarize the causes or effects and restate your big idea?

4. Proofread and Publish

Give Your Explanation the Finishing Touch

- Make sure transitional words and phrases connect causes and effects as clearly as possible.
- Check for capitalization of proper nouns, such as the names of countries and regions.
- Have someone else read your paper.

5. Practice and Apply

Use the steps and strategies outlined in this workshop to write your cause-and-effect paper. Share your paper with other students who wrote on the same topic. Compare your lists of causes or effects.

References

Available @

↗ **hmhsocialstudies.com**

- Facts About the World
- Regions of the World Handbook
- Standardized Test-Taking Strategies
- Economics Handbook

Categorizing

READING SOCIAL STUDIES

FOCUS ON READING

When you sort things into groups of similar items, you are categorizing. Think of folding laundry. First you might sort into different piles: towels, socks, and T-shirts. The piles—or categories—help you manage the laundry because towels go to a different place than socks. When you read, categorizing helps you to manage the information by identifying the main types, or groups, of information. Then you can more easily see the individual facts and details in each group. Notice how the information in the paragraph below has been sorted into three main groups.

> The subjects of Egyptian paintings vary widely. Some of the paintings show important historical events, such as the crowning of a new king or the founding of a temple. Others show major religious rituals. Still other paintings show scenes from everyday life, such as farming or hunting.
>
> *From Section 4, Egyptian Achievements*

Subjects of Egyptian Paintings		
Category 1: Important historical events	**Category 2:** Major religious rituals	**Category 3:** Everyday life

YOU TRY IT!

Read the following sentences. Then use a graphic organizer like the one above to categorize the natural barriers in ancient Egypt. Create as many categories as you need.

> In addition to a stable food supply, Egypt's location offered another advantage. It had natural barriers, which made it hard to invade Egypt. To the west, the desert was too big and harsh to cross. To the north, the Mediterranean Sea kept many enemies away. To the east, more desert and the Red Sea provided protection. Finally, to the south, cataracts in the Nile made it difficult for invaders to sail into Egypt that way.
>
> *From Section 1, Geography and Early Egypt*

Asking Questions

FOCUS ON READING

When newspaper reporters want to get to the heart of a story, they ask certain questions: who, what, when, where, why, and how. When you are reading a textbook, you can use these same questions to get to the heart of the information you are reading. Notice how asking and answering questions about the passage below gets at the important information.

When?
751 BC

Where?
Egypt

What?
Conquered Upper Egypt

As Kush was growing stronger, Egypt was losing power. A series of weak pharaohs left Egypt open to attack. In the 700s BC a Kushite king, Kashta, took advantage of Egypt's weakness. Kashta attacked Eqypt. By about 751 BC he had conquered Upper Egypt.

From Section 1, Kush and Egypt

Why?
To gain more power

Who?
Kashta

How?
Attacking during reign of weak pharaoh

YOU TRY IT!

Read the following passage carefully. Review the information in the passage by asking and answering the questions below.

By the AD 300s, Kush had lost much of its wealth and military might. Seeing that the Kushites were weak, the king of Aksum sent an army to conquer his former trade rival. In AD 350, the army of Aksum's King Ezana destroyed Meroë and took over the kingdom of Kush.

From Section 2, Later Kush

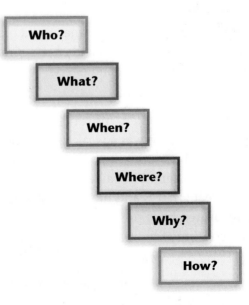

Who?

What?

When?

Where?

Why?

How?

READING SOCIAL STUDIES

Understanding Cause and Effect

FOCUS ON READING

To understand a country's history, you should look for cause and effect chains. A cause makes something happen, and an effect is what happens as a result of a cause. The effect can then become a cause and create another effect. Notice how the events below create a cause-and-effect chain.

> As the trade in gold and salt increased, Ghana's rulers gained power. Over time, their military strength grew as well. With their armies they began to take control of this trade from the merchants who had once controlled it. Merchants from the north and south met to exchange goods in Ghana. As a result of their control of trade routes, the rulers of Ghana became wealthy.
>
> *From Section 1, Empire of Ghana*

| **First Cause**
Increase in gold and salt trade | → | **Effect**
Ghana's rulers became powerful | → | **Effect**
More military strength | → | **Effect**
Took control of trade routes | → | **Final Effect**
Rulers of Ghana became wealthy |

YOU TRY IT!

Read the following sentences, and then use a graphic organizer like the one above to analyze causes and effects. Create as many boxes as you need to list the causes and effects.

> When Mansa Musa died, his son Maghan took the throne. Maghan was a weak ruler. When raiders from the southeast poured into Mali, he couldn't stop them. The raiders set fire to Timbuktu's great schools and mosques. Mali never fully recovered from this terrible blow. The empire continued to weaken and decline.
>
> *From Section 2, Mali and Songhai*

Summarizing

FOCUS ON READING

Learning about countries means understanding a lot of information. Summarizing is one way to help you handle large amounts of information. A summary is a short restatement of the most important ideas in a text. The example below shows three steps you can use to write a summary. First underline important details. Then write a short summary of each paragraph. Finally, combine these paragraph summaries into a short summary of the whole passage.

> With more than 10 million people, Cairo is the largest urban area in North Africa. The city is crowded, poor, and polluted. Cairo continues to grow as people move into the city from Egypt's rural areas in search of work. For centuries, Cairo's location at the southern end of the Nile Delta helped the city grow. The city also lies along old trading routes.
>
> Today the landscape of Cairo is a mixture of modern buildings, historic mosques, and small, mud-brick houses. However, there is not enough housing in Cairo for its growing population. Many people live in makeshift housing in the slums or boats along the Nile. Communities have even developed in cemeteries, where people convert tombs into bedrooms and kitchens.
>
> *From Section 3, North Africa Today*

Summary of Paragraph 1
The crowded city of Cairo is North Africa's largest city and continues to grow.

Summary of Paragraph 2
Without enough housing, people in Cairo live in slums, boats and cemeteries.

Combined Summary
Cairo is North Africa's largest city, and it is so crowded that people live in houses, boats and cemeteries.

YOU TRY IT!

Read the following paragraphs. First, write a summary for each paragraph and then write a combined summary of the whole passage.

> Even though Egypt is a republic, its government is heavily influenced by Islamic law. Egypt's government has a constitution and Egyptians elect their government officials. Power is shared between Egypt's president and the prime minister.
>
> Many Egyptians debate over the role of Islam in the country. Some Egyptian Muslims believe Egypt's government, laws, and society should be based on Islamic law. However, some Egyptians worry that such a change in government would mean fewer personal freedoms.
>
> *From Section 3, North Africa Today*

READING SOCIAL STUDIES

Understanding Comparison-Contrast

FOCUS ON READING

Comparing shows how things are alike. Contrasting shows how things are different. You can understand comparison-contrast by learning to recognize clue words and points of comparison. Clue words let you know whether to look for similarities or differences. Points of comparison are the main topics that are being compared or contrasted. Notice how the passage below compares and contrasts life in rural and urban areas.

> Rural homes are small and simple. Many homes in the Sahel and savanna zones are circular. Straw or tin roofs sit atop mud, mud-brick, or straw huts. Large extended families often live close together in the same village . . .
>
> In urban areas, also, members of an extended family may all live together. However, in West Africa's cities you will find modern buildings. People may live in houses or high rise apartments.
>
> *From Section 2, History and Culture*

Highlighted words are points of comparison.

Underlined words are clue words.

Clue Words

Comparison	Contrast
share, similar, like, also, both, in addition, besides	however, while, unlike, different, but, although

YOU TRY IT!

Read the following passage about Liberia and Sierra Leone. Use a diagram like the one here to compare and contrast the two countries.

> Now, both Liberia and Sierra Leone are trying to rebuild. They do have natural resources on which to build stronger economies. Liberia has rubber and iron ore while Sierra Leone exports diamonds.
>
> *From Section 3, West Africa Today*

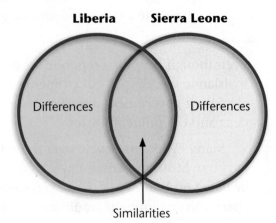

Liberia   Sierra Leone

Differences   Differences

Similarities

Identifying Supporting Details

FOCUS ON READING

Why believe what you read? One reason is because of details that support or prove the main idea. These details might be facts, statistics, examples, or definitions. In the example below, notice what kind of proof or supporting details help you believe the main idea.

> The landscape of East Africa has many high volcanic mountains. The highest mountain in Africa, Mount Kilimanjaro, rises to 19,340 feet. Despite Kilimanjaro's location near the equator, the mountain's peak has long been covered in snow. This much colder climate is caused by Kilimanjaro's high elevation.
>
> *From Section 1, Physical Geography*

Main Idea
The landscape of East Africa has many high volcanic mountains.

Supporting Details			
Example	**Statistic**	**Fact**	**Fact**
The highest mountain is Mount Kilimanjaro.	Mount Kilimanjaro is 19,340 feet high.	Kilimanjaro has a cold climate.	It is near the equator, but its peak is snow covered.

YOU TRY IT!

Read the following sentences, and then use a graphic organizer like the one above to identify the supporting details.

> Somalia is less diverse than most other African countries. Most people in the country are members of a single ethnic group, the Somali. In addition, most Somalis are Muslims and speak the same African language, also called Somali.
>
> *From Section 3, East Africa Today*

Using Word Parts

FOCUS ON READING

Many English words are made up of several word parts: roots, prefixes, and suffixes. A root is the main part of the word. A prefix is a letter or syllable added before the root. A suffix is a word part added after the root. Knowing the meanings of common prefixes and suffixes may help you figure out unfamiliar words. Below are some common prefixes and suffixes along with their meanings and examples of their use.

Common Prefixes		
Prefix	**Meaning**	**Sample Words**
en-	to cause to be	enforce
in-	not	ineffective
inter-	between, among	interpersonal
mal-	bad	malfunction
pro-	for, in front	proclaim
re-	again	rerun, rebuild

Common Suffixes		
Suffix	**Meaning**	**Sample Words**
-al	relating to	directional
-dom	state, condition	freedom
-ion	action, condition	rotation, selection
-ous	characterized by	victorious
-ment	result, action	development, entertainment

YOU TRY IT!

Read the following words from the chapter. Underline any prefixes or suffixes. Use the chart above to find the meaning of the prefix or the suffix. Then come up with a definition for each word.

independence,	instability,	malnutrition,
interact,	re-elected,	enslaved,
industrial,	endanger,	migration

Making Generalizations

FOCUS ON READING

As you read about different people and cultures, you probably notice many similarities. Seeing those similarities may lead you to make a generalization. A generalization is a statement that applies to many different situations or people even though it is based on a few specific situations or people. In the following example, a generalization is made from combining new information with information from personal experience. Sometimes you might also make a generalization from reading about several new situations, even though you don't have personal experience with the situation.

Several large rivers cross Southern Africa's plains. The Okavango River flows from Angola into a huge basin in Botswana. This river's water never reaches the ocean. Instead it forms a swampy inland delta that is home to crocodiles, zebras, hippos, and other animals. Many tourists travel to Botswana to see these wild animals in their natural habitat.

From Section 1, Physical Geography

1. What you read:
Tourists will travel a long way to see wild animals.

2. What you know from personal experience:
My family loves to see wild animals in the zoo.

Generalization:
Many people enjoy seeing wild animals in person.

YOU TRY IT!

Read the following sentences about four South African countries. Then make a generalization from these four situations about political instability and a country's economy.

Zimbabwe has suffered from a poor economy and political instability.

Mozambique is one of the world's poorest countries. The economy has been badly damaged by civil war, but it is improving.

Comoros suffers from a lack of resources and political instability. The government of Comoros is struggling to improve education and promote tourism.

Madagascar was ruled for more than 20 years by a socialist dictator. Today the elected president is working to improve the struggling economy.

From Section 3, Southern Africa Today

ATLAS

Strait of
Juan de Fuca

45°N

Puget
Sound

Mount Rainier
14,410 ft
(4,392 m)

Franklin D.
Roosevelt Lake

Pend
Oreille
Lake

Flathead River

Lewis Range

Flathead Lake

Milk River

R O C K Y

Missouri River

Lake
Sakakawea

G R E A T

Columbia River

Willamette River

C A S C A D E   R A N G E

Columbia
Plateau

Bitterroot
Range

Salmon River

CONTINENTAL

Salmon
River
Mts.

Sawtooth
Mts.

Grand
Tetons

Yellowstone
River

Yellowstone
Lake

Bighorn Mts.

Bighorn River

Powder River

Yellowstone River

Fort Peck
Lake

Lake
Oahe

M O U N T A I N S

C O A S T   R A N G E S

Klamath
River

Goose
Lake

Snake River

40°N

Cape
Mendocino

Shasta
Lake

Pyramid
Lake

Wasatch Range

Gannett Peak
13,804 ft
(4,207 m)

Wind River Range

Wind River

DIVIDE

Front Range

South Platte River

North Platte River

Black
Hills

Cheyenne River

White River

Niobrara - River

I N T E R

San Francisco Bay

S I E R R A   N E V A D A

Central Valley

Sacramento River

Lake Tahoe

Great
Salt
Lake

Great
Salt Lake
Desert

Utah
Lake

Uinta
Mts.

Green River

Colorado River

Mount Elbert
14,433 ft
(4,400 m)

Platte River

35°N

G R E A T

B A S I N

San Joaquin River

Mount Whitney
14,494 ft
(4,419 m)

Death Valley

Mojave
Desert

C O L O R A D O

Lake
Powell

Pikes Peak
14,110 ft
(4,301 m)

Republican River

Smoky Hill River

Monterey
Bay

Coast Ranges

Colorado River

Lake
Mead

Grand
Canyon

P L A T E A U

San Juan River

San Luis
Valley

Sangre De Cristo Mts.

P L A I N S

125°W

120°W

PACIFIC

OCEAN

Channel

Islands

Salton
Sea

Imperial
Valley

Painted Desert

DIVIDE

Rio Grande

Canadian   River

30°N

Gila River

Sonoran
Desert

CONTINENTAL

Pecos River

Colorado

To understand the relative locations of Alaska and
Hawaii, as well as the vast distances separating them
from the rest of the United States, see the world map.

Gulf of
California

Amistad
Reservoir

Rio Grande

Kauai

Niihau

Oahu

22°N

HAWAII

155°W

ARCTIC OCEAN

BROOKS RANGE

Molokai

PACIFIC
OCEAN

Lanai

Maui

Kahoolawe

160°W

RUSSIA

Bering Strait

Arctic Circle

Yukon River

CANADA

Nueces R.

Mauna Kea
13,796 ft
(4,206 m)

Hawaii

0   75   150 Miles

0   75   150 Kilometers

Projection: Mercator

19°N

St. Lawrence
Island

St. Matthew
Island

Tanana River

ALASKA   RANGE

Mount McKinley
20,320 ft
(6,194 m)

170°E

55°N

Bering Sea

Nunivak
Island

Kuskokwim River

MEXICO

50°N

Attu Island

W   N
E   S

ALEUTIAN
ISLANDS

180°

170°W

0   250   500 Miles

0   250   500 Kilometers

Projection: Albers Equal Area

Gulf of Alaska

Kodiak Island

160°W

150°W

40°W

Alexander
Archipelago

55°N

PACIFIC
OCEAN

CANADA

Isle
Royale

Mesabi Range

Lake Superior

St. John River

St. Lawrence Seaway

St. Lawrence River

Longfellow Mts.

Penobscot River

Minnesota River

Mississippi River

Wisconsin River

Lake Michigan

Lake Huron

Lake
Champlain

Adirondack
Mts.

Green
Mts.

White
Mts.

Hudson River

Connecticut River

Cape Cod

Des Moines River

Missouri River

Lake Erie

Lake Ontario

ALLEGHENY PLATEAU

Catskill
Mts.

Susquehanna
River

Allegheny R.

Delaware River

Long Island Sound

Long Island

40°N

70°W

P L A I N S

Illinois River

Wabash River

Scioto River

Monongahela R.

Potomac River

APPALACHIAN MOUNTAINS

Delaware
Bay

Chesapeake
Bay

ATLANTIC
OCEAN

nsas R.

Lake of the
Ozarks

OZARK PLATEAU

Ohio River

Kanawha
River

James River

Roanoke River

Pamlico
Sound

Cape Hatteras

35°N

Keystone
Lake

Lake Barkley

Cumberland River

Cumberland Plateau

Great Smoky
Mts.

BLUE RIDGE MOUNTAINS

P I E D M O N T

ula
ake

Arkansas River

White River

Kentucky
Lake

exoma

Ouachita
Mts.

Tennessee River

Coosa River

Oconee River

Savannah River

ELEVATION

Feet		Meters
13,120		4,000
6,560		2,000
1,640		500
656		200
(Sea level) 0		0 (Sea level)
Below sea level		Below sea level

ake

Trinity River

Saline River

Red River

Mississippi River

Pearl River

Tombigbee River

Alabama R.

Chattahoochee River

Altamaha River

Sea Islands

Okefenokee
Swamp

0   100   200 Miles

0   100   200 Kilometers

Projection: Albers Equal Area

Toledo
Bend
Reservoir

G U L F   C O A S T A L   P L A I N

Chandeleur
Islands

Mississippi
Delta

FLORIDA PENINSULA

Cape
Canaveral

80°W

N
W   E
S

95°W

90°W

85°W

Gulf of Mexico

Lake
Okeechobee

BAHAMAS

25°N

The
Everglades

Cape Sable

Florida Keys

Straits of Florida

75°W

Strait of Juan de Fuca

Puget Sound

Franklin D. Roosevelt Lake

Pend Oreille

Seattle

Tacoma

Olympia ★

Spokane

WASHINGTON

Flathead Lake

Great Falls

Fort Peck Lake

Missouri River

NORTH DAKOTA

Lake Sakakawea

Portland

Columbia River

Helena ★

MONTANA

Yellowstone River

Bismarck ★

Salem ★

Eugene ●

OREGON

IDAHO

Boise ★

Sun Valley ●

Billings ●

SOUTH DAKOTA

Lake Oahe

Cape Mendocino

Goose Lake

Shasta Lake

Snake River

Pocatello ●

Yellowstone Lake

WYOMING

Pierre ★

Rapid City ●

Pyramid Lake

Sacramento River

Ogden ●

Great Salt Lake

Salt Lake City ★
Provo ●

Cheyenne ★

NEBRASKA

Berkeley ●

Reno ●

Carson City ★

NEVADA

Lake Tahoe

Sacramento ★

Oakland ●
San Francisco ●

San Francisco Bay

San Jose ●

San Joaquin River

Utah Lake

Green River

Platte River

Monterey Bay

Fresno ●

CALIFORNIA

UTAH

Boulder ●

Vail ●

Denver ★

COLORADO

Aspen ●

Colorado Springs ●

KANSAS

Lake Powell

Pueblo ●

Arkansas River

Las Vegas ●

Lake Mead

Santa Barbara ●

Ventura ●

Los Angeles ●

Riverside ●

Palm Springs ●

Long Beach ●
Anaheim ●
Santa Ana ●

Channel Islands

Salton Sea

Flagstaff ●

Taos ●

Santa Fe ★

OKLAHOMA

Canadian River

San Diego ●

ARIZONA

Albuquerque ●

Oklahoma ●

Amarillo ●

Law

PACIFIC OCEAN

Phoenix ★

NEW MEXICO

Gila River

Casa Grande ●

Tucson ●

Las Cruces ●

Lubbock ●

Brazos River

Abilene ●

Fort W

El Paso ●

Midland ●
Odessa ●

TEXAS

Gulf of California

Pecos River

Colorado R

Austi

To understand the relative locations of Alaska and Hawaii, as well as the vast distances separating them from the rest of the United States, see the world map.

Amistad Reservoir

Rio Grande

San Antonio ●

ARCTIC OCEAN

Arctic Circle

RUSSIA

Corpus Chris

Laredo ●

Pa Isla

MEXICO

Kauai

Niihau

Oahu

HAWAII

Molokai

Honolulu ★

PACIFIC OCEAN

Lanai

Maui

Kahoolawe

Bering Strait

St. Lawrence Island

Nome ●

Yukon River

Hilo ●

Hawaii

St. Matthew Island

Fairbanks ●

CANADA

| 0 | 75 | 150 Miles |
| 0 | 75 | 150 Kilometers |

Projection: Mercator

Nunivak Island

ALASKA

Anchorage ●
Valdez ●

Bering Sea

Skagway ●

Attu Island

Juneau ★

Gulf of Alaska

ALEUTIAN ISLANDS

| 0 | 250 | 500 Miles |
| 0 | 250 | 500 Kilometers |

Projection: Albers Equal Area

Kodiak Island

Alexander Archipelago

PACIFIC OCEAN

CANADA

MAINE

MINNESOTA
Duluth
Superior
Marquette
Sault Ste. Marie

Lake Superior

WISCONSIN

MICHIGAN

Fargo
and ks

Minnesota River

Sioux Falls

Sioux City

IOWA

Minneapolis
St. Paul

Green Bay

Madison
Milwaukee

Grand Rapids
Lansing

Saginaw

Lake Michigan

Lake Huron

Burlington
Montpelier
Augusta

Portland

VT
NH
Concord
Manchester

Lake Champlain

Hudson R.

St. Lawrence River

Connecticut R.

Lake Ontario

Rochester
Syracuse
Albany
Springfield

Boston
Worcester
Providence

MA
CT RI

Cape Cod

NEW YORK

Buffalo

Hartford

New Haven

Bridgeport

Yonkers

Long Island Sound

Long Island

Cedar Rapids
Davenport
Des Moines

Rockford

Chicago

Gary
South Bend
Fort Wayne

Toledo

Lake Erie

Cleveland
Youngstown
Akron

PENNSYLVANIA

Pittsburgh

Susquehanna River

Harrisburg

Allentown

Jersey City
Newark

New York City

Trenton

Camden

NJ

Mississippi River

Illinois River

Peoria

Springfield

INDIANA

Indianapolis

OHIO

Columbus

Dayton
Cincinnati

WEST VIRGINIA

Philadelphia

Baltimore

DE
Dover

Atlantic City

Delaware Bay

MO

Missouri River

MISSOURI

Kansas City
Kansas City

ka

ILLINOIS

St. Louis
East St. Louis

Louisville
Evansville

Lexington

Frankfort

Charleston

Washington, D.C.

Annapolis

Chesapeake Bay

ATLANTIC OCEAN

40°N

70°W

Jefferson City

Lake of the Ozarks

Ohio River

KENTUCKY

VIRGINIA

Richmond

Newport News
Norfolk

Virginia Beach

Keystone Lake

Springfield

Lake Barkley

Kentucky Lake

Nashville

Knoxville

Greensboro
Durham
Raleigh

35°N

Cape Hatteras

Tulsa

nita

Fayetteville

Kentucky River

Chattanooga

TENNESSEE

Asheville

Winston-Salem

NORTH CAROLINA

Charlotte

ula ke

ARKANSAS

Memphis

Huntsville

Greenville

SOUTH CAROLINA

Columbia

Charleston

ke exoma

Little Rock

Pine Bluff

Atlanta

Savannah River

Sea Islands

allas

Shreveport

Vicksburg

MISSISSIPPI

Jackson

Meridian

Montgomery

ALABAMA

Birmingham

Columbus

GEORGIA

Macon

Savannah

Chattahoochee R.

30°N

co

Red River

Toledo Bend Reservoir

LOUISIANA

Beaumont
Houston

Baton Rouge

New Orleans

Biloxi

Mobile

Pensacola

Chandeleur Islands

Tallahassee

Jacksonville

Galveston

Gulf of Mexico

FLORIDA

Gainesville

Orlando

Cape Canaveral

80°W

Tampa
St. Petersburg

Lake Okeechobee

Fort Myers

Fort Lauderdale

Miami

BAHAMAS

25°N

Cape Sable

Florida Keys

Straits of Florida

75°W

N
W E
S

95°W
90°W
85°W

National capital
State capitals
Other cities

0   100   200 Miles
0 100   200 Kilometers

Projection: Albers Equal Area

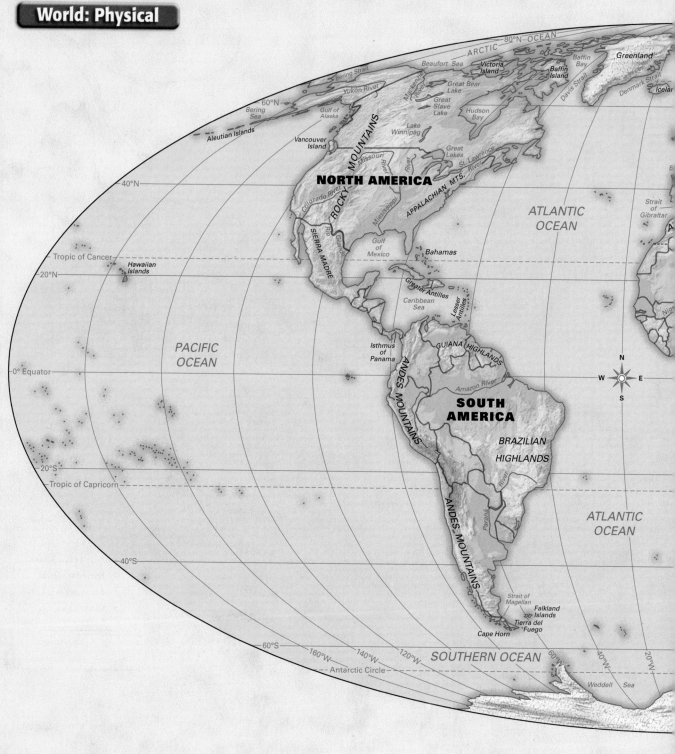

ARCTIC 80°N OCEAN

Beaufort Sea
Victoria Island
Baffin Island
Baffin Bay
Greenland
Davis Strait
Denmark Strait
Iceland

Bering Strait
Yukon River
Mackenzie River
Great Bear Lake
Great Slave Lake
Hudson Bay

60°N
Bering Sea
Gulf of Alaska
ROCKY MOUNTAINS
Lake Winnipeg
Great Lakes
St. Lawrence River
Aleutian Islands
Vancouver Island
Missouri River

NORTH AMERICA

40°N
Colorado River
Mississippi
APPALACHIAN MTS.

ATLANTIC OCEAN

Strait of Gibraltar

SIERRA MADRE
Rio Grande
Gulf of Mexico
Bahamas

Tropic of Cancer
Hawaiian Islands
20°N

Greater Antilles
Caribbean Sea
Lesser Antilles

PACIFIC OCEAN

Isthmus of Panama
GUIANA HIGHLANDS

ANDES MOUNTAINS
Amazon River

0° Equator

N
W   E
S

SOUTH AMERICA

BRAZILIAN HIGHLANDS

20°S
Tropic of Capricorn

Paraná River

ANDES MOUNTAINS

ATLANTIC OCEAN

40°S

Strait of Magellan
Falkland Islands
Tierra del Fuego
Cape Horn

60°S
160°W 140°W 120°W
SOUTHERN OCEAN
60°W 40°W 20°W
Antarctic Circle
Weddell Sea

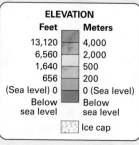

ELEVATION

Feet		Meters
13,120		4,000
6,560		2,000
1,640		500
656		200
(Sea level) 0		0 (Sea level)
Below sea level		Below sea level

Ice cap

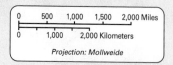

0   500   1,000   1,500   2,000 Miles
0   1,000   2,000 Kilometers

Projection: Mollweide

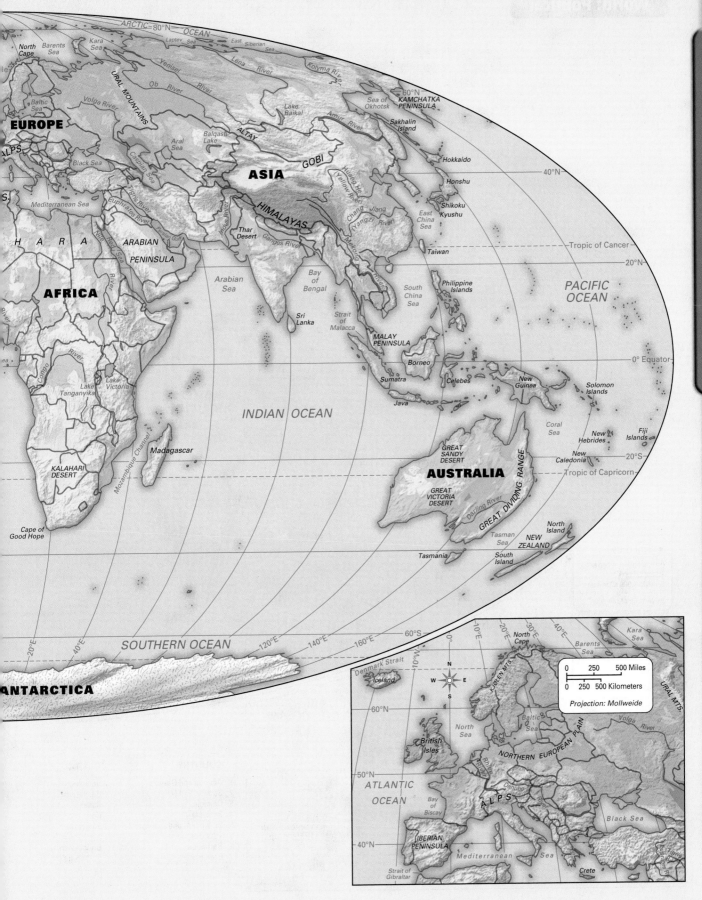

EUROPE

ARCTIC 80°N OCEAN

North Cape
Barents Sea
Kara Sea
Laptev Sea
East Siberian Sea

URAL MOUNTAINS

Ob River
Yenisei River
Lena River
Kolyma River

Volga River

60°N

Sea of Okhotsk

KAMCHATKA PENINSULA

Aral Sea
Balqash Lake

Lake Baikal

ALTAY

Amur River

Sakhalin Island

Black Sea

Caspian Sea

ASIA

GOBI

40°N

Hokkaido

Honshu

Mediterranean Sea

Tigris River
Euphrates River

Persian Gulf

ARABIAN PENINSULA

HIMALAYAS

Huáng He (Yellow River)

Chang Jiang (Yangzi) River

East China Sea

Shikoku
Kyushu

SAHARA

Nile River
Red Sea

Thar Desert

Ganges River

Indus River

Mekong River

Tropic of Cancer

20°N

Taiwan

AFRICA

Arabian Sea

Bay of Bengal

South China Sea

Philippine Islands

PACIFIC OCEAN

Sri Lanka

Strait of Malacca

MALAY PENINSULA

0° Equator

Congo River

Lake Tanganyika
Lake Victoria

Borneo

Sumatra

Celebes

New Guinea

Solomon Islands

Java

INDIAN OCEAN

Coral Sea

New Hebrides

Fiji Islands

Madagascar

Mozambique Channel

GREAT SANDY DESERT

GREAT DIVIDING RANGE

New Caledonia

20°S

KALAHARI DESERT

AUSTRALIA

Tropic of Capricorn

GREAT VICTORIA DESERT

Darling River

Cape of Good Hope

North Island

Tasman Sea

NEW ZEALAND

SOUTHERN OCEAN

60°S

120°E
140°E
160°E

Tasmania

South Island

ANTARCTICA

20°E
40°E

ATLAS

Denmark Strait
Iceland

North Cape

Barents Sea

Kara Sea

10°E
20°E
30°E
40°E

60°N

KJØLEN MTS.

Baltic Sea

Volga River

URAL MTS.

0 250 500 Miles
0 250 500 Kilometers

Projection: Mollweide

British Isles

North Sea

NORTHERN EUROPEAN PLAIN

Rhine River

50°N

ATLANTIC OCEAN

Bay of Biscay

ALPS

Danube

Black Sea

40°N

IBERIAN PENINSULA

Mediterranean Sea

Strait of Gibraltar

Crete

ATLAS

ARCTIC OCEAN

Greenland
(DENMARK)

ALASKA
(U.S.)

60°N

CANADA

Godthåb

ICELA

Aleutian Islands

Vancouver

Winnipeg

NORTH
AMERICA

Ottawa   Montreal

40°N

Chicago

Toronto

New York City

UNITED
STATES

Washington,
D.C.

ATLANTIC
OCEAN

Raba

Casablanca

MOROCC

Los Angeles

Houston

Bermuda
(U.K.)

Western
Sahara
(Claimed by
Morocco)

MEXICO

Tropic of Cancer

20°N

Mexico
City

MAURITANIA

Nouakchott

HAWAII
(U.S.)

CAPE VERDE

SENEGAL

Dakar

GAMBIA

Bam

Be

GUINEA-BISSAU

GUINEA

PACIFIC
OCEAN

Caracas

VENEZUELA   GUYANA

Georgetown   SURINAME

SIERRA
LEONE

CÔ
D'IV

Bogotá

Paramaribo   French Guiana
(FRANCE)

LIBERIA

COLOMBIA

0° Equator

Quito

N

KIRIBATI

Galápagos
Islands
(ECUADOR)

ECUADOR

W   E

PERU

SOUTH
AMERICA

S

SAMOA

American
Samoa

Lima

BRAZIL

Brasília

20°S

BOLIVIA

La Paz

TONGA

Sucre

Tropic of Capricorn

PARAGUAY

Rio de Janeiro

São Paulo

ATLANTIC
OCEAN

CHILE

Asunción

⊕ National capital

URUGUAY

● Other city

Santiago

Buenos
Aires

Montevideo

0   500   1,000 Miles

ARGENTINA

0 500 1,000 Kilometers

40°S

Projection: Mollweide

Falkland
Islands
(U.K.)

South
Georgia
(U.K.)

South Sandwich
Islands

60°S

SOUTHERN OCEAN   60°

Antarctic Circle

160°W   140°W   120°W

40°

20°

90°W   80°W

FLORIDA
(U.S.)

Tropic of Cancer

0   200   400 Miles

Nassau

70°W

60°W

20°N

0 200 400 Kilometers

BAHAMAS

Projection: Mercator

ATLANTIC   OCEAN

Havana

Gulf of
Mexico

CUBA

Turks and Caicos Is.
(U.K.)

Cayman Is.
(U.K.)

HAITI

DOMINICAN
REPUBLIC

Virgin Islands
(U.S. and U.K.)

1

MEXICO

BELIZE

Port-au-Prince

20°N

2

JAMAICA

Santo
Domingo

Guadeloupe (FRANCE)

Belmopan

Kingston

Puerto Rico
(U.S.)

3

GUATEMALA

HONDURAS

Caribbean   Sea

Martinique (FRANCE)

Guatemala City

Tegucigalpa

4

6

San Salvador

NICARAGUA

Netherlands
Antilles
(NETHERLANDS)

5

EL SALVADOR

Managua

Aruba
(NETHERLANDS)

7

Port-of-
Spain

N

COSTA RICA

Panama
City

TRINIDAD AND
TOBAGO

W   E

San Jose

10°N

S

PANAMA

VENEZUELA

PACIFIC   OCEAN

COLOMBIA

GUYANA

COUNTRY	CAPITAL
1 Antigua and Barbuda	St. Johns
2 St. Kitts and Nevis	Basseterre
3 Dominica	Roseau
4 St. Lucia	Castries
5 St. Vincent and the Grenadines	Kingstown
6 Barbados	Bridgetown
7 Grenada	St. George's

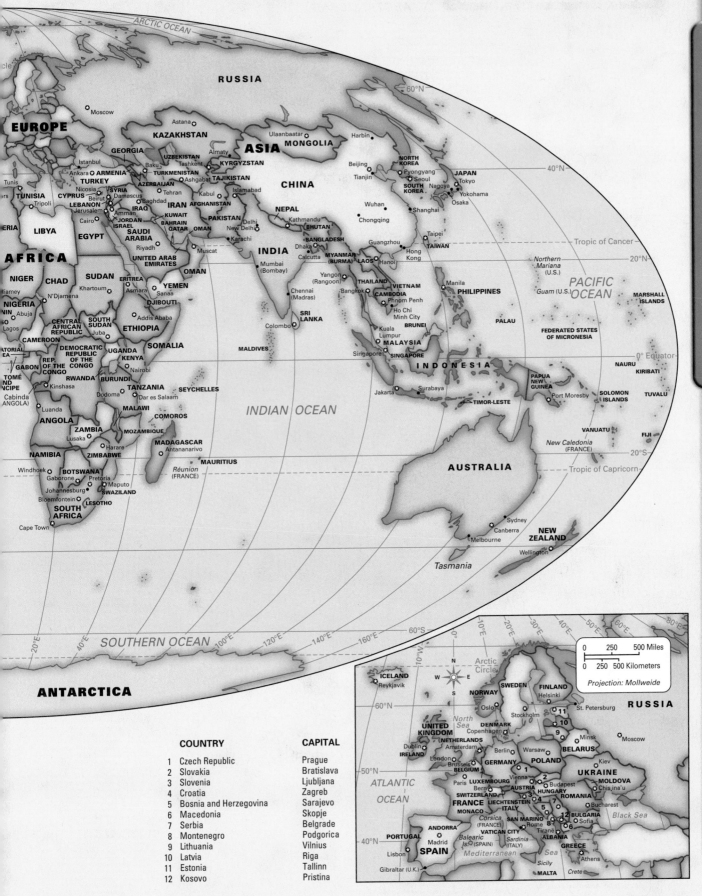

COUNTRY	CAPITAL
1 Czech Republic	Prague
2 Slovakia	Bratislava
3 Slovenia	Ljubljana
4 Croatia	Zagreb
5 Bosnia and Herzegovina	Sarajevo
6 Macedonia	Skopje
7 Serbia	Belgrade
8 Montenegro	Podgorica
9 Lithuania	Vilnius
10 Latvia	Riga
11 Estonia	Tallinn
12 Kosovo	Pristina

Projection: Mollweide

North America: Physical

ASIA

EUROPE

ARCTIC OCEAN

+North Pole

POLAR ICE PACK

160°E

170°E

10°E

0°

10°W

20°W

30°W

St. Lawrence Island

Bering Strait

Nunivak Island

Bering Sea

180°

170°W

Queen Elizabeth Islands

Ellesmere Island

Greenland

Denmark Strait

BROOKS RANGE

Beaufort Sea

Banks Island

Baffin Bay

40°W

Victoria Island

Baffin Island

Davis Strait

Cape Farewell

Mt. McKinley 20,320 ft (6,194 m)

ALASKA RANGE

Yukon River

Mackenzie River

Great Bear Lake

50°N

50°N

Gulf of Alaska

Kodiak Island

YUKON PLATEAU

Peace River

Southampton Island

Hudson Strait

Labrador Sea

Alexander Archipelago

Athabasca River

Lake Athabasca

Coats Island

Queen Charlotte Islands

Mansel Island

Vancouver Island

R O C K Y

Saskatchewan River

Nelson River

CANADIAN

Hudson Bay

S H I E L D

Anticosti Island

Newfoundland

Mount Rainier 14,410 ft (4,392 m)

CASCADE RANGE

COAST RANGE

Lake Winnipeg

Prince Edward Island

Gulf of St. Lawrence

Cape Breton Island

40°N

40°N

Columbia River

G R E A T

St. Lawrence River

PACIFIC OCEAN

Cape Mendocino

Snake River

M O U N T A I N S

Missouri River

BLACK HILLS

Superior

Lake Michigan

Lake Huron

MOUNTAINS

Cape Cod

Long Island

ATLANTIC OCEAN

SIERRA NEVADA

GREAT BASIN

Great Salt Lake

P L A I N S

Lake Ontario

APPALACHIAN

CENTRAL VALLEY

DEATH VALLEY

Platte River

Mississippi River

INTERIOR PLAINS

Ohio R.

PIEDMONT

Cape Hatteras

30°N

30°N

Bermuda

CENTRAL VALLEY RANGES

Mount Whitney 14,494 ft (4,419 m)

Colorado River

COLORADO PLATEAU

OZARK PLATEAU

Cumberland R.

Tennessee River

ATLANTIC COASTAL PLAIN

Guadalupe Island

Arkansas River

Red River

Mississippi River

Cape Canaveral

BAJA CALIFORNIA

Gulf of California

Rio Grande

Brazos River

GULF COASTAL PLAIN

FLORIDA PENINSULA

Tropic of Cancer

20°N

20°N

SIERRA MADRE OCCIDENTAL

Gulf of Mexico

Florida Keys

Straits of Florida

Bahamas

SIERRA MADRE ORIENTAL

Cuba

Popocatépetl 17,887 ft (5,452 m)

YUCATÁN PENINSULA

Greater Antilles

Jamaica

Hispaniola

Puerto Rico

Lesser Antilles

10°N

SIERRA MADRE DEL SUR

Caribbean Sea

Trinidad

CENTRAL AMERICA

Lake Nicaragua

ISTHMUS OF PANAMA

0° Equator

SOUTH AMERICA

160°W 150°W 140°W 130°W 120°W 110°W 100°W 90°W 80°W 70°W 60°W

ELEVATION

Feet		Meters
13,120		4,000
6,560		2,000
1,640		500
656		200
(Sea level) 0		0 (Sea level)
Below sea level		Below sea level
	Ice cap	

0   300   600 Miles

0   300   600 Kilometers

Projection: Azimuthal Equal Area

ASIA

ARCTIC OCEAN

North Pole

EUROPE

St. Lawrence Island
Bering Sea
Nunivak Island

Point Barrow

Queen Elizabeth Islands

Ellesmere Island

Greenland (DENMARK)

ICELAND

Beaufort Sea

Banks Island

Baffin Bay

ALASKA (U.S.)

Anchorage

Kodiak Island

Gulf of Alaska

Victoria Island

Great Bear Lake

Baffin Island

Davis Strait

Denmark Strait

Arctic Circle

Cape Farewell

Juneau

Alexander Archipelago

Queen Charlotte Islands

Great Slave Lake

Southampton Island
Coats Island
Mansel Island

Hudson Strait

Labrador Sea

PACIFIC OCEAN

Vancouver Island

Edmonton

CANADA

Hudson Bay

Anticosti Island

Newfoundland

St. Pierre and Miquelon (FRANCE)

Vancouver
Seattle
Portland

Calgary

Lake Winnipeg

Winnipeg

Lake Superior
Lake Huron
Lake Michigan

Prince Edward Island
Gulf of St. Lawrence

Cape Breton Island

Quebec
Montreal
Ottawa
Toronto

Lake Ontario
Lake Erie

Boston
Cape Cod
New York City
Philadelphia

ATLANTIC OCEAN

Minneapolis
Milwaukee
Chicago

Detroit
Cleveland
Columbus

Baltimore
Washington, D.C.

San Francisco
San Jose

Great Salt Lake

Salt Lake City

Denver
Kansas City

Indianapolis
St. Louis

Norfolk

UNITED STATES

Bermuda (U.K.)

Los Angeles
San Diego
Tijuana

Memphis

Atlanta
Birmingham

Phoenix

Dallas

Jacksonville

Austin
San Antonio

Houston

New Orleans

Tropic of Cancer

Monterrey

Gulf of California

Gulf of Mexico

Florida Keys

Miami
Nassau

BAHAMAS

Turks and Caicos Islands (U.K.)

Puerto Rico (U.S.)

DOMINICAN REPUBLIC

ST. KITTS & NEVIS

ANTIGUA & BARBUDA

MEXICO

Guadalajara
Mexico City
Puebla

Mérida

Havana
CUBA

Straits of Florida

San Juan

Guadeloupe (FRANCE)

DOMINICA

Cayman Is. (U.K.)

Kingston
JAMAICA

HAITI
Port-au-Prince

Santo Domingo

Virgin Is. (U.S. U.K.)

Martinique (FRANCE)

ST. LUCIA

BARBADOS

ST. VINCENT AND THE GRENADINES

GRENADA

Belmopan
BELIZE

Caribbean Sea

Netherlands Antilles (NETHERLANDS)

GUATEMALA
HONDURAS

Guatemala City
San Salvador
EL SALVADOR

Tegucigalpa
NICARAGUA
Managua

Aruba (NETHERLANDS)

TRINIDAD AND TOBAGO

San José

Panama Canal

Panama City

COSTA RICA

PANAMA

SOUTH AMERICA

Equator

N
W E
S

National capital
Other city

0   300   600 Miles
0   300   600 Kilometers

Projection: Azimuthal Equal-Area

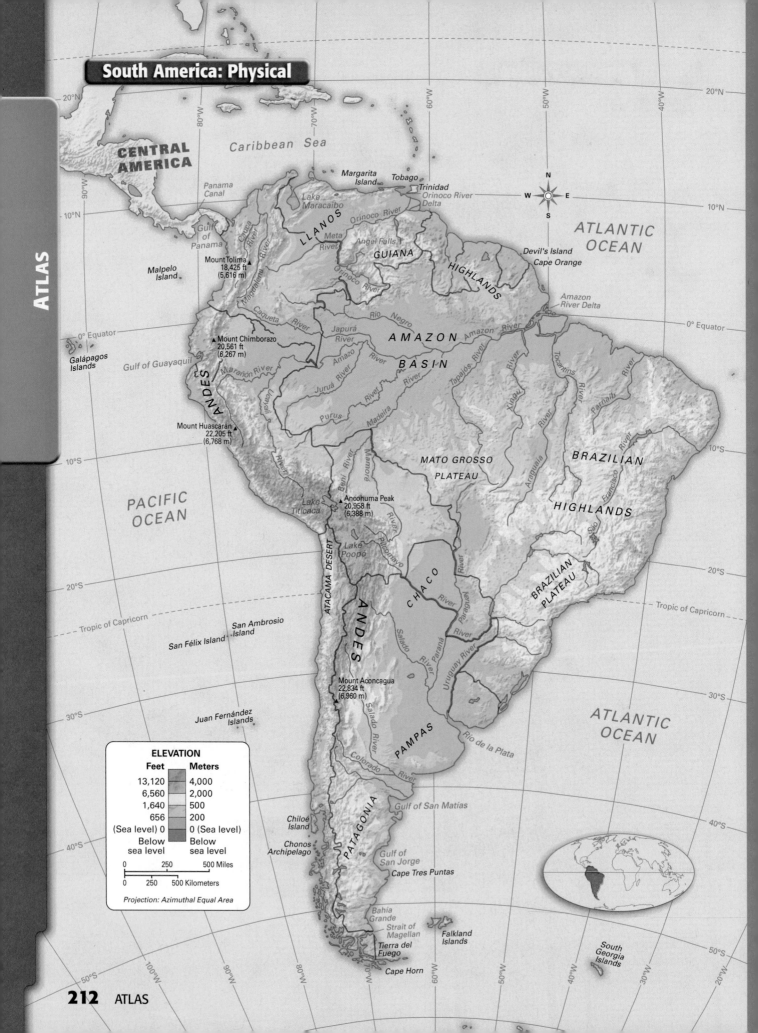

South America: Physical

CENTRAL
AMERICA

Caribbean Sea

Panama
Canal

20°N

20°N

Margarita
Island   Tobago

Trinidad

Orinoco River
Delta

Gulf of
Panama

LLANOS

Lake
Maracaibo

Orinoco River

Meta
River

Angel Falls

GUIANA

HIGHLANDS

ATLANTIC
OCEAN

10°N

10°N

Devil's Island
Cape Orange

Malpelo
Island

Mount Tolima
18,425 ft
(5,616 m)

Caquetá

River

Orinoco River

Río

Negro

Amazon
River Delta

Galápagos
Islands

Gulf of Guayaquil

Mount Chimborazo
20,561 ft
(6,267 m)

Japurá
River

AMAZON

Amazon

River

BASIN

0° Equator

0° Equator

Marañón River

Amazo

River

Juruá

River

Tapajós River

Tocantins

River

River

ANDES

Purus

River

Madeira

River

Xingú

Parnaíba

River

BRAZILIAN

River

10°S

10°S

Mount Huascarán
22,205 ft
(6,768 m)

Beni River

MATO GROSSO

PLATEAU

Araguaia

River

São

Francisco

HIGHLANDS

Lake
Titicaca

Ancohuma Peak
20,958 ft
(6,388 m)

Mamoré

River

PACIFIC
OCEAN

Lake
Poopó

Pilcomayo

River

BRAZILIAN
PLATEAU

ATACAMA DESERT

CHACO

River

20°S

20°S

San Ambrosio
Island

Paraguay

River

Tropic of Capricorn

Tropic of Capricorn

San Félix Island

ANDES

Salado

River

Paraná

Uruguay River

River

Juan Fernández
Islands

Mount Aconcagua
22,834 ft
(6,960 m)

30°S

ATLANTIC
OCEAN

30°S

Salado

River

PAMPAS

Río de la Plata

Colorado

River

ELEVATION

Feet		Meters
13,120		4,000
6,560		2,000
1,640		500
656		200
(Sea level) 0		0 (Sea level)
Below sea level		Below sea level

Gulf of San Matías

Chiloé
Island

PATAGONIA

Chonos
Archipelago

Gulf of
San Jorge

Cape Tres Puntas

0   250   500 Miles

0   250   500 Kilometers

Projection: Azimuthal Equal Area

40°S

40°S

Bahía
Grande

Strait of
Magellan

Falkland
Islands

Tierra del
Fuego

South
Georgia
Islands

Cape Horn

50°S

50°S

South America: Political

CENTRAL AMERICA

Caribbean Sea

Barranquilla
Cartagena

Caracas

Lake Maracaibo

VENEZUELA

Georgetown
Paramaribo
Cayenne

ATLANTIC OCEAN

Medellín

Bogotá

GUYANA

SURINAME

French Guiana (FRANCE)

Malpelo Island (COLOMBIA)

COLOMBIA

Cali

Quito

ECUADOR

Guayaquil

Galápagos Islands (ECUADOR)

Belém

0° Equator

PERU

Trujillo

BRAZIL

Recife

Callao

Lima

PACIFIC OCEAN

Lake Titicaca

La Paz

Arequipa

Lake Poopó

BOLIVIA

Sucre

Brasília

Salvador

Belo Horizonte

PARAGUAY

Campinas
São Paulo

Asunción

Rio de Janeiro

Curitiba

Tropic of Capricorn

San Ambrosio Island (CHILE)

San Félix Island (CHILE)

Pôrto Alegre

CHILE

Juan Fernández Islands (CHILE)

Córdoba

Valparaíso
Santiago

Rosario

Buenos Aires

URUGUAY

Montevideo

ATLANTIC OCEAN

ARGENTINA

⊛ National capital
• Other city

0   250   500 Miles
0 250   500 Kilometers

Projection: Azimuthal Equal-Area

Strait of Magellan

Falkland Islands (U.K.)

Tierra del Fuego

South Georgia Island (U.K.)

Europe: Physical

ASIA

SOUTHWEST ASIA

AFRICA

URAL MOUNTAINS

NORTHERN EUROPEAN PLAIN

PLAINS

Caspian Sea

Mt. Elbrus (5,642 m)
18,510 ft

CAUCASUS MTS.

Sea of Azov

CRIMEAN PENINSULA

Black Sea

Sea of Marmara

Aegean Sea

Rhodes

Crete

BALKAN PENINSULA

TRANSYLVANIAN ALPS

CARPATHIAN

DINARIC ALPS

Adriatic Sea

APENNINES

Tyrrhenian Sea

Sicily

Malta

Mediterranean Sea

Corsica

Sardinia

Balearic Islands

PYRENEES

IBERIAN PENINSULA

Cape Finisterre

Strait of Gibraltar

Bay of Biscay

ATLANTIC OCEAN

ALPS

Mont Blanc (4,810 m)
15,781 ft

Lake Geneva

ARCTIC OCEAN

KJØLEN MOUNTAINS

Norwegian Sea

Arctic Circle

North Cape

Barents Sea

KOLA PENINSULA

White Sea

Lake Onega

Lake Ladoga

Rybinsk Reservoir

Gulf of Finland

Gulf of Bothnia

Lake Vänern

Lake Vättern

Kattegat

Skagerrak

BALTIC

Baltic Sea

North Sea

Iceland

Faeroe Islands

Shetland Islands

Orkney Islands

Hebrides

British Isles

Irish Sea

PENNINES

English Channel

Thames River

Seine River

Loire River

Garonne River

Rhine River

Elbe River

Oder River

Vistula River

Danube River

Po River

Tiber River

Ebro River

Tagus River

Guadiana River

Guadalquivir River

Duero River

Rhône River

Dniester River

Nistru River

Dnipro River

Don River

Volga River

Kama River

Dvina River

North Dvina River

Pechora River

Vistula River

Vardava R.

Daugava R.

Pechora

White Sea

70°N

60°N

50°N

40°N

70°E

50°E

40°E

30°E

20°E

10°E

0°

10°W

20°W

30°W

40°W

50°W

30°E

20°E

30°E

10°W

20°W

N
E
S
W

ELEVATION

Feet	Meters
13,120	4,000
6,560	2,000
1,640	500
656	200
(Sea level) 0	0 (Sea level)
Below sea level	Below sea level

Ice cap

0   150   300 Miles

0   150   300 Kilometers

Projection: Azimuthal Equal Area

Europe: Political

ATLAS

National capital
Other city

| 0 | 150 | 300 Miles |
| 0 | 150 | 300 Kilometers |

Projection: Azimuthal Equal-Area

ASIA

URAL MOUNTAINS

RUSSIA

Nizhny Novgorod

Moscow

Barents Sea

White Sea

FINLAND

St. Petersburg

Helsinki

Gulf of Finland

Tallinn

ESTONIA

Riga

LATVIA

LITHUANIA

Vilnius

Minsk

BELARUS

RUSSIA

Kiev

UKRAINE

MOLDOVA

Chişinău

Caspian Sea

Black Sea

SOUTHWEST ASIA

North Cape

SWEDEN

Stockholm

Göteborg

Baltic Sea

Gulf of Bothnia

Warsaw

POLAND

Kraków

SLOVAKIA

Bratislava

Budapest

HUNGARY

Bucharest

ROMANIA

Sofia

BULGARIA

Skopje

MACEDONIA

Tirana

ALBANIA

Pristina

KOSOVO

MONTENEGRO

Podgorica

Aegean Sea

Athens

GREECE

Rhodes

Crete

ARCTIC OCEAN

NORWAY

Oslo

Bergen

DENMARK

Copenhagen

Hamburg

GERMANY

Berlin

Dresden

Prague

CZECH REPUBLIC

Vienna

AUSTRIA

LIECHTENSTEIN

Vaduz

SLOVENIA

Ljubljana

Zagreb

CROATIA

BOSNIA AND HERZEGOVINA

Sarajevo

Belgrade

SERBIA

SAN MARINO

San Marino

Adriatic Sea

Rome

VATICAN CITY

ITALY

Naples

Sicily

MALTA

Valletta

Mediterranean Sea

Sardinia (ITALY)

Corsica (FRANCE)

Cologne

Bonn

Luxembourg

Munich

SWITZERLAND

Bern

Lake Geneva

Milan

Monaco

Monaco

Lyon

Marseille

Amsterdam

THE NETHERLANDS

Brussels

BELGIUM

LUXEMBOURG

Paris

FRANCE

North Sea

UNITED KINGDOM

Edinburgh

SCOTLAND

Liverpool

ENGLAND

London

WALES

NORTHERN IRELAND

Belfast

Dublin

IRELAND

British Isles

English Channel

Channel Islands (U.K.)

Shetland Islands

Faeroe Islands (DENMARK)

ICELAND

Reykjavik

ATLANTIC OCEAN

Bay of Biscay

PYRENEES

ANDORRA

Andorra la Vella

Barcelona

Balearic Islands (SPAIN)

Valencia

SPAIN

Madrid

Seville

Gibraltar (U.K.)

Strait of Gibraltar

AFRICA

PORTUGAL

Lisbon

Arctic Circle

North Cape

70°N

60°N

50°N

40°N

30°W

20°W

10°W

0°

10°E

20°E

30°E

40°E

50°E

60°E

Asia: Physical

ELEVATION

Feet	Meters
13,120	4,000
6,560	2,000
1,640	500
656	200
0 (Sea level)	0 (Sea level)
Below sea level	Below sea level

Ice cap

0 250 500 750 Miles
0 250 500 750 Kilometers

Projection: Two-Point Equidistant

EUROPE

AFRICA

AUSTRALIA

North Pole

Arctic Circle

Wrangel Island
New Siberian Islands
Aleutian Islands
KAMCHATKA PENINSULA
Bering Sea
Sea of Okhotsk
Sakhalin Island
Kuril Islands
Hokkaido
CENTRAL RANGE
KOLYMA MTS.
CHERSKIY RANGE
VERKHOYANSKY RANGE
STANOVOY MOUNTAINS
Aldan River
Lena River
Amur River
GREATER KHINGAN RANGE
YABLONOVY RANGE
Shilka River
Lake Baykal
MONGOLIAN PLATEAU
GOBI
QIN LING
He Huang (Yellow River)
NORTH CHINA PLAIN
Yellow Sea
Sea of Japan (East Sea)
Honshu
Shikoku
Kyushu
Korea Strait
Ryukyu Islands
Okinawa
East China Sea
Taiwan
Luzon Strait
Luzon
Philippines
Mindanao
Celebes Sea
Borneo
Celebes
Banda Sea
Molucca
New Guinea
MACKE MOUNTAINS
Arafura Sea
PACIFIC OCEAN

SIBERIA
CENTRAL SIBERIAN PLATEAU
Tunguska River
Angara River
Yenisey River
Lower Tunguska River
TAYMYR PENINSULA
North Land
Franz Josef Land
Novaya Zemlya
Kara Sea
Barents Sea
WEST SIBERIAN PLAIN
Ob River
Irtysh River
Ishim River
SAYAN MOUNTAINS
ALTAY MOUNTAINS
TIAN SHAN
KAZAKH UPLANDS
Balqash Lake
TARIM BASIN
TAKLIMAKAN DESERT
KUNLUN MOUNTAINS
PLATEAU OF TIBET
Mount Everest 29,035 ft (8,850 m)
HIMALAYAS
Brahmaputra River
Nu River
Chang Jiang (Yangtze) River
Mekong River
Hong River
Gulf of Tonkin
Xi River
Hainan
South China Sea
INDOCHINA PENINSULA
Chao Phraya River
MALAY PENINSULA
Gulf of Thailand
Sumatra
Bangka
Java Sea
Java
Mentawai Islands
BOHEA HILLS

URAL MOUNTAINS
USTYURT PLATEAU
TURAN LOWLAND
KYZYL KUM
KARA KUM
Aral Sea
Amu Darya
Syr Darya
HINDU KUSH
INDO-GANGETIC PLAIN
THAR DESERT
Ganges River
Indus River
Sutlej River
DECCAN PLATEAU
Godavari River
WESTERN GHATS
EASTERN GHATS
Irrawaddy River
Bay of Bengal
Andaman Islands
Nicobar Islands
Sri Lanka
Lakshadweep Islands
Maldives
INDIAN OCEAN

Caspian Sea
CAUCASUS MTS.
Mount Ararat 16,945 ft (5,165 m)
ANATOLIAN PLATEAU
Black Sea
Bosporus
Cyprus
Mediterranean Sea
SINAI PENINSULA
Red Sea
SYRIAN DESERT
AN-NAFUD
Tigris River
Euphrates River
Persian Gulf
ZAGROS MTS.
GREAT SALT DESERT
RUB' AL-KHALI
Arabian Sea
Gulf of Oman
Gulf of Aden
Socotra Island

Tropic of Cancer
Equator

Asia: Political

National capitals
Other cities

750 Miles
250   500   750 Kilometers

Projection: Two-Point Equidistant

PACIFIC OCEAN

AUSTRALIA

New Guinea

Arafura Sea

TIMOR-LESTE

Dili

Celebes Sea

PHILIPPINES

Manila

Luzon Strait

Taipei

TAIWAN

East China Sea

Ryukyu Islands (JAPAN)

JAPAN

Tokyo
Yokohama
Kyoto
Osaka
Hiroshima
Nagasaki
Sapporo

Kuril Islands (RUSSIA)

Sakhalin Island

Sea of Okhotsk

Bering Sea

Aleutian Islands

North Pole

Arctic Circle

RUSSIA

Yakutsk

Laptev Sea

Kara Sea

Barents Sea

Novosibirsk
Omsk
Yekaterinburg

URAL MOUNTAINS

Moscow

EUROPE

RUSSIA

Black Sea

Istanbul
Ankara
Izmir

TURKEY

GEORGIA
Tbilisi
ARMENIA
Yerevan

CYPRUS
Nicosia
LEBANON
Beirut
ISRAEL
Tel Aviv
Jerusalem

SYRIA
Damascus
Amman
JORDAN

Mediterranean Sea

AFRICA

Red Sea

Jidda
Mecca

SAUDI ARABIA

Riyadh

YEMEN
Sanaa

Gulf of Aden

Socotra (YEMEN)

Mosul
Baghdad
Basra
IRAQ

KUWAIT
Kuwait City

BAHRAIN
Manama
QATAR
Doha

UNITED ARAB EMIRATES

Abu Dhabi

OMAN
Masqat (Muscat)

Persian Gulf

Arabian Sea

IRAN
Tehran
Shiraz

AZERBAIJAN
Baku

Caspian Sea

TURKMENISTAN
Ashgabat

Astana

KAZAKHSTAN

Lake Balkhash

Aral Sea

UZBEKISTAN
Tashkent

Almaty

Bishkek
KYRGYZSTAN
TAJIKISTAN
Dushanbe

AFGHANISTAN
Kabul

Chelyabinsk

Irkutsk

Lake Baykal

Ulaanbaatar

MONGOLIA

CHINA

Harbin
Fushun
Beijing
Dalian
Qingdao

NORTH KOREA
Pyongyang
SOUTH KOREA
Seoul
Pusan

Yellow Sea

Shanghai
Nanjing
Wuhan
Chongqing
Chengdu

Guangzhou
Hong Kong
Macao
Hainan (CHINA)

South China Sea

Hanoi
VIETNAM
Vientiane
LAOS
THAILAND
Bangkok
CAMBODIA
Phnom Penh

MYANMAR (BURMA)
Mandalay
Yangon (Rangoon)

Gulf of Thailand

Ho Chi Minh City

BRUNEI
Bandar Seri Begawan

MALAYSIA
Kuala Lumpur
SINGAPORE
Singapore

INDONESIA

Medan

Jakarta
Bandung

Java Sea
Ujung Pandang
Surabaya

PAKISTAN
Islamabad
Lahore
Karachi

Delhi
New Delhi
Jaipur
Ahmadabad

NEPAL
Kathmandu
BHUTAN
Thimphu

BANGLADESH
Dhaka

Kolkata (Calcutta)

INDIA

Mumbai (Bombay)
Bangalore
Chennai (Madras)

Bay of Bengal

Andaman Islands (INDIA)

Andaman Sea

Nicobar Islands (INDIA)

SRI LANKA
Colombo

Male
MALDIVES

Lakshadweep Islands (INDIA)

INDIAN OCEAN

Tropic of Cancer

Equator

EUROPE

SOUTHWEST ASIA

Azores

Madeira Islands

Strait of Gibraltar

ATLAS MOUNTAINS

Mediterranean Sea

Gulf of Sidra

Suez Canal

Persian Gulf

Canary Islands

Tropic of Cancer

Cape Blanc

EL DJOUF

S A H A R A

AHAGGAR MOUNTAINS

AIR MTS.

LIBYAN DESERT

QATTARA DEPRESSION

Nile River

Lake Nasser

Red Sea

NUBIAN DESERT

TIBESTI MOUNTAINS

Cape Verde Islands

Cape Verde

Niger River

Senegal R.

S A H E L

S U D A N

CHAD BASIN

Lake Chad

Blue Nile

White Nile

Lake Tana

Gulf of Aden

FOUTA DJALLON

White Volta R.

Black Volta R.

Benue River

Lake Volta

SUDAN BASIN

ETHIOPIAN HIGHLANDS

HORN OF AFRICA

SOMALI PENINSULA

Cape Palmas

Gulf of Guinea

ADAMAWA MTS.

Ubangi River

Congo River

Lake Albert

Lake Edward

RIFT VALLEY

Lake Turkana

Mount Kenya 17,058 ft (5,199 m)

Cape Lopez

CONGO BASIN

Kasai River

Lake Kivu

Lake Victoria

SERENGETI PLAIN

Mount Kilimanjaro 19,340 ft (5,895 m)

INDIAN OCEAN

Equator

Lake Tanganyika

MASAI STEPPE

Zanzibar

Seychelles

MITUMBA MOUNTAINS

WESTERN RIFT VALLEY

EASTERN RIFT VALLEY

Lake Rukwa

Ascension

ATLANTIC OCEAN

Cuanza River

Lake Mweru

Lake Malawi (Nyasa)

Cape Delgado

Comoro Islands

Madagascar

Lake Kariba

Zambezi River

Mozambique Channel

Okavango Delta

Victoria Falls

Mauritius

Réunion

NAMIB DESERT

KALAHARI BASIN

KALAHARI DESERT

Impopo River

Tropic of Capricorn

Orange River

Vaal River

DRAKENSBERG MOUNTAINS

GREAT KARROO

Cape of Good Hope

ELEVATION

Feet		Meters
13,120		4,000
6,560		2,000
1,640		500
656		200
(Sea level) 0		0 (Sea level)
Below sea level		Below sea level

0   250   500 Miles

0   250   500 Kilometers

Projection: Azimuthal Equal-Area

ATLAS

EUROPE

SOUTHWEST ASIA

Azores
(PORTUGAL)

Strait of
Gibraltar

Mediterranean Sea

Madeira
(PORTUGAL)

Algiers • Tunis ★ Tripoli

Casablanca• •Rabat

MOROCCO

TUNISIA

Canary Islands
(SPAIN)

Alexandria

Giza •Cairo

El Aaiún •

WESTERN
SAHARA
(Claimed by
Morocco)

ALGERIA

LIBYA

EGYPT

Tropic of Cancer

Red Sea

MAURITANIA

MALI

NIGER

CHAD

SUDAN

ERITREA

CAPE
VERDE

Nouakchott

Khartoum ★

•Asmara

Gulf of Aden

DJIBOUTI

•Praia

SENEGAL

Dakar★

GAMBIA

BURKINA
FASO

Niamey

Djibouti •

Banjul★ •Bamako

*Lake
Chad*

Bissau★

Ouagadougou

N'Djamena
•

ETHIOPIA

GUINEA-
BISSAU

GUINEA

BENIN

NIGERIA

Addis Ababa
•

Conakry★

TOGO

•Abuja

Freetown★

CÔTE
D'IVOIRE

GHANA

SOUTH
SUDAN

SOMALIA

SIERRA LEONE

Monrovia•

Yamoussoukro
•

Lomé

CENTRAL AFRICAN
REPUBLIC

LIBERIA

Abidjan•

Accra★

Lagos
•

Juba
•

Porto-
Novo

CAMEROON

Bangui•

*Gulf of
Guinea*

Malabo★

UGANDA

Mogadishu •

EQUATORIAL GUINEA

•Yaoundé

KENYA

SÃO TOMÉ AND PRÍNCIPE

São Tomé★

REPUBLIC
OF THE
CONGO

Kisangani
•

Kampala★

0° Equator

Libreville★

Nairobi
•

GABON

RWANDA

Kigali★

*Lake
Victoria*

DEMOCRATIC
REPUBLIC
OF THE CONGO

Bujumbura★

BURUNDI

Mombasa•

Brazzaville★

*INDIAN
OCEAN*

Victoria★

Kinshasa★

Pemba•

TANZANIA

Zanzibar•

SEYCHELLES

CABINDA
(ANGOLA)

Dodoma★
*Lake
Tanganyika*

Dar es Salaam
•

*ATLANTIC
OCEAN*

Luanda★

COMOROS

•Lubumbashi

Moroni•

MALAWI

St. Helena
(U.K.)

ANGOLA

ZAMBIA

Lilongwe★

Antananarivo

Lusaka★

MOZAMBIQUE

★

MAURITIUS

Harare★

ZIMBABWE

MADAGASCAR

Port Louis★

Réunion
(FRANCE)

Tropic of Capricorn

NAMIBIA

BOTSWANA

•Bulawayo

Windhoek★

Gaborone★

Pretoria★

Johannesburg•

Maputo★

Mbabane

SWAZILAND

Bloemfontein•

Maseru★

LESOTHO

SOUTH AFRICA

Cape Town•

✪ National capital

• Other city

|0 | 250 | 500 Miles|

|0 | 250 | 500 Kilometers|

Projection: Azimuthal Equal-Area

The Pacific: Political

NORTH AMERICA

ASIA

NORTH PACIFIC OCEAN

SOUTH PACIFIC OCEAN

INDIAN OCEAN

AUSTRALIA

Philippine Sea

South China Sea

Timor Sea

Arafura Sea

Coral Sea

Tasman Sea

Tropic of Cancer

Equator

Tropic of Capricorn

International Date Line

MICRONESIA

MELANESIA

POLYNESIA

KIRIBATI

MARSHALL ISLANDS

NAURU

SOLOMON ISLANDS

TUVALU

VANUATU

FIJI

SAMOA

TONGA

PALAU

FEDERATED STATES OF MICRONESIA

PAPUA NEW GUINEA

NEW ZEALAND

Hawaiian Islands
Hawaii (U.S.)

Midway Island (U.S.)

Johnston Island (U.S.)

Wake Island (U.S.)

Eniwetok I.

Kwajalein Island

Majuro

Gilbert Islands

Tarawa

Palikir

Truk Is.

Agana
Guam (U.S.)

Northern Marianas (U.S.)

Bonin Islands (JAPAN)

Volcano Islands (JAPAN)

Melekeok

New Guinea

Bismarck Archipelago

Port Moresby

Honiara

Guadalcanal I.

Espíritu Santo I.

Malekula I.

Port-Vila

New Caledonia (FRANCE)

Nouméa

Loyalty Islands (FRANCE)

Funafuti

Kingman Reef (U.S.)

Palmyra Island (U.S.)

Washington Island

Fanning Island

Howland I. (U.S.)

Baker I. (U.S.)

McKean I.

Gardner I.

Phoenix Islands

Jarvis I. (U.S.)

Starbuck Island

Tokelau (N.Z.)

Wallis & Futuna (FR.)

Suva

American Samoa

Pago Pago

Apia

Nuku'alofa

Niue (N.Z.)

Manihiki Island

Cook Islands (NEW ZEALAND)

Rarotonga Island

Society Islands (FRANCE)

Papeete

Tahiti (FRANCE)

French Polynesia

Tuamotu Archipelago (FRANCE)

Marquesas Islands (FRANCE)

Tubuai Islands (FRANCE)

Rapa Island (FRANCE)

Pitcairn (U.K.)

Ducie Island

Easter Island (CHILE)

Kermadec Islands (N.Z.)

Norfolk Island (AUSTRALIA)

North Island

South Island

Auckland

Wellington

Christchurch

Chatham Islands (N.Z.)

Bounty Islands (N.Z.)

Auckland Islands (NEW ZEALAND)

Darwin

Perth

Adelaide

Melbourne

Hobart

Sydney

Canberra

Brisbane

Christmas Island (AUSTRALIA)

Map Legend

⊕ National capital
● Other city

| 0 | 500 | 1,000 Miles |
| 0 | 500 | 1,000 Kilometers |

Projection: Azimuthal Equal-Area

N E S W

30°N 15°N 0° Equator 15°S 30°S 45°S

135°W 150°W 165°W 180° 165°E 150°E 135°E 120°E 120°W

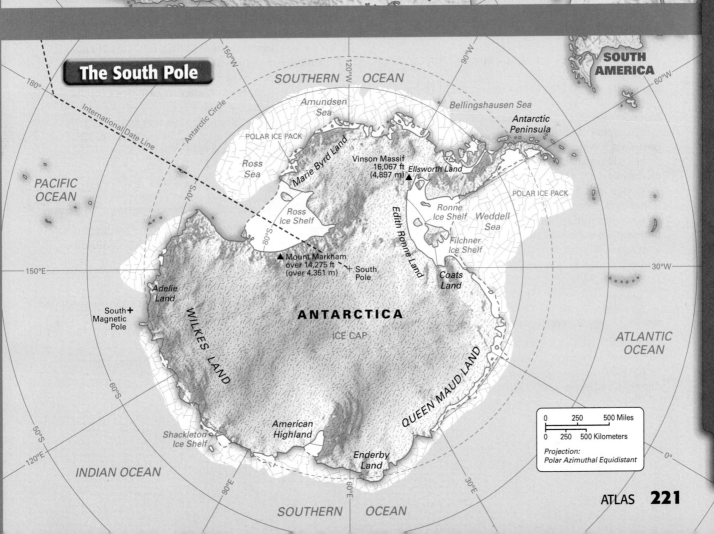

The North Pole

ASIA

Laptev
Sea

120°E

80°N

70°N

60°N

50°N

150°E

180°

Bering
Sea

90°E

3.09

30°E

150°W

120°W

ARCTIC
OCEAN

POLAR ICE PACK

North
Pole

North
Magnetic
Pole

Beaufort
Sea

NORTH
AMERICA

International Date Line

0°

Barents
Sea

EUROPE

Norwegian
Sea

Kara
Sea

Arctic Circle

Greenland
Sea

30°W

Greenland
(DENMARK)

ATLANTIC
OCEAN

Baffin
Bay

60°W

The South Pole

SOUTHERN   OCEAN

SOUTH
AMERICA

180°

150°W

120°W

90°W

60°W

International Date Line

Antarctic Circle

Amundsen
Sea

Bellingshausen Sea

Antarctic
Peninsula

PACIFIC
OCEAN

POLAR ICE PACK

Ross
Sea

70°S

Marie Byrd Land

Vinson Massif
16,067 ft
(4,897 m)

Ellsworth Land

POLAR ICE PACK

80°S

Ross
Ice Shelf

Edith Ronne Land

Ronne
Ice Shelf

Weddell
Sea

150°E

Mount Markham
over 14,275 ft
(over 4,351 m)

South
Pole

Filchner
Ice Shelf

30°W

Adelie
Land

South
Magnetic
Pole

WILKES   LAND

ANTARCTICA

ICE CAP

Coats
Land

QUEEN MAUD LAND

ATLANTIC
OCEAN

60°S

Shackleton
Ice Shelf

American
Highland

Enderby
Land

0°

120°E

INDIAN OCEAN

90°E

60°E

30°E

SOUTHERN   OCEAN

ATLAS **221**

ATLAS

Gazetteer

A

Abuja (ah-BOO-jah) (9°N, 7°E) the capital of Nigeria (p. 107)

Accra (6°N, 0°) the capital of Ghana (p. 107)

Addis Ababa (AH-dis AH-bah-bah) (9°N, 39°E) the capital of Ethiopia (p. 129)

Alexandria an ancient city in Egypt built by Alexander the Great (p. 85)

Algeria a country in North Africa between Morocco and Libya; it is the largest country in Africa (p. 85)

Algiers (37°N, 3°E) the capital of Algeria (p. 85)

Angola a country in Central Africa that borders the Atlantic Ocean (p. 149)

Antananarivo (19°S, 48°E) the capital of Madagascar (p. 171)

Asmara (15°N, 39°E) the capital of Eritrea (p. 129)

Atlas Mountains a high mountain range in northwestern Africa (p. 87)

B

Bamako (BAH-mah-koh) (13°N, 8°W) the capital of Mali (p. 107)

Bangui (bahn-GEE) (4°N, 19°E) the capital of the Central African Republic (p. 149)

Banjul (BAHN-jool) (13°N, 17°W) the capital of Gambia (p. 106)

Benin a country in West Africa between Togo and Nigeria (p. 107)

Bissau (bis-OW) (12°N, 16°W) the capital of Guinea-Bissau (p. 106)

Bloemfontein (BLOOM-fahn-tayn) (29°S, 26°E) the judicial capital of South Africa (p. 171)

Botswana a country in Southern Africa between Namibia and Zimbabwe (p. 171)

Brazzaville (4°S, 15°E) the capital of the Republic of the Congo (p. 149)

Bujumbura (booh-juhm-BOOHR-uh) (3°S, 29°E) the capital of Burundi (p. 129)

Burkina Faso (boor-KEE-nuh FAH-soh) a landlocked country in West Africa (p. 107)

Burundi (buh-ROON-dee) a landlocked country in East Africa (p. 129)

C

Cairo (30°N, 31°E) the capital of Egypt (p. 85)

Cameroon a country in Central Africa south of Nigeria (p. 149)

Cape of Good Hope a cape at the southern tip of Africa (p. 173)

Cape Town (34°S, 18°E) the legislative capital of South Africa (p. 171)

Cape Verde (VUHRD) an island country off the coast of West Africa (p. 106)

Central African Republic a landlocked country in Central Africa south of Chad (p. 149)

Chad a landlocked country in West Africa located east of Niger (p. 107)

Comoros (KAH-muh-rohz) an island country in the Indian Ocean off the coast of Africa (p. 171)

Conakry (KAH-nuh-kree) (10°N, 14°W) the capital of Guinea (p. 106)

Congo Basin a large flat area on the Congo River in Central Africa (p. 151)

Congo, Democratic Republic of the the largest and most populous country in Central Africa (p. 149)

Congo, Republic of the a country in Central Africa on the Congo River (p. 149)

Congo River the major river of Central Africa (p. 151)

copper belt a region rich in copper that stretches from Zambia to Democratic Republic of the Congo (p. 153)

Côte d'Ivoire (KOHT dee-VWAHR) a country in West Africa between Liberia and Ghana (p. 107)

D

Dakar (15°N, 17°W) the capital of Senegal (p. 106)

Dar es Salaam (7°S, 39°E) the capital of Tanzania (p. 129)

Darfur a region in western Sudan; because of genocide, millions of people have fled from Darfur (p. 141)

Djenné (14°N, 5°W) city in Mali (p. 74)

Djibouti (ji-BOO-tee) a country in East Africa on the Horn of Africa (p. 129)

Djibouti (12°N, 43°E) the capital of Djibouti (p. 129)

Dodoma (6°S, 36°E) the capital of Tanzania (p. 129)

Drakensberg a mountain range in Southern Africa (p. 173)

E, F

Egypt a country in North Africa on the Mediterranean Sea; home to one of the world's oldest civilizations (p. 85)

Equatorial Guinea a country in Central Africa between Cameroon and Gabon (p. 149)

Eritrea (er-uh-TREE-uh) an East African country north of Ethiopia (p. 129)

Ethiopia an East African country located on the Horn of Africa (p. 129)

Freetown (9°N, 13°W) the capital of Sierra Leone (p. 106)

G, H

Gabon (gah-BOHN) a country in Central Africa between Cameroon and the Democratic Republic of the Congo (p. 149)

Gaborone (24°S, 26°E) the capital of Botswana (p. 171)

Gambia a country in West Africa surrounded on three sides by Senegal (p. 106)

Gao (16°N, 0°) the capital of the Songhai Empire (p. 71)

Ghana a country in West Africa between Côte d'Ivoire and Togo (p. 107)

Ghana an ancient empire in West Africa (p. 63)

Great Rift Valley a series of valleys in East Africa caused by the stretching of Earth's crust (p. 131)

Great Zimbabwe an ancient walled town in Southern Africa (p. 177)

Guinea a country in West Africa north of Sierra Leone (p. 106)

Guinea-Bissau a country in West Africa north of Guinea (p. 106)

Harare (hah-RAH-ray) (18°S, 31°E) the capital of Zimbabwe (p. 171)

J, K

Juba (5°N, 32°E) the capital of South Sudan (p. 129)

Kampala (0°, 32°E) the capital of Uganda (p. 129)

Kenya a country in East Africa south of Ethiopia (p. 129)

Khartoum (16°N, 33°E) the capital of Sudan (p. 129)

Kigali (2°S, 30°E) the capital of Rwanda (p. 129)

Kinshasa (4°S, 15°E) the capital of the Democratic Republic of the Congo (p. 149)

Kongo Kingdom a powerful kingdom that once ruled much of Central Africa (p. 156)

Kush a powerful kingdom that ruled Nubia from about 2000 BC to AD 350 (p. 47)

L

Lagos (6°N, 3°E) a city in Nigeria; the most populous city in West Africa (p. 107)

Lake Victoria the largest lake in Africa (p. 131)

Lesotho (luh-SOH-toh) a country completely surrounded by South Africa (p. 171)

Liberia a country in West Africa between Sierra Leone and Côte d'Ivoire (p. 107)

Libreville (0°, 9°E) the capital of Gabon (p. 149)

Libya a country in North Africa between Egypt and Algeria (p. 85)

Lilongwe (li-LAWN-gway) (14°S, 34°E) the capital of Malawi (p. 149)

Lomé (6°N, 1°E) the capital of Togo (p. 107)

Lower Egypt the northern part of ancient Egypt, downriver from Upper Egypt (p. 15)

Luanda (9°S, 13°E) the capital of Angola (p. 149)

Lusaka (15°S, 28°E) the capital of Zambia (p. 149)

M

Madagascar a large island country off the southeastern coast of Africa (p. 171)

Maghreb a region in North Africa that includes western Libya, Tunisia, Algeria, and Morocco; it means "west" in Arabic (p. 100)

Malabo (mah-LAH-boh) (4°N, 9°E) the capital of Equatorial Guinea (p. 149)

Malawi a landlocked country in Central Africa located south of Tanzania (p. 149)

Mali a country in West Africa on the Niger River (p. 107)

Mali an ancient empire in West Africa (p. 71)

Maputo (27°S, 33°E) the capital of Mozambique (p. 171)

Maseru (29°S, 27°E) the capital of Lesotho (p. 171)

Mauritania a country in West Africa located between Mali and the Atlantic Ocean (p. 107)

Mauritius (maw-RI-shuhs) an island country east of Madagascar (p. 219)

Mbabane (uhm-bah-BAH-nay) (26°S, 31°E) the capital of Swaziland (p. 171)

Memphis (30°N, 31°E) the ancient capital of Egypt (p. 15)

Meroë (MER-oh-wee) (17°N, 34°E) an ancient capital of Kush (p. 52)

Mogadishu (2°N, 45°E) the capital of Somalia (p. 129)

Monrovia (6°N, 11°W) the capital of Liberia (p. 107)

Morocco a country in North Africa south of Spain (p. 84)

Moroni (12°S, 43°E) the capital of Comoros (p. 171)

Mount Kilimanjaro (3°S, 37°E) the highest mountain in Africa at 19,341 feet (5,895 m); it is in Tanzania near the Kenya border (p. 131)

Mozambique a country in Southern Africa south of Tanzania (p. 171)

N

Nairobi (1°S, 37°E) the capital of Kenya (p. 129)

Namib Desert a desert in southwestern Africa (p. 173)

Namibia a country on the Atlantic coast of Southern Africa (p. 171)

N'Djamena (uhn-jah-MAY-nah) (12°N, 15°E) the capital of Chad (p. 107)

Niamey (14°N, 2°E) the capital of Niger (p. 107)

Niger (NY-juhr) a country in West Africa north of Nigeria (p. 107)

Niger River the major river of West Africa (p. 109)

Nigeria a country on the Atlantic coast of West Africa (p. 107)

Nile River the longest river in the world; located in North Africa (p. 15)

Nouakchott (nooh-AHK-shaht) (18°N, 16°W) the capital of Mauritania (p. 106)

Nubia a region in North Africa located on the Nile River south of Egypt (p. 47)

O, P, R

Ouagadougou (wah-gah-DOO-goo) (12°N, 2°W) the capital of Burkina Faso (p. 107)

Port Louis (20°S, 58°E) the capital of Mauritius (p. 219)

Porto-Novo (6°N, 3°E) the capital of Benin (p. 107)

Praia (PRY-uh) (15°N, 24°W) the capital of Cape Verde (p. 106)

Pretoria (26°S, 28°E) the administrative capital of South Africa (p. 171)

Rabat (34°N, 7°W) the capital of Morocco (p. 84)

Rwanda a country in East Africa between Tanzania and the Democratic Republic of the Congo (p. 129)

S

Sahara the world's largest desert; it dominates much of North Africa (p. 87)

Sahel a semiarid region between the Sahara and wetter areas to the south (p. 110)

São Tomé (sow too-MAY) (1°N, 6°E) the capital of São Tomé and Príncipe (p. 149)

São Tomé and Príncipe (PREEN-see-pee) an island country located off the Atlantic coast of Central Africa (p. 149)

Senegal a country in West Africa south of Mauritania (p. 106)

Serengeti Plain a large plain in East Africa that is famous for its wildlife (p. 131)

Seychelles an island country located east of Africa in the Indian Ocean (p. 219)

Sierra Leone a West African country located south of Guinea (p. 106)

Somalia an East African country located on the Horn of Africa (p. 129)

Songhai an ancient empire in West Africa (p. 71)

South Africa a country located at the southern tip of Africa (p. 171)

South Sudan a country in East Africa, newly independent in 2011 (p. 141)

Sudan a country in East Africa (p. 129)

Suez Canal a canal in Egypt that links the Mediterranean and Red seas (p. 87)

Swaziland a country in Southern Africa almost completely surrounded by South Africa (p. 171)

T, U, V

Tanzania (tan-zuh-NEE-uh) an East African country south of Kenya (p. 129)

Timbuktu (17°N, 3°W) a major cultural and trading city in the Mali and Songhai empires (p. 71)

Togo a country in West Africa between Ghana and Benin (p. 107)

Tripoli (33°N, 13°E) the capital of Libya (p. 85)

Tunis (37°N, 10°E) the capital of Tunisia (p. 85)

Tunisia a country in North Africa on the Mediterranean Sea (p. 85)

Uganda a country in East Africa located west of Kenya (p. 129)

Upper Egypt the southern region of ancient Egypt, upriver of Lower Egypt (p. 15)

Victoria (1°S, 33°E) the capital of Seychelles (p. 219)

W, Y, Z

Windhoek (VINT-hook) (22°S, 17°E) the capital of Namibia (p. 171)

Yamoussoukro (yah-moo-SOO-kroh) (7°N, 5°W) the capital of Côte d'Ivoire (p. 107)

Yaoundé (yown-DAY) (4°N, 12°E) the capital of Cameroon (p. 149)

Zambezi River a river in Central Africa that flows into the Indian Ocean (p. 151)

Zambia a country in Central Africa east of Angola (p. 149)

Zanzibar an island in Tanzania; once a major trading center (p. 131)

Zimbabwe a country in Southern Africa between Botswana and Mozambique (p. 171)

English and Spanish Glossary

MARK	AS IN	RESPELLING	EXAMPLE
a	alphabet	a	*AL-fuh-bet
ā	Asia	ay	AY-zhuh
ä	cart, top	ah	KAHRT, TAHP
e	let, ten	e	LET, TEN
ē	even, leaf	ee	EE-vuhn, LEEF
i	it, tip, British	i	IT, TIP, BRIT-ish
ī	site, buy, Ohio	y	SYT, BY, oh-HY-oh
	iris	eye	EYE-ris
k	card	k	KAHRD
kw	quest	kw	KWEST
ō	over, rainbow	oh	OH-vuhr, RAYN-boh
ů	book, wood	ooh	BOOHK, WOOHD
ȯ	all, orchid	aw	AWL, AWR-kid
ȯi	foil, coin	oy	FOYL, KOYN
aů	out	ow	OWT
ə	cup, butter	uh	KUHP, BUHT-uhr
ü	rule, food	oo	ROOL, FOOD
yü	few	yoo	FYOO
zh	vision	zh	VIZH-uhn

*A syllable printed in small capital letters receives heavier emphasis than the other syllable(s) in a word.

Phonetic Respelling and Pronunciation Guide

Many of the key terms in this textbook have been respelled to help you pronounce them. The letter combinations used in the respelling throughout the narrative are explained in this phonetic respelling and pronunciation guide. The guide is adapted from Webster's Tenth New College Dictionary, Merriam-Webster's New Geographical Dictionary, and Merriam-Webster's New Biographical Dictionary.

A

Afrikaners (a-fri-KAH-nuhrz) Dutch, French, and German settlers and their descendants in South Africa (p. 178)
  afrikaners colonizadores holandeses, franceses y alemanes y sus descendientes en Sudáfrica (pág. 178)

afterlife life after death (p. 22)
  la otra vida vida después de la muerte (pág. 22)

animism the belief that bodies of water, animals, trees, and other natural objects have spirits (p. 114)
  animismo creencia de que las masas de agua, los animales, los árboles y otros objetos de la naturaleza tienen espíritu (pág. 114)

apartheid South Africa's government policy of separation of races that was abandoned in the 1980s and 1990s; apartheid means "apartness" (p. 178)
  apartheid política gubernamental de Sudáfrica de separar las razas, abandonada en las décadas de 1980 y 1990; apartheid significa "separación" (pág. 178)

B

basin a generally flat region surrounded by higher land such as mountains and plateaus (p. 150)
  cuenca región generalmente llana rodeada de tierras más altas, como montañas y mesetas (pág. 150)

Berbers members of an ethnic group who are native to North Africa and speak Berber languages (p. 93)
  bereberes miembros de un grupo étnico del norte de África que hablan lenguas bereberes (pág. 93)

Boers Afrikaner frontier farmers in South Africa (p. 178)
  bóers agricultores afrikaners de la frontera en Sudáfrica (pág. 178)

C

cataracts rapids along a river, such as those along the Nile in Egypt (p. 15)
  rápidos fuertes corrientes de un río, como las del Nilo en Egipto (pág. 15)

delta a triangle-shaped area of land made from soil deposited by a river (p. 15)
delta zona de tierra triangular creada a partir de la tierra que deposita un río (pág. 15)

desertification the spread of desert-like conditions (p. 110)
desertización ampliación de las condiciones desérticas (pág. 110)

dialect a regional variety of a language (p. 158)
dialecto variedad regional de una lengua (pág. 158)

dictator a ruler who has almost absolute power (p. 101)
dictador gobernante que tiene poder casi absoluto (pág. 101)

droughts periods when little rain falls and crops are damaged (p. 132)
sequías períodos en los que los cultivos sufren daños por la falta de lluvia (pág. 132)

dynasty a series of rulers from the same family (p. 17)
dinastía serie de gobernantes pertenecientes a la misma familia (pág. 17)

ebony a dark, heavy wood (p. 48)
ébano madera oscura y pesada (pág. 48)

elite (AY-leet) people of wealth and power (p. 23)
élite personas ricas y poderosas (pág. 23)

enclave a small territory surrounded by foreign territory (p. 184)
enclave territorio pequeño rodeado de territorio extranjero (pág. 184)

engineering the application of scientific knowledge for practical purposes (p. 24)
ingeniería aplicación del conocimiento científico para fines prácticos (pág. 24)

escarpment a steep face at the edge of a plateau or other raised area (p. 172)
acantilado cara empinada en el borde de una meseta o de otra área elevada (pág. 172)

exports items sent to other regions for trade (p. 52)
exportaciones productos enviados a otras regiones para el intercambio comercial (pág. 52)

extended family a family group that includes the father, mother, children, and close relatives (p. 115)
familia extendida grupo familiar que incluye al padre, la madre, los hijos y los parientes cercanos (pág. 115)

famine an extreme shortage of food (p. 121)
hambruna grave escasez de alimentos (pág. 121)

free port a city in which almost no taxes are placed on goods sold there (p. 101)
puerto libre ciudad en la que se pagan muy pocos impuestos por los bienes que allí se venden (pág. 101)

genocide the intentional destruction of a people (p. 141)
genocidio destrucción intencional de un grupo de personas (pág. 141)

geothermal energy energy produced from the heat of Earth's interior (p. 139)
energía geotérmica energía generada por el calor del interior de la Tierra (pág. 139)

griot (GREE-oh) a West African storyteller (p. 76)
griot narrador de cuentos de África occidental (pág. 76)

hieroglyphics (hy-ruh-GLIH-fiks) the ancient Egyptian writing system that used picture symbols (p. 34)
jeroglíficos sistema de escritura del antiguo Egipto, en el cual se usaban símbolos ilustrados (pág. 34)

I

imperialism an attempt to dominate a country's government, trade, and culture (p. 135)
imperialismo intento de dominar el gobierno, el comercio y la cultura de un país (pág. 135)

imports goods brought in from other regions (p. 52)
importaciones bienes que se traen a un país de otras regiones (pág. 52)

inflation the rise in prices that occurs when currency loses its buying power (p. 163)
inflación aumento de los precios que ocurre cuando la moneda de un país pierde poder adquisitivo (pág. 163)

ivory a white material made from elephant tusks (p. 48)
marfil material blanco procedente de los colmillos de los elefantes (pág. 48)

kente (ken-TAY) a hand-woven, brightly colored West African fabric (p. 79)
   kente tela de África occidental, tejida a mano y muy colorida (pág. 79)

malaria a disease spread by mosquitoes that causes fever and pain (p. 164)
   malaria enfermedad transmitida por los mosquitos que causa fiebre y dolor (pág. 164)

malnutrition a condition of not getting enough nutrients from food (p. 165)
   desnutrición estado producido al no obtener suficientes nutrientes de los alimentos (pág. 165)

merchant a trader (p. 52)
   mercader comerciante (pág. 52)

Middle Kingdom the period of Egyptian history from about 2050 to 1750 BC marked by order and stability (p. 28)
   Reino Medio período de la historia de Egipto desde aproximadamente 2050 a 1750 a. C., caracterizado por el orden y la estabilidad (pág. 28)

mosque (MAHSK) a building for Muslim prayer (p. 73)
   mezquita edificio musulmán para la oración (pág. 73)

mummy a specially treated body wrapped in cloth for preservation (p. 22)
   momia cadáver especialmente tratado y envuelto en tela para su conservación (pág. 22)

New Kingdom the period from about 1550 to 1050 BC in Egyptian history when Egypt reached the height of its power and glory (p. 28)
   Reino Nuevo período de la historia egipcia desde aproximadamente 1550 a 1050 a. C., en el que Egipto alcanzó el punto máximo de su poder y su gloria (pág. 28)

noble a rich and powerful person (p. 20)
   noble persona rica y poderosa (pág. 20)

O

oasis a wet, fertile area in a desert where a spring or well provides water (p. 88)
   oasis zona húmeda y fértil en el desierto con un manantial o pozo que proporciona agua (pág. 88)

obelisk (AH-buh-lisk) a tall, pointed, four-sided pillar in ancient Egypt (p. 36)
   obelisco pilar de cuatro caras, alto y puntiagudo en el antiguo Egipto (pág. 36)

Old Kingdom the period from about 2700 to 2200 BC in Egyptian history that began shortly after Egypt was unified (p. 19)
   Reino Antiguo período de la historia egipcia desde aproximadamente 2700 a 2200 a. C. que comenzó poco después de la unificación de Egipto (pág. 19)

oral history a spoken record of past events (p. 76)
   historia oral registro hablado de hechos ocurridos en el pasado (pág. 76)

papyrus (puh-PY-ruhs) a long-lasting, paper-like material made from reeds that the ancient Egyptians used to write on (p. 34)
   papiro material duradero hecho de juncos, similar al papel, que los antiguos egipcios utilizaban para escribir (pág. 34)

periodic market an open-air trading market that is set up once or twice a week (p. 153)
   mercado periódico mercado al aire libre que funciona una o dos veces a la semana (pág. 153)

pharaoh (FEHR-oh) the title used by the rulers of Egypt (p. 17)
   faraón título usado por los gobernantes de Egipto (pág. 17)

proverb a short saying of wisdom or truth (p. 77)
   proverbio refrán breve que expresa sabiduría o una verdad (pág. 77)

pyramid a huge triangular tomb built by the Egyptians and other peoples (p. 24)
   pirámide tumba triangular y enorme construida por los egipcios y otros pueblos (pág. 24)

R

rift valleys places on Earth's surface where the crust stretches until it breaks (p. 130)
   valles de fisura puntos de la superficie de la Tierra en los que la corteza se estira hasta romperse (pág. 130)

Rosetta Stone a huge stone slab inscribed with hieroglyphics, Greek, and a later form of Egyptian that allowed historians to understand Egyptian writing (p. 35)
   piedra Roseta gran losa de piedra con inscripciones en jeroglíficos, en griego y en una forma tardía del idioma egipcio que permitió a los historiadores entender la escritura egipcia (pág. 35)

ENGLISH AND SPANISH GLOSSARY

safari an overland journey to view African wildlife (p. 139)
safari excursión por tierra con el fin de ver animales salvajes en África (pág. 139)

Sahel (SAH-hel) a strip of land that divides the Sahara from wetter areas (p. 110)
Sahel franja de tierra que divide el Sahara de zonas más húmedas (pág. 110)

sanctions economic or political penalties imposed by one country on another to try to force a change in policy (p. 182)
sanciones penalizaciones económicas o políticas que un país impone a otro para obligarlo a cambiar su política (pág. 182)

savanna an area of tall grasses and scattered trees and shrubs (p. 110)
sabana zona de pastos altos con arbustos y árboles dispersos (pág. 110)

secede to break away from the main country (p. 118)
separarse dividirse del territorio principal del país (pág. 118)

silent barter a process in which people exchange goods without contacting each other directly (p. 64)
trueque silencioso proceso mediante el cual las personas intercambian bienes sin entrar en contacto directo (pág. 64)

silt finely ground fertile soil that is good for growing crops (p. 86)
cieno tierra fértil de partículas finas que es buena para el crecimiento de los cultivos (pág. 86)

souk (SOOK) a marketplace or bazaar in the Islamic world (p. 101)
zoco mercado o bazar del mundo islámico (pág. 101)

sphinx (sfinks) an imaginary creature with a human head and the body of a lion that was often shown on Egyptian statues (p. 36)
esfinge criatura imaginaria con cabeza humana y cuerpo de león que se representaba a menudo en las estatuas egipcias (pág. 36)

townships crowded clusters of small homes in South Africa outside of cities where black South Africans live (p. 179)
distritos segregados grupos de pequeñas viviendas amontonadas ubicadas en las afueras de las ciudades de Sudáfrica, donde vivían los sudafricanos negros (pág. 179)

trade network a system of people in different lands who trade goods back and forth (p. 52)
red comercial sistema de personas en diferentes lugares que comercian productos entre sí (pág. 52)

trade route a path followed by traders (p. 29)
ruta comercial camino seguido por los comerciantes (pág. 29)

veld (VELT) open grassland areas in South Africa (p. 174)
veld praderas descampadas en Sudáfrica (pág. 174)

zonal organized by zone (p. 110)
zonal organizado por zonas (pág. 110)

ENGLISH AND SPANISH GLOSSARY

Index

INDEX

INDEX

INDEX

Credits and Acknowledgments

Unless otherwise indicated below, all video reference screens are © 2010 A&E Television Networks, LLC. All rights reserved.

For permission to reproduce copyrighted material, grateful acknowledgment is made to the following sources:

Random House, Inc., www.randomhouse.com:
AKE: The Years of Childhood by Wole Soyinka. Copyright © 1981 by Wole Soyinka.

Scribner, an imprint of Simon & Schuster Adult Publishing Group: "The Snows of Kilimanjaro" from *The Short Stories of Ernest Hemingway.* Copyright 1938 by Ernest Hemingway; copyright renewed © 1966 by Mary Hemingway.

Sources used by The World Almanac® for charts and graphs:

Geographical Extremes: Africa: *The World Almanac and Book of Facts, 2005; The World Factbook, 2005;* Africa: *The World Factbook, 2005;* U.S. Bureau of the Census, International Database; United Nations Statistical Yearbook; Africa's Growing Population: International Programs Center, U.S. Census Bureau; Africa and the World: *The World Factbook, 2005;* U.S. Bureau of the Census, International Database; Egypt's Population, 2003: United Nations Population Division; Africa's Largest Cities: Britannica Book of the Year 2005; United Nations Population Division; Population Density in East Africa: International Programs Center, U.S. Census Bureau; *The World Factbook, 2005;* Major Religions of Central Africa: www.worldchristiandatabase.org; Kinshasa's Growing Population: United Nations Population Division; Tourism in Southern Africa: World Tourism Organization

Illustrations and Photo Credits

Cover: (l), Denny Allen/Gallo Images/Getty Images; (r), Doug Armand/Getty Images.

Frontmatter: ii, Victoria Smith/HMH Photo; iv, Egyptian National Museum, Cairo, Egypt/SuperStock; v, Steve Vidler/SuperStock; vi, Staff/Reuters/Corbis; vii, Ognen Teofilovski/Reuters; viii, NASA/Photo Researchers, Inc.; H16 (t), Earth Satellite Corporation/Photo Researchers, Inc.; H16 (tc), Frans Lemmens/Getty Images; H16 (c), London Aerial Photo Library/Corbis; H16 (bc), Harvey Schwartz/Index Stock Imagery/Fotosearch; H16 (b), Tom Nebbia/Corbis.

Introduction: A, Celia Mannings/Alamy; B (bkgd), Planetary Visions; B (tl), Digital Vision/Getty Images; B (b), Photodisc Red/Getty Images; 1 (cl), Joseph Van Os/The Image Bank/Getty Images; 3, Sharna Balfour/Corbis.

Chapter 1: 12, Anders Blomqvist/Lonely Planet Images; 13 (tr), 2010 A&E Television Networks, LLC. All rights reserved; 13 (bl), SIME s.a.s/eStock Photo; 13 (br), Erich Lessing/Art Resource, NY; 16 (b), Erich Lessing/Art Resource, NY; 17 (c), Reza/Webistan/Corbis; 21 (br), Rèunion des Musèes Nationaux/Art Resource, NY; 21 (bcl), Araldo de Luca/Corbis; 21 (bcr), Erich Lessing/Art Resource, NY; 21 (bl), Scala/Art Resource, NY; 22 (t), Musèe du Louvre, Paris/SuperStock; 23 (br), British Museum, London, UK/Bridgeman Art Library; 23 (tl), Archivo Iconografico, S.A./CORBIS; 23 (tr), The Trustees of The British Museum/Art Resource, NY; 30 (br), Gianni Dagli Orti/Corbis;

30 (bl), Bildarchiv Preussischer Kulturbesitz/Art Resource, NY; 31 (bl), Gianni Dagli Orti/Corbis; 33 (br), HIP/Scala/Art Resource, NY; 35 (tr), Robert Harding Picture Library; 38 (tl), Time Life Pictures/Getty Images; 38 (tr), Scala/Art Resource, NY; 39 (tr), Egyptian National Museum, Cairo, Egypt/SuperStock; 39 (tl), Royalty-Free/Corbis; 41 (r), Robert Harding Picture Library; 41 (c), Egyptian National Museum, Cairo, Egypt/SuperStock; 41 (tl), Reza/Webistan/Corbis.

Chapter 2: 44 (bl), Robert Caputo/Aurora Photos; 45 (br), Sandro Vannini/CORBIS; 45 (bl), Bildarchiv Preussischer Kulturbesitz/Art Resource, NY; 47, Le Tourneur D'Ison Cyril/Gamma Press, Inc.; 48 (bl), The Art Gallery Collection/Alamy; 48-49, Erich Lessing/Art Resource, NY; 49 (br), Erich Lessing/Art Resource, NY; 50 ,Erich Lessing/Art Resource, NY; 51 (bl), Nubian, Meroitic Period, 100 B.C.-A.D. 300. Object Place: Sudan, Nubia. Iron. Width x length: 1.5 x 7.6 cm (9/16 X 3 in.), Museum of Fine Arts, Boston. MFA-University of Pennsylvania Exchange. 1991.1116; 51 (br), Egyptian, Ram's Head Amulet, ca. 770-657 B.C.E; Dynasty 25; late Dynastic period, gold; 1 5/8 x 1 3/8 in. (4.2 x 3.6 cm): The Metropolitan Museum of Art, Gift of Norbert Schimmel Trust, 1989 (1989.281.98). Image The Metropolitan Museum of Art/Art Resource, NY; 51 (bc), Nubian, Meroitic Period, 100 B.C.-A.D. 300. Object Place: Sudan, Nubia. Iron. Length: 9.7 cm (3 13/16 in.), Museum of Fine Arts, Boston. MFA-University of Pennsylvania Exchange. 1991.1119; 57 (r), with respect to 1989.281.98 Egyptian, Ram's Head Amulet, ca. 770-657 B.C.E; Dynasty 25; late Dynastic period, gold; 1 5/8 x 1 3/8 in. (4.2 x 3.6 cm): The Metropolitan Museum of Art, Gift of Norbert Schimmel Trust, 1989 (1989.281.98). Image The Metropolitan Museum of Art/Art Resource, NY; 57 (c), Erich Lessing/Art Resource, NY; 57 (l), The Art Gallery Collection/Alamy.

Chapter 3: 60, Nik Wheeler/CORBIS; 325 (br), PhotoDisc; 61 (bl), ISSOUF SANOGO/AFP/Getty Images; 64, John Elk III Photography; 65 (cl), obert Estall photo agency/Alamy; 68, Steve McCurry/Magnum Photos; 68 (tr), Nik Wheeler/CORBIS; 68 (tl), Musee du Quai Branly/Scala/Art Resource, NY; 68 (cl), Aldo Tutino/Art Resource, NY; 68 (br), B. Christopher/Alamy; 69 (tr), HIP/Scala/Art Resource, NY; 69 (cr), Reza; Webistan/CORBIS; 71 (tr), Private Collection, Credit: Heini Schneebeli/Bridgeman Art Library; 75 (br), The Granger Collection, New York; 77, Pascal Meunier/Cosmos/Aurora Photos; 78 (tl), Reuters/Corbis; 78 (tr), AFP/Getty Images; 81 (r), AFP/Getty Images; 81 (c), The Granger Collection, New York; 81 (l), obert Estall photo agency/Alamy.

Chapter 4: 84, Jon Arnold/DanitaDelimont.com; 85 (tr), 2010 A&E Television Networks, LLC. All rights reserved; 85 (bl), Age Fotostock/SuperStock; 85 (br), Claudia Adams/DanitaDelimont.com; 87, Steve Vidler/eStock Photo; 90, Age Fotostock/SuperStock; 91 (t), Sandro Vannini/CORBIS; 92 (t), Kenneth Garrett/National Geographic Image Collection; 92 (bl), Art by Elizabeth Daynes/National Geographic Image Collection; 92 (br), Kenneth Garrett/National Geographic Image Collection; 94, Patrick Ward/CORBIS; 95 (l), Karim Selmaoui/EPA/Landov; 95 (r), Abbas/Magnum Photos; 98, Age Fotostock/SuperStock; 99, NASA/Photo Researchers, Inc.; 101 (tl), Moritz Steiger/The Image Bank/Getty Images; 101 (cl), Frans Lemmens/Alamy; 102, Andrew Gunners/

Getty Images; 103 (r), Andrew Gunners/Getty Images; 103 (c), Age Fotostock/SuperStock.

Chapter 5: 106, David Else/Lonely Planet Images; 107 (br), David Else/Lonely Planet Images; 107 (bl), Owen Franken/CORBIS; 109, Bruno Morandi/Robrt Harding World Imagery/Getty Images; 110, M. ou Me. Desjeux/CORBIS; 111 (tl), © LucynaKoch/iStockPhoto.com; 111 (tr), Christopher Herwig/Aurora/Getty Images; 113, Bettmann/CORBIS; 114 (bc), Face mask with plank, Bwa People, Burkina Faso (wood & pigment), African, (20th century)/Indianapolis Museum of Art, USA, Gift of Mr and Mrs Harrison Eiteljorg/Bridgeman Art Library; 114 (bl), Imagestate/PictureQuest/Jupiter Images; 115, Margaret Courtney-Clarke/CORBIS; 116 (bl), HIP/Art Resource, NY; 117 (t), Michael Dwyer/Alamy Photos; 119, Reuters/CORBIS; 121 (b), Staff/Reuters/Corbis; 122, Yann Arthus-Bertrand/CORBIS; 123, Michael Juno/Alamy; 125 (c), Imagestate/PictureQuest; 125 (l), M. ou Me. Desjeux/CORBIS; 125 (tr), Staff/Reuters/Corbis.

Chapter 6: 128, Bildarchiv Preussischer Kulturbesitz/Art Resource, NY; 129 (bl), Jack Dykinga/The Image Bank/Getty Images; 129 (br), Tim Davis/CORBIS; 131, Robert Preston/Alamy; 132, NASA/Photo Researchers, Inc.; 133, Goran Goransson; 135 (tl), Dave Bartruff/CORBIS; 136, Gideon Mendel/CORBIS; 140 (cr), Age Fotostock/SuperStock; 141, Scott Nelson/Getty Images; 142 (cl), Frances Linzee Gordon/Lonely Planet Images; 142 (bl), Liba Taylor/CORBIS; 142 (tl), Network Photograhers/Alamy; 144, David Else/Lonely Planet Images; 145 (c), Dave Bartruff/CORBIS; 145 (r), Liba Taylor/CORBIS; 145 (l), Robert Preston/Alamy.

Chapter 7: 148, Roger Turley/Alamy; 149 (br), Christie's Images/CORBIS; 149 (bl), Robert Caputo/Aurora; 151, Frans Lemmens/The Image Bank/Getty Images; 152 (tr), © Digital Vision/Getty Images; 152 (cr), © Photodisc/Getty Images; 155 (tr), Michael Nichols/National Geographic Image Collection; 155 (tl), Michael Nichols/National Geographic Image Collection; 157 (tl), Bojan Brecelj/CORBIS; 157 (tr), The Trustees of the British Museum/Art Resource, NY; 158 (bl), Jorgen Schytte/Photolibrary; 159, Christopher Calais/In Visu/CORBIS; 161, Robert Caputo/Aurora; 162 (cr), Didier Ruef/Pixsil/Aurora; 162-163 (b), Age Fotostock/SuperStock; 163 (cl), David Else/Lonely Planet Images; 164, Ian Berry/Magnum Photos; 167 (r), Ian Berry/Magnum Photos; 167 (l), © Digital Vision/Getty Images; 167 (tc), The Trustees of the British Museum/Art Resource, NY.

Chapter 8: 170, Yann Arthus-Bertrand/CORBIS; 171 (bl), Hein von Horsten/Getty Images; 171 (br), Owen Franken/CORBIS; 173, Steve Vidler/SuperStock; 174, Worldsat; 177 (cr), Colin Hoskins/Corbis; 177 (bl), Ariadne Van Zanderbergen/Lonely Planet Images; 178, The Art Gallery Collection/Alamy; 179, Ognen Teofilovski/Reuters; 180–181 (b), © Iconotec/Alamy; 181 (tl), Lindsay Hebberd/CORBIS; 183 (cr), Walter Dhladhla/AFP/Getty Images; 183 (t), Sophie Elbaz/CORBIS; 184-185, Chris Harvey/Getty Images; 186, Luke Hunter/Lonely Planet Images; 187, imagebroker/Alamy; 189 (r), Chris Harvey/Getty Images; 189 (c), Ognen Teofilovski/Reuters; 189 (l), Steve Vidler/SuperStock.

Staff Credits

The people who contributed to *Holt McDougal: Africa* are listed below. They represent editorial, design, production, emedia, and permissions.

Melanie Baccus, Angela Beckmann, Julie Beckman-Key, Genick Blaise, Ed Blake, Jennifer Campbell, Henry Clark, Grant Davidson, Nina Degollado, Rose Degollado, Christine Devall, Michelle Dike, Lydia Doty, Chase Edmond, Mescal Evler, Susan Franques, Stephanie Friedman, Bob Fullilove, Matthew Gierhart, Bill Gillis, Ann Gorbett, Janet Harrington, Betsy Harris, Wendy Hodge, Tim Hovde, Cathy Jenevein, Carrie Jones, Kadonna Knape, Laura Lasley, Sarah Lee, Sean McCormick, Joe Melomo, Richard Metzger, Andrew Miles, Debra O'Shields, Jarred Prejean, Paul Provence , Shelly Ramos, Curtis Riker, Michelle Rimsa, Michael Rinella, Jennifer Rockwood, Carole Rollins, Beth Sample, Annette Saunders, Jenny Schaeffer, Kay Selke, Chris Smith, Jeremy Strykul, Jeannie Taylor, Terri Taylor, Joni Wackwitz, Mary Wages, Diana Holman Walker, Nadyne Wood, Robin Zaback